Above the Shots

Above

THE SHOTS

An Oral History of the

Kent State Shootings

CRAIG S. SIMPSON AND
GREGORY S. WILSON

The Kent State University Press
Kent, Ohio

© 2016 by The Kent State University Press, Kent, Ohio 44242
All rights reserved
Library of Congress Catalog Number 2015036107
ISBN 978-1-60635-291-5

Library of Congress Cataloging-in-Publication Data
Names: Simpson, Craig S., author. | Wilson, Gregory S., author.
Title: Above the shots : an oral history of the Kent State shootings /
    Craig S. Simpson and Gregory S. Wilson.
Description: Kent, Ohio : Kent State University Press, [2016] |
    Includes bibliographical references and index.
Identifiers: LCCN 2015036107 | ISBN 9781606352915 (pbk. : alk. paper) ∞
Subjects: LCSH: Kent State Shootings, Kent, Ohio, 1970. | Kent State University--History.
Classification: LCC LD4191.O72 S56 2016 | DDC 378.771/37--dc23
LC record available at http://lccn.loc.gov/2015036107

20 19 18 17 16   5 4 3 2 1

Contents

Acknowledgments

T hroughout the process of researching and writing this book, we benefited from the insights and assistance of several people and organizations.

Steve Paschen and Amanda Faehnel at Kent State University Special Collections and Archives were exceedingly accommodating as we navigated the voluminous May 4 Collection. Also at KSU, Lori Boes at the May 4 Visitors Center gave valuable time and shared her insights on the events of May 4th, 1970, and their meaning. A long-standing member of the Kent community, Sandra Perlman Halem not only recorded the first official series of interviews for the Kent State Shootings Oral History Project but also generously helped forge connections for subsequent interviews. In Columbus, the staff at the Ohio Historical Society provided great assistance in locating records relevant to the shootings. At Indiana University, Joel Silver and Lori Dekydtspotter made several helpful suggestions to overcome periods of stasis and uncertainty.

At KSU Press, Joyce Harrison and Will Underwood exhibited Job-like patience as we worked through many drafts and took longer than we anticipated in seeing this volume through to production. Tom Grace was incredibly generous with his time as an official reader of our manuscript, a historian who combines a deep academic background with firsthand experience of these events and who is a valued friend. Thanks as well to the anonymous reader for KSU Press for his or her thoughts on our manuscript. Additionally, Bill Childs and David Steigerwald read portions of the text and aided our thinking about the material and its context.

We had the good fortune to present early, draft portions of our research at the Oral History Association meetings in 2011 (Denver) and 2012 (Cleveland). We thank our fellow panelists, audience members, and the organizers for the opportunity to share our ideas and hear their feedback. Troy Reeves deserves special thanks for arranging CSPAN-3 to record and air our 2011 panel on campus protests in the 1960s, as does Barbara Truesdell, assistant director of the Center for the Study of History and Memory at Indiana University, for her expert moderation of that panel.

Our families deserve our deep gratitude. Laura Hilton and Kate Wilson in Ohio gave their love and support and much-needed time either for writing or for breaks away from what has been at times a difficult subject to address. Steve and Carol Simpson in Bloomington, Indiana, who lived near the Berkeley campus as the anti–Vietnam War protest movement intensified and whose own recollections of Kent State are vivid even though secondhand, demonstrated once again their indefatigable support.

Last, and most certainly not least, we thank all of our narrators for agreeing to share their memories. Without them, this book would not be possible, and we have done our best to stay true to their words and meaning.

The Narrators

Mike (Meyer) Alewitz. Undergraduate student at Kent State University in 1970, muralist and activist.

Chuck (Charles W.) Ayers. Undergraduate student at Kent State University from 1966 to 1971, former editorial cartoonist for the *Akron Beacon Journal*, and co-author of the comic strip *Crankshaft*.

Denny Benedict. Undergraduate student at Kent State University from 1969 to 1973.

Richard G. Bentley. Professor of Journalism and Technology at Kent State University in 1970.

Ellis Berns. Undergraduate student at Kent State University from 1967 to 1971.

Anita Bixenstine. Professor in the Honors College at Kent State University in 1970.

Ed (V. Edwin) Bixenstine. Professor in the Department of Psychology at Kent State University in 1970.

William Brauning. Undergraduate student at Kent State University in 1970.

Rick Byrum. Undergraduate student at Kent State University in 1970.

John Carson. Mayor of the City of Kent from 1966 to 1969; proprietor of W. H. Donaghy drugstore in downtown Kent.

Carol Cartwright. President of Kent State University from 1991 to 2006.

John Cleary. Undergraduate student at Kent State University in 1970 and one of the nine wounded students on May 4, 1970.

Linda Cooper-Leff. Undergraduate student at Kent State University from 1966 to 1970.

Joe Cullum. Undergraduate student at Kent State University in 1970, one of the Kent 25.

Timothy DeFrange. Kent, Ohio, resident and Kent State University student in 1970.

Catherine Delattre. Undergraduate student at Kent State University in 1970.

Bruce Dzeda. Kent State University senior in 1970.

Michael Erwin. Undergraduate student at Kent State University in 1970, and one of the Kent 25.

Naomi Goelman Etzkin. Undergraduate student at Kent State University in 1970.

Julio Arturo Fanjul. Undergraduate student at Kent State University in 1970.

Eldon Fender. Undergraduate student majoring in education at Kent State University in 1970.

Linda Fifer. Student at Kent State University from 1970 to 1975.

Rob Fox. Undergraduate student at Kent State University in 1970.

Joann (Peterangelo) Gavacs. Senior at Kent State University in 1970.

John Guidubaldi. Professor in the Counseling and Personnel Services Education Department at Kent State University in 1970.

Ken Hammond. Undergraduate student studying political science at Kent State University from 1967 to 1971, and one of the Kent 25.

David Hansford. Senior at Theodore Roosevelt High School (Kent, Ohio) in 1970.

William Derry Heasley. Vietnam veteran and an undergraduate student at Kent State University in 1970.

Rebecca V. Howe. Undergraduate student at Kent State University in 1970.

Peter Jedick. Undergraduate student at Kent State University from 1967 to 1971 and author of the 1998 book, *Hippies*.

Dean Kahler. Undergraduate student at Kent State University in 1970, paralyzed from the waist down after being shot on May 4.

Arthur Koushel. Undergraduate student at Kent State University in 1970.

Art (Arthur) Krummel. Member of the 145th Infantry, Ohio Army National Guard; on duty on the Kent State University campus in May 1970.

Jerry (Jerry Middleton) Lewis. Emeritus Professor of Sociology at Kent State University; faculty marshal on May 4, 1970.

Lisa Lynott. Student at Kent State University beginning in 1985 and a member of the May Fourth Task Force.

Ellen Mann. High school senior at the Kent State University School in 1970.

Carol Mirman. Senior majoring in fine arts at Kent State University in 1970, and one of the Kent 25.

Carl M. Moore. Director of Forensics and Assistant Professor of Speech at Kent State University in 1970.

Tim (Edmund Timothy) Moore. Undergraduate student at Kent State University in 1970, and later president of Black United Students (BUS); at the time of his interview, was Associate Dean of the College of Arts and Sciences at Kent State.

James Mueller. Student at the University of Akron during the 1960s and a resident of Akron in 1970.

Shirley Ohles. Wife of Kent State University professor of education John Ohles in 1970.

John Panagas. Professor in Speech and Hearing program in 1970.

John A. Peach. Chief of Police and Director of Public Safety at Kent State University at the time of his interview; native of Kent who had just started his career with the campus police force in the fall of 1970.

Murv (Murvin H.) Perry. Director of the Kent State University School of Journalism and Associate Dean of the College of Fine and Professional Arts in 1970.

Curtis Pittman. Undergraduate student at Kent State University in 1970 and member of Black United Students (BUS).

Rosann Rissland. Resident of Kent in 1970.

Michael Schwartz. President of Kent State University from 1982 to 1991.

Barry Seybert. Ninth-grade student in Cleveland Heights, Ohio, in 1970; later involved in Tent City and co-founder of May 4 Task Force.

Joseph M. Sima. Undergraduate student at Kent State University in 1970.

Ron (J. Ronald) Snyder. Captain and company commander of Company C of the 145th Infantry of the Ohio National Guard on May 4, 1970.

Nathan R. Sooy. Undergraduate student at Kent State University beginning in 1973; involved in Tent City protests in 1977.

Kathy Stafford. Undergraduate at Kent State University in 1970, involved in President's Commission on KSU Violence; retired in 2008 as Vice President for University Relations.

Ronald Sterlekar. Undergraduate student at Kent State University in 1970 and member of student organization the Mobobrious PIT.

James T. Vacarella. Undergraduate student at Kent State University in 1970.

Albert Van Kirk. Vietnam veteran and an undergraduate student at Kent State University in 1969–1970.

Winona Vannoy. Physical education instructor at Kent State University in 1970.

Janice Marie Gierman Waskco. Freshman at Kent State University in 1970.

William Wilen. PhD candidate studying at Pennsylvania State University and, in April 1970, had accepted a teaching position at Kent State University beginning in the fall.

Diane Yale-Peabody. Sophomore majoring in journalism at Kent State University in 1970.

Lowell S. Zurbuch. An instructor in the School of Technology at Kent State University in 1970.

Introduction
The Project

Craig S. Simpson

A nyone who believes the tragic events at Kent State University (KSU) on May 4, 1970, are no longer relevant needs only to have been where I was a few years ago to deduce otherwise. It was a beautiful spring day not unlike that infamous afternoon forty years earlier, and I was taking a lunchtime stroll along the southwest side of campus, where the Liquid Crystals Institute and the burned-out remnants of *Partially Buried Woodshed*—Robert Smithson's work of land art—commingle. Up ahead, an undergraduate tour guide was shepherding a herd of middle schoolers, and his boilerplate was drowned out by the kids' boisterous chant,

> If you go to this school, you'll get shot!
> If you go to this school, you'll get shot!
> If you go to this school, you'll get shot!

The guide, clearly rattled, tried explaining that the campus was safe, that the shootings had happened a long time ago, but to no avail. The four-decades-old deaths of four KSU students from gunshots fired by members of the Ohio National Guard have offered the most tragic kind of name recognition, the sort that eclipses all the university's fine citizens, programs, contributions, and communities. *If you go to this school, you'll get shot*: it's for what Kent State is known, and the story of the institution has been, in many ways, a struggle to come to terms with how this perception has shaped reality.

When I arrived in 2004 as Assistant Curator (eventually Special Collections Librarian, although my duties were the same), I had at most a rudimentary understanding of Kent State and even less concerning Jackson State, where two students had been killed only ten days after the tragic events at Kent. Having specialized in medieval history, I did know that campus violence was not a modern phenomenon. Crime was rampant at European universities in the Middle Ages. Riots broke out sporadically, as when students at the University of Paris in 1229 protested a strike by their instructors, shutting down the university for two years. Town vs. gown tensions festered and occasionally erupted into conflict: in 1355, townspeople attacked the University of Oxford with bows and arrows. In my coursework, I learned the difference between medieval revolts and the later European and American revolutions; strictly speaking, that the former tended to be spontaneous bursts of violence borne out of a sense of injustice, while the latter were governed by an underlying ideology.

This distinction may be obvious, but it has been one source of contention among many when attempting to describe what happened at Kent State. During my first year at KSU Special Collections and Archives, which climaxed with the thirty-fifth annual commemoration in May 2005, my colleague, Kathleen Siebert Medicus (Special Collections Cataloger), successfully petitioned the Library of Congress to change the subject heading "Kent State University—Riot, May 4, 1970" to "Kent State Shootings, Kent, Ohio, 1970." ("May 4," while a common regional term, was correctly considered by the Library of Congress to be less familiar on a national level.) Has the revision from "Riot" to "Shootings" signaled a change in the American cultural perspective—a shift in focus from those who initiated the protest to those who pulled the trigger? (The international perspective has always been overwhelmingly sympathetic toward the students.) Also in 2005, when I became head of the Kent State Shootings Oral History Project, it was soon apparent that opinions about what happened in 1970 varied drastically. There was a general demarcation between alumni and faculty who viewed the events as a crime, and citizens of the community who justified the actions of the National Guard.

Then, as now, Kent, Ohio, was a conservative Democratic town in a conservative Democratic county (Portage), with a student population that leaned toward liberal in a way that alumni who witnessed the events of 1970 see as vague and noncommittal. However, KSU students of the late 1960s and early 1970 were on the whole reluctant to embrace the counterculture compared to students at Berkeley; Columbia; Madison; or even Columbus, Ohio. While the majority of Kent State students in 1970 were against the Vietnam War, even more were against the immediate presence of the National Guard on campus. Out of a student population of twenty-one thousand, some two thousand protesters were actively involved in the events of May 4; others were curious onlookers. And the Guardsmen who fired their weapons did not discriminate between them.

Four Days in May

The shootings themselves, lasting all of thirteen seconds, have reverberated for more than four decades. In the lingering debate over historical memory, these shots have been regarded—depending on one's point of view—as the responsibility of either left-wing radicals or a right-wing government, as a symbol of younger- or older-generation malfeasance, as the end of the 1960s campus protest movement, or the beginning of a new protest movement entirely. To understand the historical memory of the Kent State shootings, it is essential to first become familiar with the events immediately preceding them (as well as the broader cultural time frame, which my coauthor will address). A basic chronology of these events is as follows:

- Friday, May 1, 1970: The day after President Nixon's announcement of the invasion of Cambodia by the United States, war protesters rallied on the Kent State campus, symbolically burying the Constitution. In the evening, riots spread across town, resulting in property damage for local Kent business establishments. The Kent mayor, Leroy Satrom, gave an initial estimate of $50,000 in damage; later estimates reduced this to $10,000.
- Saturday, May 2, 1970: That night, protesters set the campus ROTC building on fire. Hearing of these events, at 8:35 P.M. Mayor Satrom formally requested National Guard troops, who were already on duty in the region. They arrived on campus about 10:00 P.M., and using tear gas and bayonets, they cleared the campus of protesters.
- Sunday, May 3, 1970: Initial calm during the day was interrupted by an inflammatory speech by Governor James Rhodes (who was in the middle of a senatorial primary race), who claimed the protests were largely the work of traveling dissident groups that he likened to Nazi brownshirts, Communists, Ku Klux Klan nightriders, and vigilantes. Later that evening, a sizable crowd of students gathered on the Kent State Commons, and others staged a sit-in just off campus demanding an audience with Kent State president Robert White and Mayor Satrom. As the Guard dispersed the crowds, another hostile verbal and physical confrontation between protesters and Guardsmen occurred.

- Monday, May 4, 1970: Midterm week classes and exams were held in the morning. During the noon hour, more than two thousand protesters (and a few thousand more onlookers) gathered at the Commons on campus. Guardsmen fired tear gas canisters, fixed bayonets, and marched toward the crowd. After dispersing the demonstrators, the Guard went back up to the top of the hill that they had descended. Then, at the crest, near the sculpture known as the Pagoda, at 12:24 P.M., twenty-eight Guardsmen, mainly in Troop G, fired sixty-seven shots. Four students were killed: Allison Krause, Jeffrey Miller, Sandra Scheuer, and William Schroeder. Nine Kent students were wounded: Alan Canfora, John Cleary, Thomas Grace, Dean Kahler, Joseph Lewis, Donald Scott MacKenzie, James Russell, Robbie Stamps, and Douglas Wrentmore. Kahler was paralyzed from the waist down.

The Kent State Shootings Oral History Project

These events spawned some individually recorded oral history interviews soon after, but it wasn't until twenty years later that a formal project was developed by Sandra Perlman Halem, a citizen of the Kent community. The May 4 Oral History Project, as it was originally titled (for regional emphasis), collected sixty-nine interviews over a ten-year period, an overwhelming majority during the 1990, 1995, and 2000 commemorations on the Kent State campus. Nearly all were recorded on analog tape and have a spontaneous quality. Many begin with an introductory request (something along the lines of "Tell us your memories") and are largely narrator-driven accounts with a minimum of follow-up questions, the gathering of data being the primary objective. These accounts were all donated to the KSU's Special Collections and Archives. Those that were audible and had narrator-signed release forms were fully transcribed, given MARC (Machine-Readable Cataloging) records, and uploaded on the Special Collections website.

The Project lay dormant until the second phase began in 2005 under my management as Special Collections Librarian and continued until my departure from KSU in 2010. Approximately forty more interviews were collected during this five-year period. While some were recorded at major commemorations (namely the aforementioned thirty-fifth in 2005 and the fortieth in 2010), many were gathered individually throughout each year. This reflected the new goals of the Project, a series of objectives designed to build on the accomplishments of the previous phase:

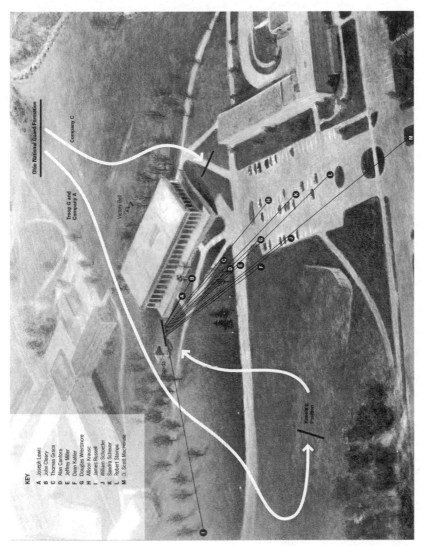

KEY

A Joseph Lewis
B John Cleary
C Thomas Grace
D Alan Canfora
E Jeffrey Miller
F Dean Kahler
G Douglas Wrentmore
H Allison Krause
I James Russell
J William Schroeder
K Sandra Scheuer
L Robert Stamps
M D. Scott MacKenzie

Ohio National Guard Formation

Troop G and Company A

Company C

Victory Bell

Pagoda

Kneeling Position

This map shows the movement of National Guard troops beginning at 12:05 P.M. on May 4, 1970. As they reached the Pagoda at approximately 12:24 P.M., one group that included members of Troop G turned and fired mainly toward students in the Prentice Hall parking lot. (May 4 Visitors Center, Kent State University)

- **A greater variety of narrators.** Because most of the interviews during phase one were conducted at the annual commemorations, most of the narrators were inevitably Kent State alumni and faculty. While it is important to emphasize the variation and nuance within these perspectives, certain elements among them remain fairly uniform. Breaking away (to an extent) from the commemoration cycle allowed for a wider range of subjects. Several citizens of the Kent community, two former KSU presidents, and a pair of retired members of the Ohio National Guard were among the narrators who contributed accounts in phase two.

- **A wider time frame.** It was decided that the Oral History Project should become a clearer reflection of the far-ranging causes and consequences of the May 4th affair. There developed a conscious effort to gather accounts from narrators who were involved in subsequent events in the 1970s, 1980s, 1990s, and 2000s: *Krause v. Rhodes* and other legal cases; the Gym Annex controversy, also known as Tent City, in which protesters demonstrated unsuccessfully against building an extension of the KSU gymnasium on part of the shooting site; the long, bitter debate over how to memorialize the shootings (if they should be memorialized at all); the debacle resulting from the Memorial Design competition and the ultimate recognition from the National Register of Historic Places; the recent controversy surrounding the Strubbe tape, a recording that some claim renders audible an order to fire; and the overall identity crisis that has faced Kent State University in the four decades since 1970.

- **A higher degree of professionalism.** Seeking a greater level of proficiency encompassed several goals, from enhanced interview techniques to more up-to-date audio technology, from developing better transcription practices to revising release forms. The project became more focused and methodical, while simultaneously opening up new avenues of research.

Common Denominators and Conflicting Interpretations

Many eyewitnesses to the shootings and the preceding events remember themselves more as bystanders than active participants, with middle-of-the-road political views, spurred to action less due to disapproval of the Vietnam War (of which most *did* disapprove) than outrage over the military occupation of their campus. Chuck Ayers, a student reporter for the *Daily Kent Stater* and *Akron Beacon Journal* who, on May 4, 1970, removed his sweater vest to reveal a Kent State T-shirt underneath, reflected that he did so as a "show of solidarity with the students and what they were going through." A more extreme case of activism was revealed by James Mueller, a University of Akron alum who, the day after the shootings, took a bus down to Columbus and tried to make a citizen's arrest of Governor Rhodes. There also are accounts from former KSU students who were in the parking lot when the Guard opened fire: one, Catherine Delattre, was pushed to safety by her boyfriend; another, Ellis Berns, tried unsuccessfully to take out of the line of fire his classmate, Sandra Scheuer, who was mortally wounded and died in his arms.

The two Guardsmen interviewed during the Project's second phase offered very diverse interpretations of the May 4 events. We each interviewed on separate occasions J. Ronald Snyder, a captain who led Company C on May 4, the group not involved in the shooting. In both interviews, he bristled at the suggestion that the Guard was unprepared for riot training. Another Guardsman, Art Krummel, stated in his interview that the Guardsmen had had very little riot training in terms of dealing with the kind of campus confrontation that Kent State presented. Additionally, Krummel discussed a haunting incident prior to the events on May 4 in which he had his finger on the trigger of his rifle. Guardsmen interviewed during the first phase of the project chose to remain anonymous.

Many narrators believe in a conspiracy of some sort, but few agree on what it was. Some believe that a circle of Guardsmen had made up their minds in advance to open fire in order to teach the students a lesson. Albert Van Kirk, a Vietnam veteran with right-wing leanings, who administered first aid to a few of the wounded, suggested that the radical organizations in town had an elaborate network that plotted a deliberate confrontation with the university administration, the town leaders, and the Guardsmen; he also implied that a bullet hole in the Pagoda sculpture shows a trajectory indicating that a sniper opened fire first. Yet another narrator, Eldon Fender, claimed to have observed one of the victims throwing stones at close range at the Guardsmen, although his memory of where the victim's body landed does not match the factual record.

It would be disingenuous for me to claim that the accounts in this book "speak for themselves." Our interview questions, responses, and editing choices all played a part in shaping the general narrative. At times we struggled in determining how much we *should* shape it: what proportion of this book should be our words, our opinions, and our interpretations compared to those of our narrators (and how to combine our individual views as coauthors—which are similar but not identical—into a unified whole). All the same, their collective memories are so vivid in detail, so thoughtful in recollection—each narrator both here and there, simultaneously in the present and the past—that there were more than a few occasions in cobbling together the succeeding chapters where the best course of action was to keep out of the way.

The events at Kent State still inspire strong emotions, to the point where opposing views frequently take the form of overheated editorials, each side arguing past each other. As authors, Greg and I struggled with an appropriate title to reflect what we hoped was a different approach to most works on the subject. ("May 4" was too regional a term; "Voices" too common among current oral history texts.) After several drafts we settled on the current one, which was the original. *Above the Shots* holds two related meanings, explicated here.

First, although certainly not without our own biases and beliefs, we as authors and historians have sought to stay above the din and present a multitude of perspectives, respecting (if not always agreeing with) the views of the narrators, and seeking to not only document our narrators' memories, but also to understand what they said, and how and why they choose to remember. Second, as a source, oral history holds a quality of being both in the present and the past. Narrators see the event as witnesses and participants. As such, narrators are both in the moment they describe and above it, looking back on the experience. Conflicting (and conflicted) as eyewitness accounts to the shootings are, one universally descriptive element they share about the May 4 confrontation is that it was *loud:* a cacophony of protesters, Guardsmen, and onlookers, followed by thirteen deafening, terrifying seconds of gunfire. By attempting to find clarity in the chaos, these narrative accounts rise above the shots—above the din—and help us, as contemporary readers, find clarity as well.

Finally, a word about the subtitle. It is *An Oral History of the Kent State Shootings: An,* not *The.* We have excerpted approximately 50 of the 121 interviews currently available online (with full audio recordings and complete transcripts) in the Kent State Shootings Oral History Project digital collection. While our choice of narrators formed a large and engaging ensemble and served a kaleidoscopic approach to the material, other voices not featured in the following pages deserve to be heard. Readers interested in more accounts (or contributing one of their own) are encouraged to explore the oral histories website of KSU Special Collections and Archives: http://www.library.kent.edu/special-collections-and-archives/kent-state-shootings-oral-histories-o. Understanding the Kent State shootings remains a work in progress, and there are many more stories that have been, can be, and should be told.

Introduction
The Memory

Gregory S. Wilson

Aftermath: A Contested Place in Collective Memory

The shootings at Kent State University on May 4, 1970, reached national and international fame as news media outlets quickly spread the story. It led to a nationwide student strike involving an estimated four million students that forced hundreds of colleges and universities to close. One of President Richard Nixon's closest advisors, H. R. Haldeman, suggested in a later book, *The Ends of Power* (1978), that the shootings helped bring about the Watergate affair that ended with Nixon's resignation in 1974 and prison terms for several Nixon aides, including Haldeman.[1] Since then, the shootings have become one of the most powerful symbols of the tumultuous years associated with the Vietnam War era. As wounded student turned historian Thomas Grace has written, the "rancorous student response" to the events "preserved the May 4 shootings in modern American memory."[2]

So, too, have the events in the aftermath of the shootings. In the wake of the events, the FBI, the Ohio State Police, and the U.S. President's Commission on Campus Unrest, informally called the Scranton Commission after its chair, former Pennsylvania governor William W. Scranton, began its own investigations. The Scranton Commission (which also investigated the killings at Jackson State College [now Jackson State University] that occurred on May 15) issued its findings in September, calling the Kent shootings "unnecessary, unwarranted and inexcusable."[3] Then, in October, a special state of Ohio grand jury meeting in Ravenna, the Portage County seat (Kent State's county), issued indictments against twenty-four then-current and some former students and one KSU faculty member (they became known as the Kent 25) on various charges coming from the events at Kent. No Guardsmen were indicted. In direct contradiction to the thrust of the Scranton Commission, the grand jury report echoed local popular opinion in Kent and placed the blame squarely on the demonstrators and the KSU administration, thereby exonerating the Guard.

Families of the dead students and the wounded filed lawsuits against the state of Ohio, but these were at first dismissed. Then, in 1973, the Justice Department, which had initially refused to empanel a federal grand jury after the Scranton Commission report, reopened its investigation, and as a result eight Guardsmen were brought to a criminal trial in 1974. Ten days into the trial, though, the judge, Frank Battisti, dismissed the case, effectively acquitting the Guardsmen. In 1975, after the Supreme Court of the United States reversed the lower court rulings to allow the parents of the slain students to sue state officials, the civil trials began against former governor James Rhodes, former KSU president Robert White, and twenty-seven Guardsmen. The suits were consolidated into one, *Krause v. Rhodes,* and in August the jury acquitted Rhodes and the Guardsmen. Courts granted an appeal in 1977, and a new trial began in December 1978. Following one day of testimony, the parties reached an out-of-court settlement in January 1979. After nearly a decade of legal battles, the plaintiffs received $675,000 (roughly $2 million in 2015 dollars) for injuries, with $350,000 going to Dean Kahler, who was paralyzed; $75,000 went to legal fees, and the remainder was divided among the other plaintiffs. This accompanied a statement from the defendants, which read in part, "In retrospect, the tragedy of May 4, 1970 should not have occurred."[4]

While the legal battles continued, tensions and confrontations erupted on the KSU campus. The university moved forward with plans to build an annex to the student gymnasium that would place the new structure on ground very close to where the students were wounded and killed. For activists, this amounted to desecration of sacred space. In May 1977, protesters pitched tents on the proposed site of the annex, creating Tent City in an effort to halt the plans. Sit-ins and other forms of civil disobedience continued through summer and fall, but construction commenced in September and was finished in 1979.

Still more controversy erupted over plans to build a memorial on campus to the dead and wounded. A set of battles began with an offer in 1977 by Cleveland's Mildred Andrews Foundation to commission a sculpture by noted artist George Segal; the university went ahead with the plan but ultimately rejected Segal's *Abraham and Isaac* bronze work as being too violent. In the early 1980s, members of KSU's May 4 Task Force, which had been created in the aftermath of the shootings and is itself an organization active in creating and preserving the history and memory of the events, approached then–KSU president Brage Golding about building a memorial on campus. The idea received support from the administration and Board of Trustees, and the university opened an official design competition in 1985. The committee chose a winner, the team of Michael G. Fahey and Ian Taberner, but Taberner, a Canadian, was disqualified because the funding came from the National Endowment for the Arts, whose rules dictated that only U.S. citizens could qualify. Fahey refused the prize, and the winning design then went to second-place finisher Bruno Ast. During the process, the university received letters condemning the idea of a memorial to the dead and wounded from the American Legion and the 37th Division of the Veterans Association, which represented Ohio veterans. Fund-raising for the design failed to reach high enough levels to help offset the initial price tag of $1.3 million. University officials requested that Ast present alternatives for a lower cost; in the end, Ast constructed a scaled-down version of his original design at a cost of around $100,000. It was dedicated on May 4, 1990.[5]

Recently, the shootings at Kent State returned to the national media spotlight. The year 2010 marked the fortieth anniversary, and that year iconic filmmaker Michael Moore broadcast the Kent State Truth Tribunal on his website, MichaelMoore.com. The Tribunal was a project consisting of a series of videotaped interviews of witnesses to the shootings conceived of and led by Laurel Krause, sister of Allison. Laurel sought a full investigation into the shootings, which she and her supporters call murder.[6] And Alan Canfora, who has dedicated much of his life to investigating the shootings, presented a tape recording that claimed to contain gunshots and an order to fire from a Guard commander prior to the National Guard barrage. The tape belonged to Terry Strubbe, who had placed a microphone attached to a tape recorder outside his dorm window near the shootings on May 4.[7]

Several events occurred in 2011 and 2012 to bring the shootings back into the popular discourse. In January 2011, a gunman opened fire at an event for Arizona representative Gabrielle Giffords. Thirteen were wounded, including Giffords, and six killed. Among the wounded was Randy Gardner, who was also a witness to the Kent shootings. His interview was added to the May 4 Collection as this book went to press. Later in 2011, a series of sit-ins spread across the nation following the lead of the Occupy Wall Street events in New York City. At one event on the University of California–Davis campus, a police officer used pepper spray on a group of demonstrators seated on the ground. During the media reports that followed this incident and other Occupy events, the shootings at Kent came up as a historical reference point for interactions between protesters and law enforcement.

In April 2012, the Department of Justice announced that it was declining to reopen the investigation of the Kent shootings after Representative Dennis Kucinich of Ohio (at the behest of Alan Canfora) made the request for a new analysis and investigation based on the 2010 finding of the copy of the Strubbe tape. The Department of Justice concluded that the sounds on the tape reported as gunfire could not be verified as such and the voice commands to fire were unintelligible. Kucinich then asked for a full report detailing the Justice Department's analysis.[8]

At the May 4 commemoration in 2013, organizers officially dedicated a new May 4 Visitors Center, located in Taylor Hall on campus and funded in part through the National Endowment for the Humanities. There are also new signs outside around the Commons and on Blanket Hill that describe and direct visitors through the events that led to the shootings. The dedication included speeches and forums involving Tom Hayden, Bill Ayers, and his wife Bernardine Dohrn, former members of Students for a Democratic Society (SDS) (and in the case of Ayers and Dohrn, the Weather Underground); a panel discussion by historians (one of whom was wounded student Tom Grace) moderated by news anchor Gwen Ifill; and a keynote speech by filmmaker Oliver Stone. After years of working to gain recognition, those committed to seeing the place as historically significant and worth remembering have achieved much. As a site listed in the National Register of Historic Places, with signs, a visitors center, a memorial sculpture by Bruno Ast, and the annual vigil and commemoration, the site of the shootings has been sanctified. In the words of geographer Kenneth E. Foote, this means it is a site that has been "publicly consecrated," incorporating a "ceremony that includes an explicit statement of the site's significance and an explanation of why the event should be remembered." The site of the shootings has been transformed into a monument.[9] This came despite early efforts by administrators at KSU to avoid memorializing the events and the opposition of some conservatives who found repugnant a memorial to students whom they considered to be radical, violent, and immoral.

But the seeming acceptance of the shootings as worthy of memorialization has not meant closure. The shootings remain embedded in the local and national memory, perhaps in part because there are still so many unanswered questions about the events and disagreements over what happened. Indeed, opinions on what happened in 1970 varied dramatically between many students, alumni, and faculty who at the time tended to view the events as a crime by the National Guard, and many citizens of the local community—and those Guardsmen willing to talk—who tended to justify the actions of the Guard. Debates remain over how and why these shootings and the events leading up to them and after should be remembered. As divided as the Kent community and the nation were at the time over the Vietnam War and the shootings, the contest over the meaning of the dead and wounded—and of the 1960s—endures.

The Interviews and Our Framework

One of the key contributions of our work is its dedicated and substantive use of oral history. Much has been written about Kent; specialists in journalism, sociology, communications, and history have all contributed their analyses and insights. The shootings at Kent have found their way into political cartoons, theater, film, and music. The effort to document the event began during May 1–4 as newspaper reporters, television crews, journalism students at Kent, and many others recorded the events. Immediately, the opinions and lines of demarcation formed over what happened, who was responsible, and how to deal with the aftermath. The key question that occupies most of these works (and one that continues to draw public interest) is, "Why did the Guard shoot?" They usually then proceed à la Perry Mason (or *Law & Order: Kent State Unit*) to put forward evidence to answer this question.

Our work is different in that, while we remain as interested in answering this question as anyone, we focus more on the memory of the events and how that memory is constructed individually and collectively. We also address the different meanings of the events for those involved and how those meanings are displayed through oral history and through the process of memorialization. The memory narratives of individuals and the process of memorialization reflect the ongoing collective and individual need to come to terms with the many salient issues exposed by the shootings. These issues include not only specific ones that address various aspects of the events during those four days in May (e.g., "Who set fire to the ROTC building?" "Why did KSU officials act as they did?") but also concerns laid bare in the 1960s, such as power and authority, cultural norms and expression, peace and violence, and war and political protest. The questions we asked of our narrators sought more clarity and detail about the events (or at least how each narrator remembers them) and to understand the conflicts and tensions that led to the shootings as part of a larger effort to understand the legacy and meaning of the 1960s more generally.

Our sources center around the oral histories conducted for the Kent State May 4 Collection at Kent State University done by Craig Simpson, Sandra

Perlman, and others. I conducted additional interviews to flesh out the story and to contribute to the collection at Kent:

- Mike Alewitz: student, eyewitness, activist, and leader of the Young Socialist Alliance at Kent.
- Rick Byrum: an eyewitness to the shootings whom I met while touring the May 4 Visitors Center.
- Joe Cullum: activist and eyewitness who gave aid to wounded student John Cleary.
- Ken Hammond: a follow-up to learn more about his background and his involvement in SDS and other activism.
- Dean Kahler: so far the only wounded student whose narrative will be housed in the KSU collection.
- Ron Snyder: a follow-up to Craig's interview to learn more about his background and views on the shootings as one of the very few Guardsmen willing to be interviewed.

I supplemented the oral histories with archival research, utilizing a variety of documents related to the shootings and their aftermath, the court cases, and the memorialization. Methodologically, we construct a narrative of the events that brings together theoretical and analytical approaches from studies of the 1960s, oral history, and memory. We tried to maintain a balance between letting the narrators speak and intervening with the authoritative voice. Mainly, we place the theory and context here in the beginning as a way to show our underlying conceptions, our methodology, and the frameworks within which we placed the oral histories. Throughout the text, we provide context and background where we felt it was needed and provide signposts back to some of the methodologies and historical interpretations we outline here.

Oral History and Narratives of Kent State and the 1960s

In the introduction to their edited collection, *Contested Pasts: The Politics of Memory* (2003), Katharine Hodgkin and Susannah Radstone assert that contests over meaning of the past are not over what actually happened but rather over "the question of who or what is entitled to speak for that past in the present."[10] However, as we show for the shootings at Kent State, the struggle is over *both* the events themselves (what actually happened) *and* their meaning. The events are yet at a moment in history when their basic truth has yet to be determined; the facts and the representation of those facts are both malleable. Their malleable state in the larger public culture is mirrored in the many continuing debates over the shootings, evidenced in the oral history testimony collected in the Kent State Archives and conducted separately for this book.

The four dead and nine wounded make the events of May 1970 significant, and they are the core of what locals call "May 4" or those outside the area call "Kent State." All the narrators are coming to terms with these dead, the manner of their death, and the wounded and the manner of their injuries. It is not simply that students were shot, but a matter of why they were shot and what the shooting, the wounding, and the dying signified then and what they mean now. Hence, the heart of the matter is contextualizing these dead and wounded, which emerges through oral history in the process of narration, recording, and analyzing. For in contextualizing, we are engaged in an effort to assign meaning to these deaths, to the series of events at Kent State, to the larger period of time we have come to call the sixties. We are also addressing power in society, as narrators and historians construct conversations about issues such as government policy, university policy, democracy, speech, behavior, and social mores.

Wounded student and now historian Tom Grace, who has maintained an active presence in the commemorations, has developed a useful framework for understanding the contested nature of the shootings. The battle over the memory of Kent State, he argues, has pitted "those who labored to highlight the political significance of May 4 against those who preferred to first enshrine it as a day for mourning and reflection and later neutralize its meaning." He goes on to note how those "who insisted on blaming the students also had a large stake in the memory war and sought to either deactivate the importance of the shootings or deny them political worth."[11] Indeed, the oral histories confirm this general pattern, as do other sources we cite for additional background. Memory in this case both follows and shapes the history.

These multiple and competing narratives regarding the shootings mirror those about the 1960s more generally. As David Steigerwald has written, for liberals and radicals, the decade was "a moment of great change abruptly ended by war and right-wing backlash." Conservatives see these years as "the beginning of a national crisis in authority and morality" that legitimized antisocial behavior.[12] This follows something Daniel Marcus pointed out in *Happy Days and Wonder Years* (2004). According to Marcus, in the recent past "various political figures, parties, and movements" have "relied upon representations of the country's cultural and political past to provide historically rooted justifications for their own present-day politics."[13] In this context, Americans gave a dichotomous meaning to the decades of the 1950s and the 1960s. In the conservative imagination, so well expressed during the presidency of Ronald Reagan, the 1950s serve as touchstone for their values; it was an era of "stable social relations, domestic prosperity, limited government, and American economic and military leadership." Conversely, the 1960s were an era of "social chaos, a turn against patriotism, and wasteful government spending." For those on the liberal-left, the opposite imaginary exists for each decade. The 1950s are seen as "socially constrictive, racist, and paranoid in the widespread embrace of McCarthyism." Activists and liberals defend the social movements of the 1960s "and many of the government programs of the Kennedy and Johnson administration as necessary and humane."[14] The oral histories remind us that the meaning of the shootings at Kent and the meaning of the sixties remain contested. Similarly, there is now greater consensus on campus regarding the memorialization of the events of May 4, yet whether they should be remembered and if so, how, remain questions for debate and disagreement among the narrators and among those active in the memorialization such as Laurel Krause and Alan Canfora. Within the town of Kent, the issue is still fraught with tension and controversy. National interest in the events during those four days in May remains high, too, signifying that the search for meaning, and perhaps justice and reconciliation, continues.

In addition to placing our work within the conversations regarding "what happened at Kent State" and a framework for understanding the meaning of the 1960s, we are also mindful of another set of conversations that involves the theory and practice of oral history and (sometimes separately, sometimes not) memory studies. Our contribution is to bring together scholarship and theories related to oral history and memory with the events at Kent State so that we may better understand the process of oral history and memory, as well as the significance of Kent at the time and since.

Oral history involves telling a narrative about oneself, about events and their meaning, and sometimes about both. These narratives are usually linear, but not always. In our interviews, we asked questions about life history: where narrators grew up, where they went to school, and why then ended up attending Kent in 1970. Besides looking for any patterns among those protesting, those in the Guard, and those residents of Kent, we were interested in examining our narrators' construction of self. In interviews done by others and other sources, we looked for that construction as well. We hoped to see how these narrators elicited a sense of self as defined by

Lynn Abrams in her work *Oral History Theory* (2010). Abrams, building on the work of Charlotte Linde, notes how oral history narratives emphasize the continuity of self through time, relate the self to others, and show the reflexivity of the self.[15] In seeing the self through time, our narrators either volunteered or were asked about their background, including where they grew up and their family history. It helped to build connections between the past and events of 1970 and the present. Knowing something of the narrator's life may shed light on how each came to be part of the events of May 1970 and the meaning each has derived from that experience.

Our narrators also showed a second sense of self in creating a unique identity through comparison with others who were there in May 1970 or with groups or individuals who have since become involved with or have written about those events. As Abrams notes, this style of remembering is often associated with men and with Western notions of time and the self; however, it is clear from our interviews that both women and men tend to set themselves apart in many ways. Finally, the narrators often maintained a reflexivity of the self, being able to talk and reflect about their past selves. They could often create a distinction between the current self as narrator of a story and the past self as participant in the story. They told not only their memory of the specific events but also reflected on their past selves as actors in events.

In crafting this sense of self through dialogue between the narrator and the interviewer, oral histories also reveal levels of subjectivity. Oral history shows how the self is presented to different people and groups at different times and how narrators use a range of available subject identities to do so.[16] Given this, we see the "the self as the outcome of a dialogic process as an individual's consciousness of subjectivity engages with existing discourses in society."[17] In our interviews, we aimed to reveal more than the telling of the events, but rather, something of each narrator, a piece of his or her story, that narrator's self. The interview is a process, conducted between the narrator and the interviewer, by which the narrator constructs an identity. Indeed, as Abrams notes, the "interview itself is a means by which" the "sense of self is constructed and reconstructed."[18] And in order to achieve this narrative, we adopted an "open, informal, semi-structured" style to encourage lengthy replies.[19] We asked questions related to life experiences but were willing to allow the narrator to move the narrative beyond the specific questions and topics that we prepared. To quote Alessandro Portelli, in answering our questions and constructing these narratives, it became quite clear that our sources told us "not just what people did but what they wanted to do, what they believed they were doing, and what they now think they did." In thinking about subjectivity, then, oral sources might tell us "less about *events* than about their *meaning*."[20] The meaning that comes from oral history combines this sense of self through narration and subjectivity.

Subjectivity leads into the notion of credibility. Again, as Portelli suggests, the "importance of oral testimony may lie not in its adherence to fact, but rather in its departure from it, as imagination, symbolism, and desire emerge." While statements may be factually incorrect, they may be "psychologically true," and this may be "equally as important as factually reliable accounts."[21] We endeavor to note those discrepancies but also to examine the importance of believing certain things occurred and the meaning derived from those beliefs. One brief example: some narrators who were involved in the May 4 demonstration insist that protesters pummeled Guardsmen with a barrage of rocks as the Guard ascended the hill and then turned to fire into the crowd; others dispute this. While, like so many events related to the shootings, the facts in this particular case are in dispute (although most accounts contend there were few rocks thrown and photographic evidence shows the closest group of students to be from about sixty to seventy-five yards away), the important point may be in the meaning of each narrative. One exonerates the Guard and the other holds the Guardsmen accountable for unwarranted use of force.

When dealing with memory and veracity, we emphasize how "memory is the site of struggle for competing meanings."[22] The interviews demonstrate the emotions, views, and perspectives of the respondents regarding the shootings. They also help us see how the memory of individuals translates to larger narratives. As Abrams notes, oral histories are "memory documents" that provide "a conduit to the meaning of an event to individuals, peoples, or entire nations."[23] According to Ron Grele, oral history interviews tell us "not just what happened but what people thought happened and how they have internalized and interpreted what happened."[24] Following Grele, if the oral histories dealing with the shootings at Kent are any guide, then the struggle over the meaning and legacy of the shootings and the 1960s more generally is a contest over what happened, what people thought happened, and how people and institutions have internalized and interpreted what happened.

Alongside narrative and subjectivity, these interviews demonstrate how, as a speech act for an audience, oral history is a performance. As such, we must pay attention to the storytelling or narrative act as well as the content of each interview. As a performance, it is "a social bonding exercise" that allows individuals to talk about themselves while also reaffirming identities within a community—family, friends, or nation. This identity constructed through storytelling can of course shift depending on the situation and the presence of others. Moreover, as a performance, oral history puts "private memory into public consciousness, thus creating new historical memory."[25] In our interviews, our narrators certainly reaffirmed their various identities, whether as wounded student or victim, as protester, as citizens of the nation or the city of Kent, as upholder of law and order, or perhaps as observer. Some had new information when we spoke to them or had never spoken publicly about the shootings; for others, it was clear they relied upon a set of stock responses, either from performance stories they had told before or through practiced ways of answering. In addition, we see another bridge between performance and oral history through the interviews in that these individual conversations are part of a larger set of performances that include the annual May 4 commemorative activities, the memorial on campus, and the new signs and visitor center. In other words, oral histories are part of a collective memory event, the meaning of which continues to be contested.

The oral histories also reveal how, for those wounded or sympathetic to the wounded, the question of empowerment is important. The reemergence in the United States of oral history within the academy came as a result of the social movements of the 1960s. Together, both oral history and the movements sought empowerment of those then marginalized from American society and from the narratives of American history researched, taught, and presented in the halls of academia, in schools, and in settings such as museums and historic sites. Power and empowerment served as the linchpins for the movements associated with the New Left, such as the civil rights and Black Power movements, the feminist movement, the antiwar movement, the student movement, the Native American movement, and the GLBT movement. The shootings themselves and the contested memory over them fit well within the themes so prevalent in oral history of power and empowerment. At root, oral history made clear "that the control of memory (and therefore history) is the subject of a power struggle between those who wish to claim the right to the 'truth' about the past and those who challenge that interpretation."[26] This clearly applies to the shootings at Kent. Our narrators were witnesses to (and in many cases participants in) the power struggles of the 1960s that included the shootings in May 1970; those struggles remain salient within each of our narrators and reflect that ongoing struggle to define the legacy of Kent and the Vietnam War era more generally.

Memory

Using oral history also allows for a richer methodology to analyze memory and its application to the events at Kent. Current studies on memory trace back to the work of sociologist Maurice Halbwachs, who coined the phrase *collective memory* in his pathbreaking work from the 1920s.[27] Halbwachs followed two theorists, Henri Bergson and Émile Durkheim. Rejecting the turn to objectivist and centralizing methodologies of history, Bergson argued instead that individual memory served as the key to seeing the variability of the individual experience of time. Building on this, Durkheim showed that different societies produce different concepts of time. Durkheim, in the words of Jeffrey Olick, connected "cognitive order (time perception) with social order (division of labor)" to show the sociological aspects to memory variability.[28]

Halbwachs (or perhaps those who followed Durkheim more directly) may have emphasized the collective memory over the individual by claiming that individuals cannot remember outside their group context; hence, the danger in this line of reasoning is to emphasize the collective over the individuals who compose it. But we are careful to understand that whatever collective memory of the shootings and of the 1960s exists, it does not operate independently through the media and other institutions. Astrid Eril and Ansgar Nünning remind us that just as social contexts "shape individual memories, a 'memory' which is represented by media and institutions must be actualized by individuals, by members of a community of remembrance."[29] We should also note that collective memory includes several memories or versions of the past operating simultaneously. And to further complicate this, these collective memories have been constructed from individual experiences, internal mnemonic operations that recall lived events, as well as public representations of the past, visible over time in cultural and political artifacts such as movies, television, advertisements, books, monuments, commemorations, and speeches.

Oral history is at the nexus of the two notions of memory as individual and collective, between history as lived and history as written. To capture the sense of memory as an interactive process at work on both the individual and collective scales, we use Geoffrey Cubitt's definition, which states that memory is "the means by which a conscious sense of the past, as something meaningfully connected to the present, is sustained and developed within human individuals and human cultures."[30] Following this, we are concerned both with the individual memories of those whose oral histories we use and collective memory together, or "the cultural history of remembering, a complex interweaving of personal memory with historical memory."[31] Collective memory (also called *cultural memory or social memory*) may be considered as "the interplay of present and past in socio-cultural contexts."[32] Going further, in his work on the events of Watergate and American memory, sociologist Michael Schudson defines collective memory as "the preservation of the past for current use in a variety of cultural forms and formulae."[33] Collective memory is located in institutions, through laws, records, and procedures, as well as practices "through which people in the present recognize a debt to the past" that includes items such as financial obligations (e.g., debt itself), "punishment, retribution, restitution, restoration, reform," and inheritance. Collective memory is located as well in more historical items such as monuments, markers, "books, holidays, statues," and souvenirs.[34] What Schudson notes about Watergate applies to Kent as well: since Watergate is in living memory, it makes it more actionable in the present; "the preservation of a memory of Watergate has in many respects been motivated by people deeply moved or hurt by Watergate who feel a commitment to one or another version of it that they want to see others accept."[35] That the events at Kent in May 1970 were violent and yet remain in living memory means the efforts to preserve a version of events are even more deeply felt by those involved. In telling about the events at Kent in May 1970, the narrators are revealing the ways the events remain in living memory, how they are yet actionable in the present, and how the process of preservation and interpretation of what happened in May 1970—whether by protesters and their families, the National Guard, administrators at Kent, or town residents—began at the time and has continued since. We are interested in what each individual remembers but also in how these individual memories become part of a larger set of collective memories about the events in 1970 and how these in turn become part of remembrance of the sixties and illustrate ongoing social, cultural, and political tensions in the United States.

In the oral histories and in the general contest over how or whether to memorialize the shootings, it is clear that many individuals preferred to forget the events—"just move on" was a common phrase used. At the institutional level, there was a struggle over whether or not Kent State should have some type of memorial or commemoration. This struggle and the debates over the narrative contained within the visitor's center and the making of the center itself remind us that the struggle over memory is not only about the shootings; it is also about the physical space and the geography of memorialization at work in Kent. Sites offer a horizontal conceptualization of memory, whereas the mental represents vertical. Memory is tied so firmly to place. Naming is a powerful tool as well, to insist upon a certain version of the past and thus present. Places also change. Sites of oppression, resistance, can become museums—to be what they are only because of what they were before.[36] Places can also be altered, transformed, and thus the meaning of the past changed or its memory destroyed. The oral histories confirm what other evidence has revealed, which is how the site, now sanctified, remains a contested and politically charged space. Layers of authority and meaning overlapped then and now still. One of the first efforts to sanctify the space came in 1971 with the first candlelight vigil. Begun by Professor Jerry Lewis, it started with a walk around campus on May 3, followed by an all-night vigil in the Prentice Hall parking lot where the four students were killed. The battles over the Gym Annex revealed further the concerns over remembering and forgetting, between space as sacred and space as utilitarian.

Rumor

Another issue with which we engage is rumor. As revealed in the oral history testimony housed at Kent State and in our own subsequent interviews, the collective need to make sense of these events—to comprehend, to cast blame—has led to the interpolating of rumor, allegation, and hearsay with facts among interview subjects. Reference to rumors continues to be part of the discourse surrounding the history of the shootings. Throughout we offer both an analysis of some of the major rumors and allegations that swirled around the events of May 1970 and continue to shape the history of the events, and we suggest how some of the research and theory on rumors might apply to the oral histories of the shootings and to oral history more generally.

Our working definition of rumor comes from Nicholas DiFonzo in *The Watercooler Effect* (2008), where he argues rumors are "unverified information statements that circulate about topics that people perceive as important; arise in situations of ambiguity, threat, or potential threat; and are used by people attempting to make sense or to manage risk."[37] Psychologists and sociologists have pioneered most of the scholarly work on rumors. The beginning reference point for most recent work on rumors is Gordon W. Allport and Leo Postman's *The Psychology of Rumor*. Appearing in 1947, their work grew out of the World War II era, during which thousands of rumors spread and had the potential to disrupt the Allied war effort. They argued for two basic conditions of rumors: "the theme of the story must be important to the speaker and listener; and the true facts must be shrouded in some kind of ambiguity."[38] Rumors thrive, they noted, "in absence of secure standards of evidence."[39] They also argued that the motivation to engage in rumors includes the needs to rationalize, protect, and justify a belief and relieve tensions over an issue, as well as the desire for closure and meaning surrounding events. Finally, individuals may pass along rumors to improve their social standing as possessors of information that others lack.

Allport and Postman also argued that within each individual mind, rumor was similar to personal testimony in that both follow a process from perception, to remembering, to reporting. Rumors, though, undergo the process numerous times as they are spread. Likewise, memory follows a similar trajectory; it is a constructive process. In this process of both memory and rumor, Allport and Postman argue that rather than expand, rumors, like memory, are sharpened, which they define as the "selective perception, retention, and reporting of a limited number of details from a larger context"; details are erased or altered. Rumors, like memory, are also leveled to become more concise and easily grasped, and they are both assimilated into the "personal and cultural contexts" of the listener and teller to make them more coherent and interesting, which may result in adjustments to details to suit the beliefs and views of the listener and teller.[40]

For our particular emphasis on the shootings at Kent, Allport and Postman also make an interesting claim about rumors and riots—"no riot ever occurs without rumors to incite, accompany, and intensify the violence."[41] Initially, these rumors of misdeeds, insults, and the like circulate and serve as a barometer of increasing social strain. Escalation occurs when rumors assume a threatening form about violence: some action that is to occur or is said to have occurred. Once violence is occurring, rumors fly faster than ever, often reflecting "acute fanaticism" or even becoming hallucinatory.

Scholars since Allport and Postman have sought to challenge and add to their initial arguments. For example, Tamotsu Shibutani, in *Improvised News* (1966), argued that rather than being simply an object, rumor "is not so much the dissemination of a designated message as the process of forming a definition of a situation."[42] A rumor is something constantly being constructed; the rumor ceases when the communicative activity ceases. As a collective activity, each participant makes a different contribution; for example, in a group there may be messengers, interpreters, skeptics, agitators, auditors, and decision makers. Yet as Shibutani focused more on the collective context, he did continue the emphasis upon rumors emerging in situations of ambiguity and said that rumors are ways to make sense of such situations.

Following these works, DiFonzo noted that rumor "is a fundamental phenomenon of social beings."[43] Humans are also "sensemaking beings" with the need to put our experiences into a perspective so that they can be understood.[44] Rumor then is "shared sensemaking," part of processing the fact that we live with degrees of uncertainty. DiFonzo states that rumors can provide a ready-made explanation to help cope with situations, and that they can also legitimate prejudiced feelings or views.[45]

Lastly, in their 2010 work, *The Global Grapevine*, Gary Fine and Bill Ellis note that spreading rumors "is a fundamentally political act with the power to alter social structures."[46] They note as well that the study of rumor "uncovers the concerns—some hidden, some explicit—of citizens." Moreover, "rumor purporting to be fact permits dangerous attitudes to enter conversation."[47]

So in what ways might these various theories of rumor apply to the case of Kent and more generally to oral history? Here we offer a few suggestions. Oral history begins on an individual level as a communication usually between two people. Hence, our approach is first an analysis of the worldview and cognitive processes of individuals; we are focused on the cognitive activities of our narrators as they attempt to make sense of the events at Kent. It is an effort to understand the internal process of memory and history as revealed through the oral history. Memory and rumor, as Allport and Postman suggested in the 1940s, might share similar trajectories and elements of processing, and hence studying rumors may suggest insights into the study of memory in oral history.

Further, if we accept the idea that rumors spread because individuals needed to explain ambiguous events, then this clearly applies to the shootings at Kent. Taking a look at oral histories of the townspeople, for example, we might apply this idea to their views as they processed the events—the ambiguity of exactly who was causing the trouble, where they were from, what they were doing on campus, and what they did and might do in town all fed into the sense of uncertainty and anxiety. For students who were protesting, they were processing the activities of the National Guard, the KSU administration, and the police, as well as political leaders such as Richard Nixon and Ohio governor James Rhodes. Their ambiguity about the reason for the Guard being there, the notion that orders may have been given by Nixon or Rhodes to shoot students, or why the ROTC building burned down contributed to the processing and disseminating of rumors.

Rumors as told through oral history can serve certain needs of the narrator. Perhaps the desire on the part of the narrator to achieve social standing with the interviewer plays a part; the narrator could see himself or herself as providing something that others may not possess. Narrators may also share in relating rumors to either defend a point of view or persuade the interviewer (and by extension the larger public that might hear the interview) about actions taken in the past. It may be that sharing the rumor allows the narrator to defend the image or actions of a group in which that narrator was a member or feels a part of (e.g., the National Guard, townspeople, or Students for a Democratic Society [SDS]).

Further, if rumors are a political act, as Fine and Ellis argue, then surely those being circulated at the time and maintained since in the history and memory of the events at Kent are that. Rumors of radicals storing guns, or poisoning the water, or of snipers, or the students who were shot having sexually transmitted diseases (STDs) or using drugs all can be seen as political statements about the New Left, the counterculture, or antiwar demonstrators and can be used as mechanisms to defend the actions of the Guard. On the other side, rumors about plans to shoot students emanating from Nixon, orders to fire being given, or government-sponsored agent provocateurs starting the riots or ROTC fire served to justify protests, to attack the government as oppressive or antidemocratic, or to condemn the Guard's actions as murder. The relaying of these rumors in the present through oral history serves, then, to defend and justify past actions to shape the memory of the events.

With these two introductions in mind, one on the project and one on the memory, our analysis begins with the setting for the shootings. Part One focuses upon the city of Kent, Kent State University, and the tensions that were building prior to May 1970. Like many universities in the United States after World War II, KSU grew tremendously both in terms of its physical footprint and the number of students. Such growth meant a closer and seemingly tense relationship between the largely white and conservative community and a university population growing in diversity and political outlook. Many narrators recall a quiet sense of conformity that came undone suddenly with the shootings. Yet as other narrators note, activism had been building for many years.

Part Two focuses on the days leading up to the shootings on May 4. As noted above, President Nixon's announcement on the night of April 30 of an invasion into Cambodia prompted a reawakening of the antiwar movement. At Kent, students gathered on May 1 to bury a copy of the Constitution and called for a rally on Monday, May 4. In the meantime, violence on May 2 and May 3, including the burning of the Army ROTC building, spread fear in Kent of further violence and radical revolution and led to the arrival of the National Guard, setting the stage for the confrontation to follow on Monday, May 4.

In Part Three, we examine the memory of the shootings. A mixture of emotions comes forward in the oral testimony among the students, Guardsmen, university leaders, city officials, and Kent residents. Fear, frivolity, anger, confusion, sorrow, and disbelief swirled through the scene as the noon rally went forward, the shots rang out, and students lay dead and dying. Intervention by faculty marshals, especially Glenn Frank, prevented what may have been another round of violent confrontation just after the shootings. As ambulances came to take away the wounded and the dead, our narrators remember those moments and reflect on the myriad of reasons given for the shootings, both then and since, some to defend the Guard, others to blame them. The contested memory of the events had already begun.

How the memory of the shootings and the immediate events before began to develop in the days, months, and years after May 4 is the focus for Part Four. We examine the investigations that came in the wake of the shootings, and how they—and their various conclusions—form part of individual and collective memory of May 4. Memory, along with history, became tools used by investigative bodies like the FBI, the Scranton Commission, and the area grand jury to argue for a certain narrative of the shootings; memory and history served those fighting in the courts during the 1970s as part of civil and criminal trials that ended with a statement of regret by the National Guard. The trials and reports failed to satisfy many participants in the May 4 shootings, but especially the wounded students, the families of those killed, and their supporters.

This lack of closure and the contested nature of the memory and meaning of the shootings characterize the struggles over memorialization of the shootings on the KSU campus. We examine those struggles in Part Five. Along with an outdoor memorial by Bruno Ast and other memorial objects, there is now a May 4 Visitors Center in the lower level of Taylor Hall, the building closest to the shootings, as well as a walking tour of the site around the Commons. As geographer Kenneth Foote observes, the site of violence is now "sanctified" on the landscape, and these memorials and the museum attempt to provide some positive meaning to the shootings. Yet like the memory of the 1960s, the oral history testimony shows that the meaning of May 4 retains its liminal state, floating among narratives both individual and collective, conservative and radical, not yet finding consensus.

PART ONE

"The largest unknown university in the world"

Kent State and the 1960s

Examining even briefly the *Daily Kent Stater* (*DKS*)—Kent State University's student newspaper now for nearly a hundred years—from 1960, it is difficult to imagine all that would come in the following decade. Eisenhower was still president and in many respects, 1960 seemed much like 1950. It was Kent State's semicentennial that year and—reflecting the general optimism in much of the nation—coverage of the festivities brimmed with self-assurance and hope. It was journalism professor William Taylor who directed the campus observance and for whom the future Taylor Hall would be named. The student editorial on the semicentennial celebration boasted that "successful progress in becoming a great, established institution of higher education seems almost inevitable."[1] In his history of Kent State written for the occasion, historian Phillip Shriver boasted that Kent State was "entering its second half-century, confident and unafraid."[2]

The political situation seemed fairly mainstream as well. In April, the student mock-Democratic convention nominated two-time former presidential candidate Adlai Stevenson and not John F. Kennedy. The student Republicans lined up behind Richard Nixon. Regular announcements in the *DKS* came of speakers and forums on the perils of Communism.[3] Glancing through issues of the *DKS* also reveals the gender divide quite readily. Kent State had a dean of men and a dean of women, and housemothers (officially called resident counselors) supervised the female dorms. The semicentennial celebrations included a campus day queen and her four attendants. Female students were called "coeds" and "girls," and they could still major in home economics. And the dean of women announced a new dress code that regulated when and where Bermuda shorts could be worn; skirts were

Aerial view of campus, 1969. The Commons and Taylor Hall are visible in the center of the photograph. Just to the left of Taylor Hall are Prentice Hall and the parking lot where four students were killed. By 1970, the university's footprint had expanded and enrollment reached some 21,000 students. (Kent State University Libraries. Special Collections and Archives.)

the standard for most areas. Men could wear Bermudas at their discretion, since there were no set regulations for them regarding attire.[4] The festivities ended in May with a campus day dance, music provided by orchestras led by Sammy Kaye and Billy May. The need for two bands came after a heated debate on campus between the "squares" who "wanted the more conservative strains" of the 1940s (as played by Kaye) and the "cools" who preferred the "frantic, way out sounds" of the 1950s as done by May.[5] Indeed, when it came to music, student writers could still marvel that "stereophonic" equipment and records were here to stay—whether one liked it or not.

As Kent State celebrated its past and looked to a bright future, the campus continued to grow to meet demand. In 1960, construction was nearly done on the Music and Speech Center, which would be the site of a major confrontation between students and police in 1969. That same year, construction began on two new dormitories—Lake and Olson Halls—near what would be Blanket Hill. Like many institutions of its kind, Kent had grown tremendously in the decade before as baby boomers made their way from high schools to colleges. The university began as a normal school (a college that trained teachers) in 1910 with a tent and 47 students; by 1960, it had some 7,500 students enrolled in a full range of graduate and undergraduate programs; the campus maintained twenty-one buildings and was in the midst of expanding to meet soaring demand. Indeed, by 1970, enrollment had reached some 21,000 and about 80 percent of the students came from Ohio.[6]

Expansion of the university, combined with suburbanization, led the town of Kent to grow as well, from 8,581 in 1940 to 17,836 in 1960 and 28,183 in 1970. The university increasingly shaped the city. By the mid-1960s, 21 percent of its paid labor force worked for KSU. In the process, Kent became the largest city in Portage County, which, given the modest size of Kent, indicates the rural, small-town profile of the area surrounding the city and the university. Many local residents and officials relished the "self-image of a non-industrial, semi-pastoral environment."[7] The city and Portage County remained fairly homogeneous: by 1969, 3.1 percent of Kent's population and 2.1 percent of the county's was African American.[8] The city's newspaper, the *Kent-Ravenna Record-Courier* reflected the values of its owner, Robert C. Dix, a staunchly anti-Communist conservative who also served as president of the Kent State Board of Trustees from 1963 to 1973.

Many narrators stress the sense of quiet conformity on campus and in the town. Kent State's image during the 1960s—a selling point in the eyes of the community—is that it was an unremarkable campus in an unremarkable town. Yet administrators worked to build its reputation for research. Outside the region, it is safe to say that the university remained like much of the Midwest for so many—flyover country, a bland place referred to as the heartland.

John Peach, who in the 1980s became KSU's chief of police and then director of public safety, began as an officer there in the 1960s. "It was a very quiet campus; it was somewhat conservative. When I say conservative, there wasn't anything to look at it being any different from a college or university anywhere."[9] David Hansford, who was a "townie"—a senior at Kent Roosevelt High School in 1970—agreed that "town involvement with the University was special events, sporting activities. It was a big school, but the city of Kent and Kent State, I think, in my opinion, got along pretty well. There was good rapport between the both of them."[10] John Guidubaldi, an undergraduate at Kent in the 1960s who returned to teach there in 1969 after earning his doctorate at Harvard in psychology, felt vastly more at ease on the former campus than the latter. "When I was here in the mid-sixties . . . it was a very peaceful place. Beautiful campus. A lot of good relationships with the town members; town-gown relations were great. . . . At Harvard, I was [a] witness to the Harvard demonstration, was in fact what I consider to be a victim of it, because they shut down the university when I was doing my dissertation."[11]

James Mueller was a University of Akron student in the 1960s and often visited Kent; he later became involved in the May 4 Task Force and often speaks at the annual commemoration.

> I remember actually sitting out there at Main and Lincoln on that bench one time with a friend and we were trying to collect our thoughts before we drove back to town being responsible drinkers, if you know what I mean. And I was saying . . . I had read somewhere that Kent was the largest unknown university in the world. I said here's this university with all these thousands of students and I said—this was maybe about 1964—other than people in northeastern Ohio, nobody even knows where it is because we didn't really have premier sporting teams. I think this was before the fashion school had come into its full blossom. So it just wasn't really that well-known a place.[12]

Even those who considered themselves activists remember feeling shocked that the protests and shootings occurred at a place like Kent. Here is Diane Yale-Peabody, interviewed in 1990:

> I'm a 1972 graduate with a Bachelor of Arts in Journalism. I was a sophomore at the time of the shootings. I can remember all through my years at Kent being very active and socially aware in politics. And I had gone to peace rallies and candlelight marches, and peace vigils at Catholic churches for a long time. I marched on October 15th in 1969 at the peace march here on campus. I went to Washington, D.C. in November 1969. And we always—I guess we thought we had to go away someplace to show our protest. We never thought Kent would be the center of something like this. So when it happened in May, we were just astounded.[13]

Ellis Berns was an eyewitness to the shootings. When asked about Kent's activism, he compared it to his experience with visiting friends who attended the University of Wisconsin, which had a long history of activism and became famous for large demonstrations in the 1960s.

> I had friends who used to go to Madison, Wisconsin. I had a friend at UW; I used to go up there on weekends. There were people protesting, it was very active. And compared to University of Wisconsin, Kent seemed like just small potatoes. It really wasn't the kind of activity—although you knew there was a bit of an undercurrent that was going on. But nothing like how it crescendoed out of control, but not expecting anything severe or anything that eventually happened on the May 4th weekend.[14]

The Scranton Commission and outside newspapers like the *New York Times* reinforced this image. "Compared with other American universities of its size," the Scranton Commission report noted, "Kent State had enjoyed relative tranquility prior to May 1970, and its student population had generally been conservative or apolitical."[15] A May 7, 1970, *New York Times* article by Douglas Kneeland, "Kent State in Flux but Still Attuned to Mid-America," captured this sense of quietude and normality disrupted suddenly by the shootings. In contrast to industrial cities like Cleveland and Youngstown, Kneeland described Kent as a "a small school, little noted, caught in the rip tide of the postwar baby boom." Its primary aim was "to provide an education for the sons and daughters of the blue-collar and white-collar middle class in this crowded, industrialized corner of northeast Ohio." Kneeland concurred with the people he interviewed, who all suggested that most Kent students—and by extension all students in Middle America—were apathetic or career-oriented and that only a small percentage could be considered activists.[16]

This sense of quiet conformity may serve several functions in memory. For many narrators and others writing about the shootings, it serves as a counter to explain the shock that came with the shootings in 1970. This trope emerged in news reports after the shootings as well, emphasizing the seeming incongruity between KSU's quiet anonymity with the sudden violence that thrust the university into the spotlight. In Guidubaldi's case, he may be using the peacefulness of the campus in his mind to reinforce his negative views of student demonstrations at Harvard and his later comments on the events of May 4, which emphasized that students themselves not only disrupted an otherwise orderly system, but through their own violent actions brought about the tragedy of May 4.

Often among conservatives, the narrative of the 1960s is that of a negative, disruptive period that compares unfavorably to the peace and stability of the previous decade. In this section of the interview, Guidubaldi is putting together his personal memory with a historical memory of the events, bringing forward into the public his internalized interpretation that reinforces a larger historical narrative about the 1960s.[17] For some, it may be they simply did not see the activism or pay attention to it, at least until the later 1960s. There does appear to be a dividing line in the memory of the 1960s between calm and chaos that falls around 1967–1968. So events and issues that many people associate with the 1960s in popular memory—tie-dye, psychedelic drugs, loud rock music, antiwar demonstrations, urban violence—derive mainly from events that occurred after approximately 1965. As Bernard von Bothmer notes, the years 1960–1963 are often the Good Sixties, associated with JFK, strong national defense, peaceful civil rights protests, and traditional social mores. The years afterward are the Bad Sixties, associated with LBJ and Nixon, urban unrest, escalation in Vietnam, and the counterculture.[18]

This perception of the city of Kent and KSU is in stark contrast to the image of northeast Ohio and the lower Great Lakes as a region filled with large urban areas of the industrial belt. The World War II era and immediate postwar decades witnessed the height of the region's prowess as the manufacturing hub for the nation and for the world. Its auto plants, steel mills, and tire factories churned out the materiel for fighting fascism and for the postwar world of mass consumption. With steady employment, the region's working-class parents could afford to send their children to college, and more and more did so. The students coming to Kent in the 1950s and mid-1960s were increasingly children of the working class, first-time college families, and overwhelmingly from the surrounding counties and their larger, urban centers, including Akron, Canton, Cleveland, Lorain, and Youngstown.

Many narrators crafted this sense of self and the student body at Kent in the Vietnam era. Rick Byrum, who witnessed the shootings, commented that Akron and Kent were—and remain—"working class schools," with "blue collar families that are sending their kids off to college." He added, "I am the only person in my family that's graduated from college."[19] Many of them, especially some of the activists, came from union households whose parents had been involved in labor activism. Joe Cullum was there protesting on May 4 and is featured in a *Life* magazine photo giving aid to wounded student John Cleary. Cullum grew up in Canton and attended Catholic schools. He came from a "working class family" and lived in "housing for a lot of the manufacturing workers that lived in Canton." He went on: "My father was a union supporter and had been for a long time. . . . My parents were both dyed-in-the-wool Democrats."[20]

Whether of activist backgrounds or not, these working-class students made up the bulk of the student body, but KSU's growth also meant more students were coming from out of state as well, particularly from the surrounding region. Although the main student population could be considered "white," that belied ethnic and class differences; there was also a growing number of African American students with about 400 in fall 1968 and 650 by spring quarter 1970. Of those in 1970, about 285 were from Cleveland or East Cleveland and another 30 from Akron.[21] And although the city of Kent remained fairly homogenous, it remained divided along its various social classes, between blue-collar and white-collar, whites and minorities of color, townies and students.

Memory Narratives: Activism and Quiet Conformity

Our narrators' memory of Kent and the university before 1970 is as divided as the memory of the shootings themselves. While some emphasize quiet conformity, others emphasize continuity between the confrontation on May 4, 1970, and earlier developments associated with student activism. They may still express shock, anger, and grief that students were killed, but they dispute the recollection of Kent as an apathetic campus that suddenly erupted in 1970.

In their view, tension between campus administrators, students, and the city of Kent had been building for some time, leading to a nascent activism on campus that has escaped most of the history of the shootings and of towns and universities outside of more prominent protest centers such as Berkeley, Wisconsin, or Columbia during the 1950s and 1960s. As Scott Bills has written, for KSU activists there exists a need to see "the four deaths as an integral part of a long and continuing struggle against militarism, imperialism, and the suppression of dissident rights at home."[22] The protests and the deaths were thus political in nature and tied directly into these activists' sense of their own political awakenings and their identity and the importance they gave to their involvement in various campus groups and causes (especially the antiwar movement), and for blacks, involvement in efforts to promote greater racial equality and recognition of African American history and culture. Even within a seemingly innocuous reflection on the atmosphere at Kent prior to 1970 are layers of meaning that reveal the struggle over control of the memory and significance of the deaths and the wounded.

A look through the 1960 *Daily Kent Stater* reveals origins of activism. The presence of ideas associated with the New Left were already present in the form of pressure over civil rights, questioning the presence of ROTC on campus, and the in loco parentis role of universities, as well as growing town-gown tensions between KSU and the city of Kent. In February 1960, readers learned that Michigan State had decided to end compulsory ROTC, which remained present on many campuses in the United States and would serve as an increasing point of tension as the Vietnam War escalated. In March 1960, Kent's mayor, Redmond Greer, requested a meeting with KSU officials to discuss the end-of-quarter celebrations—students partying at the end of the academic term—along Franklin and Erie Streets in downtown.[23] In April, the Student Council gave support to antisegregation sit-down protests in the South, which had started at the Woolworth's lunch counter in Greensboro, North Carolina, and spread to other cities.[24] Activists in the interracial campus group Kent Council on Human Affairs (KCHA) led sympathy picketing strikes against chain stores in downtown Kent. This continued into May and prompted a forum to investigate segregationist practices on campus and in Kent, organized by the KCHA.[25]

This set of protests continued into 1961, near the end of George Bowman's nineteen-year tenure as university president. Bowman, who had little tolerance for dissent and public protests, initially refused to address the issue and berated faculty and students for pressing it; finally, however, he relented and announced, with full public support from Kent State Board of Trustees president Robert Dix, that KSU would bar discrimination in university-approved commercial housing. Meanwhile, Jack Lewis, managing editor of the DKS, expressed his frustration that students were coddled, "directed and in many cases openly regimented." They were "persuaded against learning to think for themselves outside the classroom."[26] Such sentiments would become part of the outlook of the student movement of the New Left and presaged those found in the Port Huron Statement of 1962, the political manifesto adopted by SDS.

Activism continued to grow. Politicking for free speech commenced in 1963, and KSU granted students the right to form political organizations on campus. The response was immediate. In 1964, students formed what became the Kent Committee to End the War in Vietnam (KCEWV); that same year, the university recognized a student chapter of the NAACP and one for the Congress of Racial Equality (CORE). Dispute over CORE recognition grew heated; after the Student Council approved the group in a 19–18 vote, the council president resigned, claiming the group advocated violence and had Communist leanings.[27] Students in CORE would lead investigations into discrimination on campus and in the Kent area and stage protests. African

Kent State University president George Bowman with vice president Robert White, early 1960s. Bowman served Kent State as president from 1944 to 1963 and witnessed some of the earliest student protests. White, his successor, dealt with expanded unrest and the 1970 shootings during his presidency, from 1963 to 1971. (Kent State University Libraries. Special Collections and Archives.)

American students created a chapter of the Black United Students (BUS) in 1967, and white students created an active chapter of SDS in 1968. Several of the SDS students split off to become national leaders of the more radical, violence-oriented Weather Underground, known colloquially as the Weathermen.

Whether the topic was free speech, student rights, racism, or Vietnam, the university itself increasingly became a target. Kent State embodied the growth of what former University of California president Clark Kerr once called the "multiversity," a series of decentralized academic communities engaging in specialized research, having growing ties to industry and the military, and receiving government grants, all designed to promote the prestige and importance of the institution. In the context of the Cold War, large universities played an increasingly vital role in promoting U.S. interests abroad and in conducting research and publishing works that supported the nexus between government, industry, the military, and education. In 1965, Kent established the Liquid Crystals Institute with support from the Department of Defense (DoD). These crystals were used by the U.S. military to detect tanks and trucks of the North Vietnamese army along the Ho Chi Minh trail. After 1968, the DoD became Kent's largest federal benefactor.[28]

The individual who received the lion's share of credit for enhancing the university's national reputation—and, ultimately, ignominy for his handling of the events of 1970—was KSU president Robert White. A schoolteacher who became a professor of education, White's climb through Kent State's administrative ranks began as dean of the College of Education and subsequently became vice president of academic affairs; then he succeeded George Bowman as president of the school in 1963. Many remember him in positive terms. Murvin Perry, at the time director of the School of Journalism and associate dean of fine and professional arts, believed that White "was very fair to the students."[29] Joann (Peterangelo) Gavacs, a senior at Kent in May 1970, thought that White "was a very, very good man" and "anguished for him" in the wake of the shootings.[30] A resident of Kent, Rosann Rissland, recalled that her "mother had had him as an instructor, so she knew him and thought he was a wonderful man. He was a very nice person."[31]

For all his personal qualities, White's leadership abilities amid the rising protests have been roundly criticized as being largely absent. According to John Peach, White "had a difficult time being a very visible point person with all these things, relying heavily on his staff; and his staff had mixed emotions and different backgrounds. They had an 'us versus them' mentality, and that's always ripe for disaster."[32] Some scholars have noted that White centralized decision making into his office—which, Thomas Hensley wrote, "worked well enough, but in crises it placed the burden of decision making on White and left other administrators without direction."[33]

Some have been even more critical. One historian noted, "White cherished order and viewed liberal and radical students as juvenile delinquents,"[34] while viewing SDS and other liberal-left protest groups as dangerous. Testifying before the House Un-American Activities Committee in June 1969 (along with several other KSU administrators; campus and Kent city police; and senior Maggie Murvay, a reporter for the *DKS* and KSU radio), White called SDS an "enemy of democratic procedure" and "academic freedom."[35] Jerry Lewis, who was then a young faculty member in sociology and was an eyewitness to the shootings, remembers that the White administration was "not very good at responding to protest . . . was very formalistic, liked to work through committees, chains-of-commands and things like that, and certainly didn't have any flexibility."[36]

After 1965, the politics of the 1960s grew more intense, and the growing tension on campus erupted into regular confrontations and more visible activism against the war, against university rules and regulations, and against racism. Mixing with politics was the counterculture's enthusiasm for new music and mores associated with behavior, dress, language, hairstyles, and sex. Mike Alewitz, who was the leader of the Young Socialist Alliance (YSA) on campus, remembers an "array of political groups" at Kent that included the YSA, Communists, and SDS.[37] (Alewitz hoped to create a "red university" led by students and aligned with workers. A similar development had occurred in France in 1968.) Rick Byrum recalled that "whenever you walked across campus there was somebody with something; there was a rally going on for Black United Students or for the SDS." Peter Jedick, now an author and editor, recalls the shift.

> When I came in 1967, I met with Dean [Murvin] Perry, at Taylor Hall, which was the journalism school. This is where eventually the protests and the rallies were. While I was talking to him, he had a nice window over the Commons, and there was a protest going on. There were maybe ten people out there. And I was kind of stupid, because things were going on in California, I guess, and maybe New York, but we were in the middle of the country, we were always three or four years behind everybody else. I said, "What's going on out there?" He said, "Oh, they're a bunch of Communists, don't even pay attention to them." I hate to say this about Mr. Perry, because I don't know who he is, and I heard he was a great dean, but this was the attitude at the time. The

protests were just beginning against the war. Actually, we were just starting to get involved with war. It didn't really start getting big until maybe '68 and '69 when Johnson started throwing a lot more soldiers over there. So this was like a small, a little group of people protesting, and not even enough to even pay attention to when I first came here.[38]

Today, Ken Hammond is a professor of history at New Mexico State University. In 1970, he was twenty years old, married, majoring in political science, and active in the Kent student chapter of SDS. He attributes the evolution of his political consciousness to his years at Kent State and remembers it as a relatively common development among his peers.

Certainly, it felt like this was something that lots of people were just sort of waking up to, sort of getting caught up in, I suppose you could say. Especially by the Fall of '68, you'd go to meetings and there'd be sixty, eighty, a hundred, two hundred people. And everybody seemed to be going through very similar kinds of processes of figuring it out, of sort of an awakening or enlightening kind of experience that wow, this finally starts to make some sense, and it looks like there's ways that this could be—that the situations, the problems that we were seeing might be addressed.[39]

As activism increased amid areas of calm and cooperation, of student pranks, and the usual day-to-day activities, tensions between activists and the KSU administration and between town and gown grew in response. One of the most significant political organizations in this era was BUS, which had adopted the ideals of the Black Panther Party (BPP) and regularly admonished the university for its failure to acknowledge, provide instruction about, and hire African Americans. A more public confrontation that many narrators remember occurred in 1968, when members of BUS and SDS organized a protest against the appearance of recruiters on campus from the Oakland, California, police department. (Oakland was the headquarters of the Black Panther Party, and activists accused the city's police department of discriminatory practices in dealing with the BPP and black residents in general.) At the demonstration, some three hundred protesters blocked the recruiters from the Student Activities Center for five hours. When the sit-in ended, several dozen counterdemonstrators armed with motorcycle chains attacked many BUS and SDS members as they left the center. Campus police stood by and watched the attack.

In 1968, after the dispute with Kent's administration over the presence on campus of recruiters from the Oakland, California, police department, approximately 250 African American students led by Black United Students protested by leaving campus for several days. (Kent State University Libraries. Special Collections and Archives.)

At first, President White and Dean of Students Robert Matson announced that KSU would press charges against the SDS protesters. Around 250 black students led by BUS then staged a walkout in protest of the charges; after two days of exile in Akron, White rescinded the threat for fear of an investigation by the Ohio Civil Rights Commission, and the black students then returned to campus. This saved SDS for the moment, although White maintained surveillance on the group, which included faculty who attended meetings and rallies, undercover campus police, and *DKS* reporters like Murvay. The FBI was also tapping the phones of SDS and using undercover agents to report on activities. In response to demands of African American students, KSU moved forward in establishing an African American studies program and with plans to hire more persons of color as staff and faculty.

In reflecting on his involvement in forming BUS, Curtis Pittman noted that the issues which drove SDS and other groups to oppose the war in Vietnam and attend the rally were not the same as for black activists.

> I was Minister of Education. I was basically in charge of the African Liberation School. We had a food program for the kids in the Skeels-Ravenna area every Saturday. . . . The township of Skeels in Ravenna housed [black] people who had moved from the south up north to

work building weapons during World War II. And it was a shame for a town . . . to have hardly any electricity, hardly any running water, fifteen, twenty miles from a state university.

[Interviewer]: [Regarding the May 4 protest] you've stated that many of the members of the African American community on campus were told it would be better if they were not at the rally for their own safety. Was there a history of BUS being involved prior to that though in demonstrations on campus in any way related to Vietnam?

Basically just the BUS leadership [was involved], maybe Rudy Perry, Erwind Blount, Fargo—Ibrahim al-Kafiz [formerly Dwayne White] and myself indirectly. Because I had to cover myself being a scholarship athlete, and not be too much involved with the politics. At the same time, during the Vietnam War, a lot of minorities were volunteering. Even I had volunteered for the Marines prior to me coming to Kent State. The armed forces was a job opportunity for a lot of blacks between '66 and '70. . . . And at Kent State, we had our own personal concerns in terms of trying to get more black teachers onto the campus, the Black Studies program, and the Institute for African-American Affairs.[40]

Like Pittman, E. Timothy Moore was a Kent State undergraduate and a member of BUS. (At the time of the interview, he was associate dean at Kent State in the College of Arts and Sciences.) Moore saw BUS and SDS more as allies—"We supported SDS, SDS supported BUS"—while still emphasizing how racial issues affected the development of his own social consciousness.

First, having come from Cleveland and having witnessed the kinds of riots that were going on all across the country in the '67–'68 period as a result of the Civil Rights Movement from years earlier, that to my understanding evolved into what we would call the "black consciousness movement." At that point, [the slogan] "Black is Beautiful," and wearing afro hairdos, and wearing African garb was a phenomenon for all of us in Cleveland as well as when we came to Kent State. So there was a vitality in the newness of that whole new attitude about ourselves, appreciation of who we were. And then to come to Kent State and find that a Black Studies program had been created out of that same momentum was a phenomenal thing for me while I was pursuing my degrees in graphic design.

As BUS continued its critique of and activism against the administration, so too did SDS. The group received official sanction from the university in 1968. The group mirrored the national organization in its critique against KSU as a multiversity, especially the university's connections to the Cold War and the war in Vietnam and its general authoritarian structure and decision-making process. The Kent chapter also would mirror the national group in its internal divisions between militant members who demanded direct action tactics and those who advocated a mixture of radical education, patient organizing, and tactical actions that garnered broader support. Its major publication at Kent was the 1969 paper, "Who Rules Kent?" Written by Ken Hammond, who, as he wrote in 1974, then favored "educational work followed by action,"[41] the document aimed to expose "the relation between the ruling class and the university, in this case Kent State University."[42]

By January 1969, Kent had become much more politicized. Chuck Ayers, best known today as the illustrator for the *Crankshaft* comic strip, attended Kent and was there for the shootings. Citing Kent's reputation as a party school rather than a center for learning or activism—"The old joke, of course they use it for every school, but I used to hear it all the time: 'If you can't go to a real school, go to Kent'"—Ayers observed that the perception was not the reality.

> There was political activity around. The Kent Committee to End the War in Vietnam had been demonstrating for several years on campus. The spring before that, spring of '69, was the SDS thing at the Music and Speech Building. So I was sort of politically aware in those terms. I was attending some of those rallies and events. Nothing out of the ordinary. It was just a college campus.[43]

Many white narrators like Ayers cite the Music and Speech incident as a critical turning point in the poor rapport that followed between students, the town, and the administration. The incident came because of the SDS Spring Offensive. In April 1969, members of the Kent chapter organized a protest march to the administration building and presented a series of demands to the KSU Board of Trustees. These included abolition of ROTC on campus and an end to the university's connections to war-related research—in particular, the Liquid Crystals Institute—and an end to KSU cooperation with law enforcement. They also demanded to see President White. A scuffle ensued with KSU police. The next day, White and Matson announced their intention to arrest and suspend six SDS members in connection with the incident; the Kent administration also revoked the SDS charter.[44]

On April 16, disciplinary hearings were held in the Music and Speech Building for SDS member Colin Neiburger. Members of SDS and their supporters led a march to the building, demanding the hearings be open; counterdemonstrators met them when they arrived and fighting ensued. A group of over one hundred students that included members of SDS and sympathizers was able to enter the building and proceeded to occupy the third floor, where the hearing was taking place. Campus, city, county, and state police all converged on the scene; as a result, sixty students were charged with breaking and entering, and the same seven suspended earlier were charged with inciting a riot.[45]

The day after, student and faculty activists as well as some moderates and liberals formed the Concerned Citizens of the Kent State Community (CCC) to demand due process and protection of civil liberties for students on campus.[46] In the fall of 1969, four of the remaining SDS leaders who had not accepted plea deals were convicted and sentenced to six months in jail for assault and battery and inciting a riot. The combined blows of the arrests and suspensions led to the disintegration of SDS. To this day, claims differ as to whether students tried to take over the building or whether police locked them inside in order to arrest them. Nevertheless, the narrators who mention the occurrence agree that it was a major precursor to the May 4 events.

Carl Moore, director of forensics and assistant professor of speech, as well as chair of the local ACLU board, would go on to coauthor a report blasting the 1971 book by James Michener, *Kent State: What Happened and Why*.[47] In a 1973 interview, Moore stated that the KSU administrators handled the Music and Speech incident

> in every possible way as poorly as they possibly could. And I thought it was wrong in the way the University reacted after they trapped those people in the building and then summarily suspended them. It even went against their own policy. I thought that more than anything else led to the climate of discomfort that existed on this campus.[48]

Chuck Ayers concurred:

> It was a good learning experience in that I got to watch how the authorities treated protesters. I got to watch the arrests. And when the [Ohio] State Highway Patrol moved in—those guys are all about ten feet tall and shoulders about sixteen feet wide, and when they would come up to somebody and say, "You're under arrest," people would

just say, "Yes, sir," and go along with them. There really was no resistance, other than maybe a token resistance of just sitting there. I got
to watch some of that.[49]

For many students, these events on campus dovetailed with personal and
national ones to become the foundation for personal political transformation. As Catherine Delattre, an eyewitness to the shootings, recalled, "[I]
didn't have a very strong opinion about the war at that very point, except I
had lost friends in high school. . . . I never was really radical, but I did become
very much against the war after about the second year. . . . I became against
the war and changed myself."[50] For Timothy DeFrange, his own opposition
to the war stemmed from having a younger brother serving in Vietnam.

When I'd been going to school at Kent State, I was very, very upset about
the Vietnam War. During my years at Kent State, I spent a lot of energy
and time trying to learn more about it. The people who knew a lot about
Vietnam were the kids in SDS. Because they got the films and stuff
from off campus, and the stuff that they had was really, really excellent
material—film material that was not available, even on the networks. I'll
never forget going to those SDS showings of the different films.

My younger brother Mark, had joined up. Wanted to be in the Army,
right out of high school. I spent a lot of time talking to him, trying
to encourage him: "The Army's great, but stay away from Vietnam.
Whatever you do, avoid going to that zone, that combat zone." And
of course he started off in boot camp and did great, and was driving
ambulance and really enjoyed the excitement of it all. Finally ended
up agreeing to go to Vietnam as a tank commander.

He told me, "You know, Vietnam is a great short cut. I can get in
and out of the Army so fast, I get double the pay. It's just the greatest short cut in the world. I get double the pay because it will be in a
combat zone."

I said, "Mark, that's crazy. There's nothing more dangerous in the
whole world than for you to go to Vietnam. And there's no way you
can control what's going to happen to you."

He said, "Oh, now look, if you get any MIA, missing-in-action
notices, don't you believe 'em. I'll be holed up in the jungle, using my
survival techniques. I'm trained. I'm really ready for this."

He died after nineteen days there. He just never got to live, [never]
got through very much.[51]

Rather than an isolated event, the protests that led to the shootings in May 1970 were part of a longer history of dissent at Kent State. By 1969, large demonstrations like this one occurred both on campus and in the city of Kent, as seen here. (Kent State University Libraries. Special Collections and Archives.)

When the bulk of students returned to start the fall 1969 semester, they found Kent students and faculty sponsoring a local Moratorium Day on October 15 in line with national events in Washington, D.C., and on campuses across the nation. The Kent moratorium included various speakers, such as Mike Alewitz from the YSA and students from BUS and former members of SDS, as well as KSU provost Louis Harris, who called for a "fundamental reassessment of our national priorities," and a march of some 3,500 from campus through downtown Kent. The *DKS* report the next day noted some opposition from conservatives in town but also support and featured a photograph of Allison Krause collecting donations in a coffee can.[52]

Law and Order

The growing radicalism on campuses against the liberal center reflected one aspect of the polarized 1960s. Another was the growing popularity of conservatism, which, quite unexpectedly would become the most powerful political movement to emerge from the 1960s. The conservative movement, later dubbed the New Right, was driven by a small but growing core of libertarians and moral traditionalists and gained support from former Democrats and many average Americans all held together by a faith in fighting the Cold War abroad and concern about the breakdown of "law and order" at home. This was the conservative coalition that was "coalescing and preparing to become a dominant force in American society."[53] The battles at Kent outlined above and the shootings in May 1970 were part and parcel of this development and the polarized political experience of the 1960s.

In charting the shift toward conservatism, 1968 often marks a political turning point, bringing Republican Richard Nixon into the White House and witnessing the strong showing of former Alabama governor George Wallace in the presidential race. Both supported the war and railed against liberals along with various groups associated with the New Left. It opened with the Tet Offensive in January 1968. North Vietnamese forces launched a series of surprise attacks against targets in South Vietnam. News footage of the brutal battles in Hué, for example, and the fight inside the compound of the U.S. embassy in Saigon shocked the American public. The attacks were a military defeat for the North Vietnamese but a political victory for them

The history of the 1960s includes not only radical and liberal activism but also a resurgent conservative movement. At Kent State, conservatives organized their own demonstrations to counter those of groups like Students for a Democratic Society and to support the war in Vietnam, as seen here. (Kent State University Libraries. Special Collections and Archives.)

and the Vietcong guerillas operating inside South Vietnam. The American public had been led to believe the war was being won, but the attacks eroded support for Lyndon B. Johnson's presidency and added fuel to the antiwar movement. This prompted Minnesota senator Eugene McCarthy to challenge LBJ for the Democratic nomination; to the surprise of many, McCarthy came within seven percentage points of defeating the sitting president in the New Hampshire Democratic presidential primary, which then prompted a second challenge to Johnson from Robert Kennedy. Three weeks later, Johnson announced that he would not seek the nomination, opening the race up to McCarthy, Kennedy, and Vice President Hubert Humphrey, who entered once Johnson dropped out. To make things more complicated, former Alabama governor George Wallace ran as an independent. Violence plagued the spring and summer as Martin Luther King Jr. was assassinated in April, Kennedy was gunned down in June, and violent clashes occurred outside the Democratic convention in Chicago that August between police and demonstrators. Urban unrest swept most major cities as well.

It appeared that Nixon would have an easy time winning the election. But Humphrey made a strong showing as he distanced himself from LBJ and Vietnam by calling for both a halt to the bombing and peace negotiations. Wallace's support from midwestern and northeastern Democrats eroded somewhat, although he did take votes from Humphrey among the white working class. Wallace also took conservative votes from Nixon. Yet Humphrey's efforts were undermined when Nixon secretly contacted South Vietnamese president Thieu and promised him a better deal if the GOP took the White House. (Humphrey knew of this but did not disclose it.) As a consequence, the peace process stalled. Nixon won the popular vote by only 512,000 but earned 301 electoral votes, including those from Ohio.

With the exception of the landslide election of 1964, when Lyndon Johnson took Ohio on his way to capturing 486 electoral votes to Barry Goldwater's 52, Ohio went with the Republicans in each election from 1952 to 1972. Portage County shifted between liberals and conservatives in this era, no doubt reflecting the presence of the university, which pulled the mainly rural and conservative county toward the Democrats. Nixon took Portage County in 1960 over Kennedy. In 1968, Democrat Hubert Humphrey garnered 44.8 percent of the vote in Portage County, taking 16,348 votes. Nixon earned 15,064 votes and 41.3 percent of the vote. But George Wallace took 5,093 votes and 14 percent of the vote. With his platform in support of segregation and the war in Vietnam, along with his tirades against governmental "coddling" of hippies and rioters at the expense of working-class whites, Wallace appealed to Caucasians in the South and beyond. Wallace drew heavily from voters inclined to vote for Nixon; thus, without Wallace in the race, Nixon would have won more handily and likely would have taken Portage County. Two years after the shootings, Nixon, in his run for a second term, gained the majority in Portage County with 51.8 percent of the vote, on his way to taking Ohio and the presidency in a landslide. Yet the liberal George McGovern earned 46.2 percent of the vote in Portage County, a strong showing likely made possible by the expanded youth vote resulting from the Twenty-Sixth Amendment.

By the late 1960s, more and more voters were being attracted to the conservative message and seeing liberalism and student activism as wrong-headed at best and dangerous at worst. Conservative narrators involved with the Kent shootings have echoed these sentiments. For John Guidubaldi, there was a real fear that student activism threatened traditional authority and social order, as he experienced at Harvard when activists took over the administration building.

On April 9, somewhere between about thirty to seventy of the more militant members of SDS (not members of the Weathermen, a group formed in the summer of 1969) decided to take over Harvard's administration building, University Hall, forcibly removing deans and other administrators; the students even carried one dean outside. By nightfall there were somewhere between three hundred and five hundred students inside the building. The group had six demands that included ending ROTC on campus and Harvard's expansion into a predominantly black working-class neighborhood that called for demolishing homes. The administration called in local and state police, and officers moved into the building around 3 A.M. on April 10 to remove the students. In quick and violent fashion, police cleared the building; they pushed students out, hit many with billy clubs, and sprayed mace. Some one hundred students were arrested, and about forty were sent to local hospitals and campus health services; some suffered cerebral concussions, others fractured bones. The majority of students, who had been apolitical, now sided with SDS and went on strike for eleven days. Harvard did make several changes because of the demonstration and the strike, which included reducing the status of ROTC, instituting courses and programs in African American studies, adding students to university committees, and increasing Harvard's work with the lower-income communities in the area.[54]

Guidubaldi, like many traditionalists, recalls his anger at the activists. He also dismisses the violence used by the police in this case.

When they did that, the Cambridge police came in and told them to get out of the building or they would evict them. . . . And they refused to do so. They [had] published some sensitive ROTC [Reserve Officers' Training Corps] contracts and government defense contracts in the underground newspaper; they threw black paint on a number of the files; threw two deans down the steps, two deans that were fairly fragile physically; and a variety of other things that were clearly confrontation politics. The Cambridge police . . . hit some students on the back of the legs with billy clubs. That set up police brutality charges and the entire university shut down in sympathy with the quote-victim-unquote students who were hit on the back of the legs. And that's all that had taken place, but the university shut down. I, and a number of fellow students, were very upset with this behavior, and we were in the majority by far, but the majority did not rule in that situation again. So I did get the dissertation done and . . . I chose to come to Kent State at that time because of my memories of the peacefulness of this place. So the bucolic Midwest beckoned.

Nevertheless, Guidubaldi had not been at Kent State long before he started noticing similar changes.

I heard more and more feelings of empowerment in the student body, feelings of disillusionment about authority and the way the war was going in Vietnam and so on. But I sensed as a faculty member, too, a feeling and a spirit among the students that was a surprise to me. I was quite taken aback by the fact that at mid-year a number of our students were pressing us to allow them to determine their curriculum. I had never heard of such a thing. But it was part of the Zeitgeist of the time that there was kind of an inflated set of expectations and a grandiosity that I was unprepared to see in a student body in my first full-time professor job.[55]

As campus activism spread in Ohio, community and college leaders relied upon the National Guard to restore order. The Guard consisted mainly of middle- and upper-middle-class whites. Many of the men from the Ohio National Guard (ONG) on duty at Kent in May 1970 had long associations with the university and the town; some had been or were students there, others who were older had children who were students there.[56] According to one report, the First Battalion of the 145th Infantry was 98 percent white and included "factory workers, a pipefitter, a janitor, salesmen, telephone workers, advertising and P.R. men, a bank examiner, research chemists," and others of similar backgrounds. Many were working on degrees in their spare time.[57] As Tom Grace has written, "For those whom data is available, members of Troop G, 107th Armored Cavalry and Company A, 145th Infantry, along with a few men of the same infantry regiment's Company C, they were mostly residents of northeastern Ohio suburbs, small towns, or, in the case of the infantry company, rural areas. Those at the center of conflict on May 4 at Kent State were experienced guardsmen."[58]

Prior to May 4, 1970, Governor James A. Rhodes had summoned the ONG for two civil disturbances, five student disturbances, a prison riot at the Ohio Penitentiary, and a wildcat Teamsters' strike. The latter occurred on April 29, 1970, and involved some 3,200 Guard troops. The Guard's job was to keep the trucks moving from the terminals to the interstates. Two units called up for the strike would then be sent to Kent on May 2: the 107th Armored Cavalry and the 145th Infantry.[59] J. Ronald Snyder, captain and company commander in the Ohio National Guard, was on the Commons on May 4; he and his men were not involved in the shootings. Snyder, who had been in the Guard for almost fifteen years by this time, indicates the variety of men in his command and his own motivations for joining the Guard:

> Well, it was a couple of things. Number one, I come from a family who has a long history of military [service]. My dad had been in World War II. I had relatives that [were] in the Civil War. I had a Revolutionary War ancestor that was at Valley Forge and throughout the South in the Revolution. And everybody knew this; it was a patriotic kind of thing. In 1956 there wasn't much going on, as far as wars or things of that nature, and it just seemed like a logical thing to do. I could do it on a part-time basis and at the same time go on with my life.[60]

Snyder had acquired firsthand experience in dealing with racially charged riots in Cleveland in 1966 and 1968, followed by Akron in July 1968, in the predominantly African American Wooster-Hawkins neighborhood.

> The Akron riots [were] a racially-motivated riot. I was a Guard officer, and was a company commander actually. We went down and kind of took care of everything. Got the police supplemented with their duties. We took back the streets, so to speak. During that course of time, there was a lot of tear gas used. We were fired on by a group, at one time, from the area of the Akron Zoo while we were changing the guard. Just a lot of things. The usual riot stuff.[61]

For many leftists, the Guard symbolized the authoritarian system that had abused its power at home and led the nation into the unjust war in Vietnam. (About fifteen thousand National Guard troops ended up in Vietnam, most of them in 1968, and almost all were officers and went as volunteers.) Yet for many draft-eligible men, like Art Krummel, there were pressing reasons for enlisting in the Guard:

> I hadn't gone to college, had no plans at that time to go, so my mother called me one day at work and said, "A registered letter came for you, and you can pick it up at the post office. We didn't get it in time from the mailman." When she told me this, I called the National Guard and they told me there was one opening or two openings and there were four people about to interview for the openings. They told me I could come right down there and test and if I pass all of their reviews, they could swear me right in. So I said, "Great." I went down, did the tests, passed all of the requirements and was sworn in, and went back to the post office the next day and discovered to my surprise and chagrin it was a notice from my insurance company that I had money coming back from them because I just changed automobile insurance companies. So that thus explains why I was in the National Guard, otherwise I would have gone to Vietnam. And it also brings to the light the motive for many, many of the people in the National Guard as well as a lot of the kids in college.[62]

Krummel's and Snyder's varied reasons for joining the National Guard suggest that it was less of a monolithic entity than has been commonly assumed. Krummel's background and views, for example, are not dissimilar from those of many antiwar demonstrators. However, it is also important to recognize a degree of distancing: Snyder was older than the students he faced at Kent; he had made a career out of military service of some type. For all their individual differences, both men had been involved in the riots of Cleveland and Akron, and both would end up at Kent State in May 1970, where the forces of the long 1960s would come together in violent, tragic ways.

PART TWO

"An edge in the air"

Nixon's War Policy

Most memories of May 4, 1970, begin on May 1, with the protests and unrest of that day: "four days in May" has a rhythmic, easy-to-remember quality. For a few narrators, however, April 30 is where the story begins. For them, the story begins with Nixon.

Once in office in January 1969, Nixon was determined to get the United States out of Vietnam but equally committed to doing so without acknowledging an American defeat. He sought a peace deal that would allow the South Vietnamese to stand up against the North Vietnamese without the aid of U.S. soldiers. To convince the North Vietnamese to negotiate, Nixon devised what he called his Madman Theory, which entailed convincing the North Vietnamese that he would do anything—including using nuclear weapons—if the war dragged on without a peace settlement. Part of this strategy included a massive bombing campaign against North Vietnamese targets inside the neutral nation of Cambodia. The bombings that began in March 1969 remained a secret because Nixon feared the outcry if the public knew he was widening the war just as he was insisting to his domestic opponents that he was trying to end it. Despite the bombings, the North Vietnamese refused to change their position, which was that all U.S. forces needed to withdraw from South Vietnam and that a new coalition government be established there.

Rather than withdraw all troops immediately from South Vietnam, Nixon removed troops gradually while maintaining economic aid and sending military equipment. He dubbed his policy *Vietnamization,* a term coined by Nixon's secretary of defense, Melvin Laird. From a peak of 543,300 soldiers as he came into office, the number of troops in South Vietnam declined in Nixon's first year to 475,200. By December 1970, there were 334,000 troops remaining. The number fell rapidly after that, falling to 156,800 by the end of 1971 and 24,000 by December 1972. As troop numbers declined, so too did the U.S. casualty rate.

Nixon also revised but maintained the draft even as he orchestrated the withdrawal of troops. In doing this, Nixon tried to remove one of the most contentious political and moral issues associated with the war in Vietnam. Draft calls continued after World War II as part of the Cold War. Following the cease-fire in Korea in 1953, calls remained low until the war in Vietnam. Against the advice of military advisors, President Johnson chose not to call up reserves, which would have required congressional approval and debate as well as sending a clear political signal that he was expanding the war even further beyond the existing draft. Johnson tried to walk the tightrope between limiting public scrutiny and opposition to the war in Vietnam as he sought to maintain economic growth and support for his domestic policies related to the Great Society. Hence, the draft remained the only means to supply troops when Johnson escalated U.S. involvement after 1965. Between 1965 and 1969, local draft boards—made up largely of older, middle-class white men—called all men classified as 1-A between the ages of 18.5 to 25, oldest first. Various deferments were allowed, including those for certain occupations, medical conditions, religious reasons, or for men who were full-time students making satisfactory progress toward a college degree.

About 2.5 million men served in Vietnam, "representing about 10 percent of the males of the generation that reached age of eighteen during the war. The draft exempted more men than it inducted into the service. Those who went to Vietnam were, as a group, poorer and less educated than the average of young Americans at the time."[1] Blacks and Hispanics tended to be over-represented, partly because of draft inequities and partly because military service continued to be an avenue of economic and social advancement for minorities. The postwar baby boom meant that more and more young men faced the possibility of being drafted "as the war grew more deadly and more controversial."[2] Under Johnson, the Selective Service eliminated deferments for men in graduate and professional schools in 1967, drawing in more white college graduates. When Nixon came into office, he reduced draft calls and then in December 1969 introduced a lottery system based upon random selection by birthdates.

Here is how Chuck Ayers remembers the 1969 lottery announcement:

Actually, only a couple years ago, I finally put my draft card away. I carried it from the time I was eighteen until just a couple years ago, just because it was such an important thing at that time. It's like your social security card. It wasn't supposed to be for identification, but you couldn't go anywhere at that time if you were a male who was obviously over eighteen—that was your ID. You showed them your draft card. And I had a high number—mine was 263 or something like that. And the day after, on campus, the first few guys that you would run into, you'd say, "What was your number last night?" And somebody would say, "Oh, mine was 300-something." And somebody else would go, "3." And you knew he was drafted. These are the kinds of things that were leading up into that Spring.[3]

However, these revisions did not stop the antiwar movement, as Nixon had hoped. On October 15 came a nationwide moratorium on the war in which hundreds of thousands of people participated in rallies and marches across the nation, from college campuses to small towns and major cities. A second demonstration in mid-November became the largest antiwar demonstration in U.S. history as perhaps 500,000 people marched in Washington, D.C., while many smaller protests were held across the nation. In between these demonstrations, Nixon made a televised speech in which he asked for support from the "silent majority" of Americans. Nixon vowed not to let the antiwar "minority" impose its views on the majority by "mounting demonstrations in the street." He further declared that the nation would have "no future as a free society" if the vocal minority prevailed "over reason and the will of the majority." He warned that the enemy would win if Americans remained divided over the war. "Let us be united for peace. Let us also be united against defeat. Because let us understand: North Vietnam cannot defeat or humiliate the United States. Only Americans can do that."[4] The antiwar movement notwithstanding, polls indicated that most Americans approved of Nixon's handling of Vietnam at this point.[5] The following spring, in a special message to Congress on April 23, 1970, Nixon announced his support for ending the draft. Among other reasons, he saw this as a political move to undermine the antiwar movement. The draft ended in 1973.[6]

Thursday, April 30, 1970

The antiwar movement had grown considerably as the war in Vietnam escalated, and victory for the United States and South Vietnam seemed ever more remote. Nixon's Vietnam policies indicated to the public his commitment to reversing those of Lyndon Johnson and ending the war. However, as Nixon pursued his Vietnamization policy and tried to fend off his antiwar critics, events in Cambodia would again raise the stakes and precipitate the tragic events at Kent State.

Cambodia remained officially neutral, even though North Vietnam used the nation for staging attacks and incursions into South Vietnam; part of the Ho Chi Minh supply trail ran inside Cambodia just over the border with South Vietnam. As noted earlier, Nixon had ordered the secret bombing of Cambodia in March 1969—Operation Breakfast, which dropped some 540,000 tons of bombs and killed somewhere between 150,000 to 500,000 civilians. While Cambodia under Prime Minister Norodom Sihanouk had allowed the North Vietnamese and Viet Cong guerillas to operate there, Sihanouk grew increasingly alarmed by the Cambodian Communists, known as the Khmer Rouge, who threatened his own power. Sihanouk restored relations with the United States, but it was too late to satisfy those of his domestic opponents who wanted stronger action against the Communists. Under the leadership of pro-American general Lon Nol, a coup ousted Sihanouk in March 1970. Then, on April 30, without Lon Nol's knowledge, U.S. and South Vietnamese forces crossed into Cambodia to battle North Vietnamese and Viet Cong guerillas.

At Kent State, the evening of April 30 was a typical night on campus. The university was on a quarter schedule then, and midterm exams were coming up the following week. The midway point of an academic quarter is always a stressful time, and some students sought to relieve the tension. At a film festival that evening in the University Auditorium, somebody walked on stage and, without explanation, set down a portable black-and-white television. At 9 P.M. that night, President Nixon made the following announcement:

Good evening my fellow Americans.

Ten days ago, in my report to the Nation on Vietnam, I announced a decision to withdraw an additional 150,000 Americans from Vietnam over the next year. I said then that I was making that decision despite our concern over increased enemy activity in Laos, Cambodia, and in South Vietnam.

At that time, I warned that if I concluded that increased enemy activity in any of these areas endangered lives of Americans remaining in Vietnam, I would not hesitate to take strong and effective measures.

Despite that warning, North Vietnam has increased its military aggression in all these areas, and particularly in Cambodia.

After full consultation with the National Security Council, Ambassador Bunker, General Abrams, and my other advisors, I have concluded that the actions of the enemy in the last 10 days clearly endanger the lives of Americans who are in Vietnam now and would constitute an unacceptable risk to those who will be there after withdrawal of another 150,000.

To protect our men who are in Vietnam and to guarantee the continued success of our withdrawal and Vietnamization programs, I have concluded that the time has come for action.[7]

This "action," the president explained, involved a combined American–South Vietnamese operation against a North Vietnamese control center just above a place called the Parrot's Beak inside Cambodia. Emphasizing that this was not an invasion, Nixon continued, "We take this action not for the purpose of expanding the war into Cambodia but for the purpose of ending the war in Vietnam and winning the just peace we all desire." He also implicitly linked the aggression of the Viet Cong with the radicals in the United States. "My fellow Americans, we live in an age of anarchy, both abroad and at home. We see mindless attacks on all the great institutions which have been created by free civilizations in the last 500 years. Even here in the United States, great universities are being systematically destroyed." He added, "If, when the chips are down, the world's most powerful nation, the United States of America, acts like a pitiful, helpless giant, the forces of totalitarianism and anarchy will threaten free nations and free institutions throughout the world."[8]

If Nixon thought this would calm the antiwar mood, he was wrong. For Kent student Catherine Delattre, Nixon's speech conjured images of war.

My boyfriend had a very low number, and so we were constantly involved in that battle with friends or people who were not wanting to go who had low numbers and could be called up. He—my husband, he became my husband, he was my boyfriend at the time—had gone back to New York state for interviews with his draft board. That was kind of devastating news on Thursday night.[9]

Rob Fox concurred:

You gotta remember that one of the reasons Richard Nixon was elected president was the fact that he was going to end the war in Vietnam.

So from the students' standpoint, they saw this as an escalation of the war because we thought it was supposed to be wound down. People thought this was the peace candidate; he was going to broker peace with the Vietnamese, and that never happened.[10]

Chuck Ayers reported that after the film festival, he and his girlfriend walked from the University Auditorium to Taylor Hall (the offices of the *Daily Kent Stater*) and went past the ROTC building.

As we walked past the building, Karen and I both in midstep stopped and looked at each other. And I can remember saying, "You felt that too, huh?" And she said, "Yeah." And it was just this strange cold feeling that wasn't like a physical cold. . . . But we were right beside the building that within forty-eight hours would be burned.[11]

Friday, May 1, 1970

Nixon's announcement sparked a renewed series of disturbances and actions across the nation, including what would become the largest set of student protests the United States had witnessed. On May 1, students "firebombed ROTC buildings at Maryland, Michigan State, Washington, Wisconsin and Yale."[12] Other immediate actions were less violent, including the rally held at Kent State. As Ken Hammond recalled, there was renewed activism at Kent after a "rather depressing time" for members of SDS and others against the war.

The tide was clearly out that fall and winter of '69 to '70. So that when the invasion of Cambodia comes, when you get Nixon's announcement there on April 30, it really comes as a, you know, a slap upside the head. I think a lot of people were kind of holding back and keeping a low profile and then this was just like "in your face" and that's part of why people freaked out so much.[13]

Kent State history graduate students Steve Sharoff and Chris Plant awoke early that morning and began distributing flyers announcing a rally at noon that day at the Victory Bell located to the north below Taylor Hall on a large, grassy open space called the Commons. The Bell had historically been used to signal victories for the Kent football team, but now it was being used as

A group of about 500 attended the rally on May 1 during which students from the group World Historians Opposed to Racism and Exploitation (WHORE) ceremoniously buried a copy of the Constitution. Standing on the right near the speaker with his back to the camera is Ken Hammond. (May 4 Collection. Kent State University Libraries. Special Collections and Archives.)

a rallying point for protest. Friday was one of the first warm spring days that year, and under a bright blue sky, a group of history graduate students calling themselves WHORE (World Historians Opposed to Racism and Exploitation) ceremonially buried a copy of the Constitution in protest against Nixon's actions. The President's Commission *Report* noted that on a tree nearby hung a sign asking, "Why is the ROTC building still standing?" There were about five hundred people there, and the rally was peaceful. Those there called for another rally on Monday, May 4, at noon to decide on whether to join other universities in a national student strike.[14] Some, such as Rob Fox, did not give much significance to the action: "So I walked by there on my way to class, and there were maybe about 5[00]–600 students just milling around talking. . . . Somebody buried the Constitution at the corner of the Bell there. Some people talked about meeting later that evening, and really nothing happened."[15]

Chuck Ayers also had a sense of irony about the shootings having culminated from what had seemed to be a relatively innocuous event. Befitting his journalistic experience, Ayers went into more detail:

I was taking a photography class at the time as part of my require-
ments as a graphic design major, but I knew all the *Stater* people too.
I had been at the *[Akron] Beacon Journal* then for a couple of years. I
wasn't doing any kind of political cartooning, I was just a part-time
staff artist. But I was really learning what journalism was about, so I
thought this was a perfect time to take some pictures. A couple weeks
before, when Jerry Rubin had been on campus, I was kind of up front
taking photos—all for the class. So we sat right in front. I sat there
with a couple of the *Stater* and *Burr* photographers and watched the
event that went on that day, and I recall not thinking a whole lot of
it, because it was just one those gestures. It was pretty important to
the people that were really involved, but I thought, What kind of an
impact is this going to have on anybody?[16]

Ken Hammond believes that had SDS been functioning, the group may
have been able to organize and lead the protests that followed.

Then of course, I think that that contributes to the way that things
happened in May of '70, because we didn't have an effective organization that could step in and try to provide some leadership or some
guidance. When word went around, the night of April 30, the morning
of May 1, that there was going to be this rally at noon, nobody really
knew what to do with it. There was all this anger and all this outrage. I
got up at the end of that rally and said a few words. But we didn't have
a structure to crank out leaflets, or to call a meeting, or even reserve
a room for a meeting. We just didn't have organizational capacity in
place at that point.[17]

There was a separate rally organized by BUS that afternoon to hear black
students from Ohio State discuss the rallies that had been held there. The BUS
rally attracted about four hundred students and ended peacefully about 3:45
P.M.[18] With the rallies over, KSU president White made the fateful decision
that things were calm enough for him to take a planned trip to Iowa to attend
a meeting of the American College Testing Program and visit his sister-in-law.
    In contrast to the relative calm of the Friday rally was the violence in
downtown Kent that evening. In the memory narratives of the shootings,
the violence of the evening marks a key reference point for narrators, and
it became a pivotal event leading up to the shootings. For those who would
later support the actions of the National Guard, the violence on Friday, the

burning of the ROTC building on Saturday, and battles between students and National Guardsmen on Saturday and Sunday all served as evidence of the breakdown of law and order. For some, it was evidence that revolutionaries (likely led by SDS) were in Kent seeking social unrest and violence. Those who denounce the shootings, or see them as an unnecessary response, separate the events over the weekend from the shootings on Monday. The shootings, they believe, were not justified against students on Monday and certainly were not justified as a final response to a series of events in Kent and on the campus that began downtown on Friday night.

The center of much student activity in downtown Kent was North Water Street, where six popular bars were located. The bars regularly held concerts and served 3.2 beer, legal for those who were at least eighteen years old, which attracted crowds from all around the region. That night, the end of the week and warm weather combined to attract a large crowd to the bars. Carol Mirman captured some of the spirit of the evening:

> I was present on Friday night downtown when the disturbances oc-
> curred. I add this part because some people think that it was only
> just the Vietnam War that was the impetus. I believe that some of
> what happened on Friday night happened because it had really been
> a long, cold, dark winter and that weekend was the first weekend of
> real spring that year. Consequently, people were down in the bars,
> down on Water Street, and out on the streets and just in kind of one
> of those youthful hormonal party places. Lots of people were milling
> around, more and more people were gathering together. Somebody
> brought a barrel and started to put things in there and they lit a fire in
> the barrel. More and more people gathered and some started talking
> about the war and people were drinking and what I do remember is
> that people started to block off the street.
>
> It became a little scarier for me when the streets were blocked off
> and I remember distinctly an elderly couple in their car stopped in the
> traffic and they were surrounded by students. And students started to
> rock the car. And they [the couple] were scared. They would lock the
> doors, they rolled up the windows and I think people were just kind
> of feeling their oats basically.
>
> It went from there. Some people began to run down the streets and
> throw rocks and break windows. At that point I left. I wasn't in favor
> of the war. But I didn't see that the people that had the shoe store and
> the butchers had anything to do with being the cause of the war.[19]

As the disturbance grew, the Kent police force and other law enforcement personnel from surrounding communities came in to quell the disruptions. At about 12:30 A.M. Kent mayor Leroy Satrom declared a state of emergency, closing the bars, which increased the size of the crowd outside; then he declared a dusk-to-dawn curfew in Kent. Satrom also heard rumors from the police and others about members of SDS trying to take over part of Kent. He then telephoned the office of Governor Rhodes and spoke to John McElroy, the governor's assistant, asking for assistance. McElroy then contacted the National Guard office, which then sent a liaison officer, Lieutenant Charles J. Barnette, to Kent to assess the situation.

Not long after the call, as the President's Commission *Report* describes it, between 1:00 A.M. and 2:00 A.M. "a force comprised of 15 Kent city police and 15 Portage County deputies used tear gas" to clear the streets and push the crowd back to campus.[20] Meanwhile, another group of students had gathered on campus, and university police were there guarding campus buildings. This was unknown to the Kent police, who were angered by the lack of help from university officers. Once students reached campus, Kent police and deputies faced them at the main gate to the university. In the midst of the standoff, a freak traffic accident dispersed the crowd. A worker was standing on his truck repairing a traffic light when a car hit the truck and knocked the scaffolding out, leaving the worker hanging above the street by the light. The crowd then focused on the worker, and once a combination of students and police rescued him, the crowd drifted away.

John Carson was mayor of Kent from 1966 to 1969 and proprietor of Donaghy's drugstore in 1970: "I was driving in East Main Street, into the downtown area, and suddenly I was in the middle of a crowd. I was driving a brand new Buick convertible, and they were saying 'Kill the mayor'; and I'm thinking, I hope they know who the mayor is." Carson continued,

> And I wasn't sure who these guys with the shotguns were, because the sheriff came out of uniform. And it was a hot summer night, and you know, some of them have got t-shirts on with their guts hanging out from the bars where they were picked up. And they were pushing the crowd back towards the campus. The crowd got unruly by this point. They were throwing a lot of stones and things, and there were some breakage. But the drugstore I owned had 125 feet of glass—and as they pushed the crowd back up East Main Street and past my drugstore no students threw stones at my building.[21]

Ron Sterlekar, an undergraduate at the time who was in the Mobobrious PIT fraternity, explained his group's role in the riots. The PIT was a non-political student organization that specialized in elaborate practical jokes: staged assassinations in front of the library, for example, or running fake candidates for KSU student offices:

> Yeah, unfortunately, we actually had a part of this. And it was for fun. We had this guy who was a writer for the *Stater* named T. P. Waterhouse, and we were running him for president. We always had a massive parade, police escort and everything the weekend before the election to go through the campus and by all the dormitories. So we had this year T. P. Waterhouse with all these choppers. But we needed more, we needed a hundred, so we invited in two motorcycle groups, one from Youngstown, one from Akron.
>
> Well, on Friday night, May 1st, we were going from bar to bar, and everybody knew T. P. He had this costume on, dressed like Captain America, with a cape. And we had motorcycle colors on and we were going from bar to bar, because we were getting free beer. And the crowd would cheer, "T. P. Waterhouse for President!" All of a sudden the bar got shut down at midnight, and they said, "Everyone out." We went out into the street and what we saw immediately were two of the motorcycle gangs that we had called in that were beating on each other. At that time, there was a bonfire in the middle of downtown Kent, and they were breaking windows too, so there was a lot of confusion there. But even James A. Michener, in his book that came out later—and he spoke at my graduation—said that everybody was wondering why the two motorcycle groups were in town. That was because of us. So, it was just a coincidence at the time. This was a fun thing, but it turned into this.[22]

Rumors: May 1

"There was a tension in almost everything that people did at that time,"[23] Chuck Ayers observed. And along with tension, narrators also reveal how the violence that occurred on May 1 in downtown fueled rumors that formed a key part of the events then and continue to be part of the history and memory of the shootings. As revealed in the oral history testimony housed at Kent State and in our own subsequent interviews, the collective need to make sense of these events—to comprehend, to cast blame—has led to the interpolating of rumor, allegation, and hearsay with facts among the narrators' accounts.

As we noted in our introduction, key observations from the work of several scholars of rumors apply to the events at Kent. Rumors thrived during those four days in May as the situation remained ambiguous, when real and perceived threats spread in town and on campus, and then after the shootings occurred. Participants and observers may have heard, spread, and believed various rumors as ways to rationalize, protect, and justify certain beliefs and to relieve tensions over the protests, property damage, and the shootings. During the time of the shootings and the events preceding them, Kent residents, police, Guardsmen, and students all heard, believed, and spread rumors to cope with the threatening situation and to deal with events for which obtaining accurate information was often difficult at best. Rumors also reflected the perceptions and political beliefs of narrators and of other historical actors who used these statements or heard them and acted upon them. Beginning with May 1, rumors played a key role in how various individuals acted and reacted to the events that unfolded. In the occurrences that followed and in the memory narratives constructed in the days and years since, rumors remained central. Oral history opens up the possibility of understanding the cognitive activities of narrators as they attempt to make sense of the events at Kent, to see the internal process of memory and history as revealed through the oral history.

This anonymous interview with a female town resident, whose father was in Kent law enforcement, applies to several issues discussed above. For this resident, the outcome of the shootings started with the violence on Friday, May 1. In this segment, the narrator reveals many rumors that circulated regarding the actions of student radicals, including how the FBI operated, giving a rich sense of the fear and uncertainty and an indication of how police and many Kent residents regarded students and the events of that evening.

My father, having been involved in law enforcement for so many years, talked frequently about his work. And the May 4 incident of course all started, that whole episode started, on a Friday night with rioting in the downtown area. Now interestingly enough my father told me that a year to two years before violence broke out on the campus in the downtown area, that the FBI had come into the city of Kent, met with the Kent Police Department and the University Police Department to inform them that there was a groundswell of radical activity going on. And they knew that some of the universities would be targeted. They weren't sure which ones, but Kent State was a strong possibility because of the size of it. It was just very vulnerable. They couldn't tell them in what form, when it would happen, but this was just simply a pre-warning that it was a potential, potential happening.

About a week before the Friday incident, the Kent police were beginning to, and I think the University police were beginning to re-alize that something was coming down as more and more merchants called the police department to report that there were vans of what they referred to as seedy-looking characters, psychedelic paintings on vans coming in from out of state. And this was continually reported primarily by the downtown business people that knew the townspeople and knew who the students were for the most part and that this was just an unusual group of people that were coming in. And of course Friday night then things started happening in downtown Kent. Fire-works were set off that made people in the bars think that there was shooting going on and they were spilling into the streets. There were fires set. Windows broken out. Police cruisers assaulted. One elderly couple who people rocked their car and scared them to death. And it was just really a bad scene. They finally called my father out who was not on duty that night.

They finally called out all the men and to try to get the students back to the KSU campus. The one thing that didn't happen that night that should have is they tried to get ahold of the Kent State University police for some assistance, and they were nowhere to be found. It was later found out that they were holed up out at the KSU stadium in buses. The gentleman in charge of the Kent State University police at that time was dismissed not long after that whole situation. But the bottom line was we had fifteen, sixteen men trying to control in fact crowds of hundreds if not a thousand students who had been drink-ing, who were—it was just kind of like mob psychology and they were irrational about many things. And many of them were just very vul-nerable to some of the outside element that had come into Kent who were working, or you know, working within the crowds, and egging people on. And many of the students in their naïveté really did not realize what they were being sucked into. Eventually they got them back on campus.[24]

The argument that outsiders and radicals were leading otherwise apoliti-cal students toward rebellion and generally causing trouble remains strong in the memory of many narrators. While characterizing the shootings as a tragedy, this memory narrative often puts responsibility for the shootings on students. Winona Vannoy, a physical education instructor at Kent State in 1970, was among those who saw things that way. Here, she paraphrases a line Jerry Rubin, the leader of the Youth International Party or Yippies, often used at speeches, where he urged students to "kill their parents" and claims that Kent faculty told students to do the same. Of course, it is not impossible that some instructors may have uttered this. But her use of the quote came in the context of her describing and conflating several activists, including Rubin, who was part of the Chicago Seven, the group charged and put on trial in 1969–1970 for inciting a riot as a result of the violent confrontations in Chicago outside the Democratic National Convention in August 1968, and the Weathermen, a separate group of which Rubin was not a member. Rubin visited Kent State on April 10, 1970, and spoke there. Vannoy says

> students that I had in classes were very cooperative and eager to learn, but expressed fear of what was happening on campus. A few shared their anxieties about things that were being stated in some other classes—one told me that her professor told the class, "If you aren't willing to kill your mother and father to gain power and take over the government, you aren't strong enough to further your cause." From shared remarks like this, I believe that we did have a few professors or instructors that were instrumental in the tragic events of May 4th, 1970. But I also believe there were many leaders such as Jerry Rubin and members of the Weathermen, Chicago Seven, and various radical groups that were traveling from campus to campus at that time. We also had many teenage runaways, such as the girl that posed for a *Life* magazine cover, depicting herself as a Kent State University student.[25]

Vannoy's suggestion that fourteen-year-old runaway Mary Ann Vec-chio "posed" over the dead body of Jeffrey Miller for John Filo's Pulitzer Prize–winning photograph indicates, from the conservative perspective, a level of radical-orchestrated conspiracy and machination unlikely in its orchestration. Yet the remark echoes similar observations by narrators that the radical element in town and on campus was aided and abetted by the media to attain a degree of power and influence that they didn't really have.

Nevertheless, the fear was substantial enough to involve the State Patrol and the FBI before and after Rubin's visit, as recounted by John Peach.[26] The records from both groups at KSU Special Collections and Archives reveal covert surveillance and undercover infiltration of suspected radical individuals and organizations at KSU similar to nationwide methods from law-enforcement agencies at the time.

"The turmoil in the evenings was pretty unsettling . . . because there were lots of rumors of bombs and fires and all kinds of activities going on, half of which never happened or were just untrue," said David Hansford, who was a senior at Kent's Roosevelt High School in 1970. (His mother, Nancy Hansford, would become the first female mayor of Kent in 1982 and also headed the Portage County Republican Party. Nancy's father, Redmond Greer, was mayor from 1960 to 1963.[27]) "The fires in the street, that was true. But, there seemed to be a change in the feel of what was going on. There was an edge in the air. It started on May 1st and all through that entire process."[28]

Saturday, May 2: The Burning of the ROTC Building

The cleanup of downtown began on Saturday morning, and some students helped business owners and other Kent residents with the task. Despite this, the mood remained tense. Business owners reported getting threatening telephone messages telling them to post antiwar signs in their store windows or face the consequences (i.e., damage to their business establishments). All day calls came into city hall from residents about various rumors and plots. The police were dispatched to guard the city's water supply after receiving word that radicals from SDS and the Weathermen were going to dump LSD into it. Indeed, Satrom and Kent city police insisted SDS and its more radical offshoot, the Weathermen, were responsible for the violence on Friday night. However, Kent State police chief Donald Schwartzmiller later commented that he had no information about Weathermen being on campus. As summarized by the *Akron Beacon Journal* report at the time, "Weatherman [sic], the most militant wing of the SDS, seems to have become a kind of policeman's shorthand for anyone who is bearded, surly and inclined toward violence."[29]

City and university officials set about making plans to quell any future violence that weekend. Mayor Satrom began a daylong series of meetings and strategy sessions by securing additional sheriff's deputies and formalizing his curfew for the city, which lasted from 8:00 P.M. to 6:00 A.M. A later meeting with university leaders set a separate curfew on campus for 1:00 A.M.

These leaders included Robert E. Matson, vice president for student affairs; Chester A. Williams, director of safety and public services; and Richard Dunn, vice president for financial affairs. KSU president White remained in Iowa. Ohio National Guard liaison officer Lieutenant Barnette told the trio that should they or the city call for the National Guard, the troops would make no distinction between city and campus. Just after 5:00 P.M. Satrom learned that sheriff's deputies would not be available. It was then that he made a request to the governor that the Guard be sent to Kent.

At 5:35 P.M., the Ohio adjutant general, Major General Sylvester T. Del Corso, told Satrom that troops would be available that evening. Then he and the assistant adjutant general, Brigadier General Robert H. Canterbury, drove from Columbus to Kent. Del Corso left instructions that troops in the Akron area would be used but that they were not be sent to Kent until he and General Canterbury arrived. Guard troops were to assemble at Wall Elementary School on Kent's west side.

Despite Lieutenant Barnette's earlier warning, university leaders believed that the troops would only be used in Kent and not on campus. With the city curfew in effect, university leaders made plans to offer special entertainment for students that evening. They also issued an injunction against student Michael Weekly and five hundred unknown students (literally John Does) barring them from further damage to campus property. At 2 A.M. on Saturday, in the midst of the disturbances that began Friday night, Weekly broke a window in the ROTC building, for which he was arrested, tried, and sentenced to thirty days in jail. The injunction did not ban campus rallies.[30] University officials also sent faculty marshals and students around campus during the afternoon with leaflets to publicize the injunction and the city curfew. The leaflets stated that peaceful rallies were authorized but failed to mention the 1:00 A.M. campus curfew. The university also established a Rumor Control Center (RCC). But in the immediate time frame of the shootings, the spread of information—true, false, unverified, and unsubstantiated—occurred closely along the lines of the aforementioned rumor theories. Events happened so quickly, chaotically, and—soon—cataclysmically, that efforts to control the situation began to unravel.

"On May 2, I was called by Bob Matson, along with Glenn Frank and Harold Kitner, to organize faculty marshals because of the problem in downtown Kent," Jerry Lewis reflected. "What the faculty marshals did was hand out a flyer saying, don't go downtown; there's a curfew; and there's a dance on campus, and things like that. Glenn Frank tore up a blue sheet of his wife's, and that became our marshaling band." Lewis also recounted a painful decision that still haunts him:

> It was at that point, I'm embarrassed to say, I made I think, the second biggest mistake of May 4, the four days. I was asked, "Was the National Guard around?" I said, "Yes, they're off-campus." Somebody asked me, "Would they come in with loaded weapons?" And I said, "No." Which was foolish, I should have checked it out, and I'm very embarrassed by that. But I just assumed like most people, they wouldn't have loaded weapons, because I had been in the Army on guard duty, and I didn't have a loaded weapon.

Lewis also put little stock in the effectiveness of the Rumor Control Center. In his words, the center "spread more rumors than it controlled" due to lack of cooperation from the administration and the fact that President White was off campus. Lewis added that most of the phone calls that came into the RCC were from townspeople, not students. This indicates a greater reliance of the Kent community on the university than the community to this day often still admits. It also suggests that the community, frustrated in its efforts to gain factual knowledge, became predisposed to accept and circulate rumors among themselves.

The anonymous female resident, whose father was on the police force, discussed the proliferation of rumors from Saturday into Monday:

> I remember I was listening to the radio because of course all weekend things were getting worse and they had called in the National Guard. My father reported to me at the time one of the reasons they did, is that a lot of informants on campus were telling them what was happening. One [rumor] was that they were going to blow up the mill. Which if they had done that, it would have leveled the downtown and killed a great deal of people. The other rumor that they had was that LSD was going to be put in the drinking water in the water plant. They simply did not have enough men to station at all the places that were threatened. My husband owned his own professional building and it was in close proximity to City Hall and he received random telephone calls that they were going to bomb his building. He was an accountant, so that didn't hardly make sense unless it was because of his affiliation with law enforcement or because of his geographic location to City

Hall, or whether it was just random calls to various businesses in Kent with bomb threats. I remember he did go out and buy plywood and boarded up all his windows in the hopes of protecting the files that he had there for clients.[31]

However, at least one rumor that circulated among Kent State students and many in town proved accurate. Allport and Postman's connection between rumor and riot became fulfilled most clearly in the burning of the Army ROTC building on the evening of Saturday, May 2. As it was on many campuses across the nation, the ROTC building at Kent State had become synonymous with the war in Vietnam and the connections between the university and the military-industrial complex. In an interview with Scott Bills for his book, *Kent State/May 4: Echoes Through a Decade* (1982), Kent State activist Ruth Gibson called it a "symbol in everybody's mind of direct oppression; the direct threat of having to go into a war that you didn't believe in, that you didn't want, that you didn't think your country should be involved in."[32]

The ROTC building was located on the northwestern end of the Commons. Physically, it belied such powerful connections; by all accounts, it was a dilapidated, wooden, single-story barracks constructed in the days of World War II. More than a few narrators in their oral history testimony recount—almost offhandedly—preknowledge that the burning would occur. An anonymous narrator said that he had heard "from a number of sources" that the ROTC building would be burned down.[33] Catherine Delattre, an undergraduate in 1970, verifies this claim: "We knew, we were told. It was a friend who called and said, 'Hey, the ROTC building is going to burn down.' It was very hush-hush kind of thing, and so we [Delattre and her boyfriend] went there and decided that if something happened we were going to see what was going to happen, and we'd be part of it if we felt comfortable."[34]

Word about the burning spread into the Kent community as well. Former mayor John Carson's narrative is especially fascinating because of how it weaves together a rumor that "everyone" knew was going to happen, "pretty good hearsay" about the incompetence of the head of the university police, casual name-dropping of his pedigree, and unequivocal admission of his own sympathies. He claimed that

every kid in town knew [the building] was going to be burned. My kids were there and they were early teenagers, because everybody was saying, go up and watch the burning. So the locals were up there in the crowd watching. The executive administrator of the police department at the university—and this is hearsay—had detached a force who were sitting out at the stadium waiting to come in and pounce on the perpetrators of the fire. But he was known for imbibing a little too much, and I think he was drunk and failed to bring his crew in. And that's hearsay, but it's pretty good hearsay.[35]

That evening, a crowd started to form near the Victory Bell on the Commons, and by 7:30 P.M., it numbered around six hundred. Unlike the previous evening, when police guarded the ROTC building and apprehended Michael Weekly, no police were present. The crowd circled by the dormitories, picking up more students so that by about 8:00 P.M. there were one thousand to two thousand in the crowd, including both students and nonstudents. As they came back toward the Commons, the crowd stopped at the ROTC building. Some in the crowd chanted "Get it," "Burn it," and "ROTC has to go." Just after 8:00 P.M., some in the crowd began to throw rocks; others threw lighted railroad flares, but they rolled off and were ineffective. After several failed attempts, a small corner of the building began to burn somewhere between 8:30 and 8:45 P.M. Firefighters did not arrive until 9:00 P.M. As the firefighters tried to extinguish the fire, some in the crowd threw rocks; others tried to cut the fire hoses or grabbed them and tried to pull them away. Faculty marshals in the crowd did not try to stop them, stating later that they were fearful of being attacked if they had, or were not sure if their authority required them to intervene or merely observe.

Mystery surrounds the events that occurred just after this. Some have suggested that Kent State police let the building burn, or that operatives employed by local police, the National Guard, or from the FBI's COINTELPRO (Counter-Intelligence Program), set the fire in order to bring in troops or police to break up and further discredit the New Left and antiwar activism.[36] Starting in 1956, COINTELPRO began as an effort to infiltrate and subvert the Communist and Socialist Workers Parties. In 1968, FBI director J. Edgar Hoover expanded the program to include New Left groups, ending in 1971. Published reports from the FBI and the President's Commission indicate that at this point the fire subsided as the firefighters retreated. Perhaps fifteen minutes later, the fire quickly grew again, and at this point Kent State police, along with Portage County sheriff's deputies, arrived and began to push the crowd away using tear gas. A small shed not far from the ROTC building also went up in flames then, and students and faculty marshals put it out with a bucket brigade. At about 10:15 P.M., the firefighters came back again to put out the new, more dramatic ROTC fire, and by this time the National Guard had arrived, escorted the firefighters to the fire, and entered the campus to deal with the crowd. University officials Williams and Schwartzmiller had concluded they needed the Guard but had not given specific authorization or made a request before the Guard arrived on campus. General Canterbury would later state that the Guard did not need specific authorization since the campus was state property. Groups of students roamed on campus and in the nearby downtown area. One group tried to set fire to an information booth at the edge of campus; another along East Main Street wrecked a telephone booth. Other groups of students followed along and tried to prevent the damage and put fires out. Once on campus, the Guard pushed the crowd, which included students, nonstudents, and faculty marshals into the dorms to end the disturbance around midnight.[37]

Our anonymous student recalled the rumor and then the burning:

I'd heard it from a number of sources that it was going to happen that night. I went over and there it was; just a bunch of standing around and yelling at the building for a long time. What ended up happening is some people threw some rocks and broke some windows. Finally some guy ran up and with a lighter or something and lit a drape. Then somebody threw something else in a window and nothing happened. Somebody finally got something burning on one corner of the place. And the fire department arrived. Then it started getting interesting. Some kid thought . . . after the firemen had their hoses all out, going up, 'cause there was a big length of hose right by the students, go over and cut it. And that went over real big. Everybody got a kick out of that. The fire department didn't know what to do. They backed off. Then finally police came and helped them. The way I remember it, the building was barely burning at that point.

And they chased us, everybody away. And I was chased up the Blanket Hill past the . . . actually I went directly up where the old archery shed was. And a couple guys standing there on the hill 'cause when we were on the hill, we didn't have to keep running, they decided it was time to fight back already. And they broke into the archery shed and were going to get the bows and arrows out to distribute to fight back with the police. And a couple of wiser students, three or four of them, heard what was

Howard Ruffner was an Air Force veteran and second-year student at Kent State in 1970. He captured many of the most poignant moments of the events in May, including this image of the ROTC building burning on the night of May 2. (© 1970 Howard Ruffner; courtesy of Howard Ruffner)

going on, and threw everything back in the shed, dragged the guys away from the shed and burned the shed to keep the students from arming themselves with bows and arrows. . . . I've never heard anybody tell why that little shed was burned. But thank God it was! Because if a bunch of eighteen year olds start shooting bows and arrows at the police. . . .[38]

Jerry Rupe, one of the Kent 25 indicted by the Portage County grand jury in October 1970, lit the American flag on fire in the attempt to burn the building. Recent revelations also indicate that one of those involved seems to have been Devo band member Bob Mothersbaugh, who was in high school at the time. Another anonymous narrator described himself as brandishing a "big stick" and "smacking out the window frames" so that Rupe could toss the burning flag—now adjacent to the stick—into the building.[39] On the opposite side of the spectrum, bystander Ellis Berns considered the ROTC fire a turning point for the entire weekend:

I remember the fire department coming and unrolling the hoses and actually trying to put the fire out. And what really pissed me off was my peers, my [fellow] students, protesting were actually cutting the fire hose, which made absolutely no sense to me. . . . These guys didn't have anything to do with [anything] but put the fire out. I wasn't throwing rocks. Why are people throwing rocks? Why are they cutting the hoses? I understand the ROTC building what it represents. But it was just something that made no sense to me.[40]

Before coming to Kent, the men in the Ohio National Guard had been on duty at the Teamster-led truckers' strike in the region. One of the key issues in the history and memory of the Kent State shootings is the level of training of the men in the Guard on campus in May 1970. Here's Ron Snyder discussing this issue:

[Interviewer]: How much training had you and your unit had with regard to riot control?

Well, actually, quite a bit. This was something that always surprised me with the Kent State matter. They always tried to insinuate that the training was little or none, when in fact we'd had considerable training. We learned to employ tear gas and other riot-control tactics. We practiced riot-control formations. Every one of our personnel that I'm aware of—now I'm speaking of Company C of the 145th Infantry—that was at Kent State had had at least six months of training on active duty.

[Interviewer]: What was the status of your men right after the truckers' strike?

Well, my evaluation, from a personal standpoint, is we had been on the detail for some time, but we'd had relief. People had been able to take showers. Sleep. There was apprehension of course, and we got the order to go to Kent, as I recall, in an afternoon, sometime in an afternoon, and we were to load everything up and move by convoy to Kent. I do not recall that we were extremely fatigued.[41]
We had incidents all the time during that deployment. One in particular where they rolled by us shooting at us, okay?

[Interviewer]: Truckers were shooting at you?

Yeah. And we took care of that problem pretty quick. Firepower tends to make things happen.

[Interviewer]: So you were firing back at them with live ammunition?

Oh yeah, sure. We didn't go anywhere without live ammunition. Whenever we went to the riots, we issued live ammunition.[42]

Guardsman Art Krummel saw the condition and training of the men differently.

We were activated for a Teamster strike that had grown pretty violent. There [were] gunshots, there were supervisors driving trucks, the striking Teamsters were not happy about it, there was a lot of things dropped on the trucks from overpasses. So the Guard was activated to help control the Teamsters and to allow these trucks to move freely in and out of the terminals. The Teamsters were clearly very angry; they were very vocal and displayed a lot of rage. But, it was assuring to me to see that there was also this respect for the uniform and for the authority of the U.S. military and that they wouldn't violate that. We weren't terribly prepared other than some minor riot control training. We weren't prepared to confront anyone and deal with that.

While this Teamster action was going on, the weather got real bad and it was raining, it was miserable, we were sleeping in pup tents on this football field in the Richfield area. We were a pretty unhappy crew. We had gotten pretty tired, but finally got word that we were going to be released. We needed to go to the Rubber Bowl (former home field of the University of Akron football team), get our equipment cleaned up, and get it turned in. And we would be sent home.[43]

But they weren't.

Sunday, May 3, 1970

Unlike the previous evening, Sunday morning was deceptively calm. The bright orange glow in the sky that had greeted the Guard's arrival on Saturday night from Akron to Kent via Route 18 (now Tallmadge Road)—which Captain Snyder compared to images of Baghdad after the 2003 bombing, and one of Snyder's soldiers said looked as though the entire town was engulfed in flames[44]—dissipated into a clear blue sky. Students awoke to the presence of some 850 Guardsmen on campus. Some protected the remains of the ROTC building, which sightseers came to view until the ONG banned visitors at 1:00 P.M. Another 300–400 Guardsmen were also deployed throughout

Kent, many of them carrying loaded rifles with bayonets. Several narrators described tanks on the streets or on campus, although these were likely the armored personnel carriers often used by the Guard. Most townspeople were relieved to see the Guard. Narrators recalled the easy manner in which students and Guardsmen interacted; others remembered feelings of trepidation and anger. Several reflected on whether or not students were aware—or should have been—that the Guard's weapons were loaded with live rounds. Eldon Fender, who had driven back from Cincinnati, compared returning to Kent with entering Fort Knox.[45]

KSU president Robert White had called for the university airplane on Saturday, and he took off from Iowa on Sunday morning. While White was airborne, Ohio governor James Rhodes, who was in a hotly contested primary campaign for the U.S. Senate, arrived via helicopter from Cleveland, and Mayor Satrom and Ohio National Guard officials showed Rhodes the damage in the city and on campus. The primary vote was coming Tuesday, May 5, and polls showed Rhodes trailing his Republican rival, Robert A. Taft Jr. At the city fire station, Rhodes held a news conference. As the *Scranton Report* notes, among those present with Rhodes "were his chief aide McElroy, General Del Corso, Mayor Satrom, KSU Vice President Matson, Ohio Highway Patrol Superintendent Robert N. Chiaramonte, Portage County Prosecutor Ronald J. Kane, U.S. Attorney Robert Krupansky, Kent Police Chief Roy Thompson and Kent Fire Chief Fred Miller."[46] Rhodes took charge of the conference and opened with a five-minute inflammatory speech, not unlike others he had made regarding student protests in Ohio.

Rhodes began by calling the unrest in Kent "probably the most vicious form of campus-oriented violence yet perpetrated by dissident groups and their allies in the state of Ohio." Once the groups moved off campus into Kent and threatened merchants and townspeople, Rhodes said it became "a problem of the state of Ohio." Pounding his fingers and then his fist on the table as he continued, Rhodes declared "we are going to employ every force of law that we have under our authority." He supported the belief that there was a plan or at least some coordinated effort among radicals in Ohio to sow unrest. "Now," the governor said, "we're going to put a stop to this for this reason: the same group that we're dealing with here today, and there's three or four of them, they only have one thing in mind: that is to destroy higher education in Ohio. . . . We are going to eradicate the problem. We are not going to treat the symptoms." He finished with a flourish:

During the day on Sunday, May 3, across campus students and Guardsmen talked and fraternized, a scene that belied the confrontations before and those to come. (May 4 Collection. Kent State University Libraries. Special Collections and Archives.)

And these people just move from one campus to the other and terrorize a community. They're worse than the brown shirts and the communist element, and also the night-riders and the vigilantes. They're the worst type of people that we harbor in America. And I want to say this—they are not going to take over a campus and the campus now is going to be part of the county and the state of Ohio. There's no sanctuary for these people to burn buildings down of private citizens of business in a community then run into a sanctuary. It's over with in Ohio.[47]

During the news conference, a reporter asked Rhodes what size organization the governor thought he was up against. Rhodes replied, "I think that we're up against the strongest, well-trained, militant, revolutionary group that has ever assembled in America."[48] Rhodes declared that he was going to ask for "an injunction . . . similar to a state of emergency." Rhodes never followed up on this, and after he left, "widespread uncertainty regarding rules, prohibitions, and proclamations remained."[49] Some believed then and maintain in their interviews that martial law had been declared. Following Rhodes, General Del Corso stated, "We will apply whatever degree of force is necessary to provide protection for the lives of our citizens and his property." Mayor Satrom echoed this: "We will take all necessary, and I repeat, all necessary action to maintain order."[50] Rhodes met President White as the latter arrived at Kent State University Airport at noon. "Bob, you have 400 of the worst riffraff in the state from all of the campuses," White reported Rhodes as saying. "They are trying to close you down. Don't give in. Keep open."[51]

White later issued a four-point statement on WKSU radio. First, he said "Kent State University has been disastrously hurt." "We must show to the nation that Kent State University has much more to it than the ugliness it has seen in our midst." Second, he thanked students, faculty, and campus security for tempering the situation on Saturday. Third, White stated that "by order of the governor, the National Guard will remain in the Kent community and campus until its leadership decides its departure is safe. Events have taken those decisions out of university hands." Finally, White declared that the university "plans to maintain normal operations and classes will meet as scheduled."[52] The university then distributed twelve thousand leaflets that listed the curfew hours on campus as being from 1:00 A.M. to 6:00 A.M.; stated that the Guard had assumed control of campus; and declared that all rallies, peaceful or otherwise, were banned.[53] How effective these two methods were in communicating the situation remains an open question.

That afternoon, a group of twenty-three faculty members issued a statement denouncing the presence of the Guard on campus and the rock throwing and violence of the previous two days. However, they asked that burning of the ROTC building be considered in the context of the war in Vietnam and the announced invasion into Cambodia. The group asked White to call a faculty meeting. He refused.

Town resident Rosann Rissland believed that martial law had been declared, as it connected to her mother's experience in Puerto Rico, likely during the nationalist uprising there in 1950.

> I just remember all of the sirens going on all the time. And I remember when the Guardsmen came, they were parked on my front lawn. I look back at it now, and I realize how strange it seems to me, I never went out my front door during that whole thing. It was like: they were on

my front lawn, and I stayed away from it. I think it goes back to my mother. She was from Puerto Rico, and she said to me—we talked about it on the phone, what was happening—and she said, "You don't go out near them, because in martial law you can get killed." And she cited a time when she was young when that had happened to a group of people who were having a religious service and American service- men opened fire on women and children and killed people. All they were doing was doing a religious parade, okay? But it was martial law. They weren't supposed to be doing it, and so they killed them.

So I was very aware that you didn't take that lightly. Even though that was a gorgeous weekend, I did not set foot in my front yard. Backyard was fine, but I did not set foot in my front yard at all. Hav- ing them up there, you heard loudspeakers going too, and the trucks pulling up on your yard and all of that stuff. It was surreal. It was really surreal. It was a scary thing.[54]

Linda Cooper-Leff, a KSU student who lived off campus, called her friends who lived in the dorms to talk about the odd, at times contradictory, atmosphere.

They said, "Well, it was really strange. We had walked over to the library and an armored personnel carrier came up and told them that they had to disperse because there were more than three people walking across campus to go to the library." . . . But, it was interesting. They said . . . everybody was bringing the kids from out—you know, the children, small kids—to come to see the burned-out ROTC buildings. And they had picnic baskets and they were having their picnic lunches and it was like a carnival. It was just "Everybody come and see the Guard."

Students attempting to walk across campus to study for finals, however, constituted a group gathering.[55]

Guardsman Art Krummel, who was assigned to a Jeep patrol around the city, recalled friendly conversations with students and townspeople.[56] How- ever, James Vacarella—a Kent undergraduate who later received a federal indictment for refusing to be drafted into the U.S. Army—had a different remembrance from his personal encounter with Major Jones of the ONG, who would be involved in the shootings on Monday. Vacarella was irked by a half-track carrier that had parked over the official seal of the university near the intersection of Lincoln and Main.

And I told the guy, "You know, you have to move off the seal," because we felt cocky and powerful and we were going to end this war. We were met by Major Jones. This guy I'll never forget. Major Jones put a pistol right to my face. There were five other guys right around me. And there were seven or eight of us but they managed to move and they caught me. And he said, "I want your name." I gave him a fake name. And he said, "Thank you." And he left. Now we had heard all that day—that was Sunday—that they were collecting names of all the long-hairs on campus and they were just going to throw everybody out on Monday and that would be the end of the riots. And that's something they should have done. 'Cause that would've ended it! [laughs] They didn't![57]

A moving story that came out of these tragic events centers on Allison Krause, one of the four KSU students killed on Monday. The story goes that Krause and her boyfriend, Barry Levine, encountered a Guardsman who had allowed someone to put a lilac in his gun barrel. As Levine has recalled in other interviews, an officer came over and forced the soldier to take out the flower, telling the soldier to "forget all this peace stuff." Allison grabbed it from the officer and said, "What's the matter with peace? Flowers are better than bullets!"[58] After the shootings, the story changed slightly to Krause putting the flower in the barrel as she made her comment.

Carol Mirman was one of the Kent 25, those indicted by a grand jury in Portage County for a number of crimes in conjunction with the shootings and events before. She mentioned in her interview that that Sunday was "the day that they caught the picture of Allison Krause with the flower and the Guard[s]man." ("I didn't know any of these people that were shot," she added. "I only hung out with people in the Art Department."[59]) However, Mirman, in this instance, is mixing the popular memory of other photographs of antiwar protesters putting flowers into gun barrels with Allison Krause's actions at Kent. There exists a photograph of the Guardsman with a flower in his barrel—and of the encounter described by Levine—but not a photo of Krause putting the flower in the barrel. Nevertheless, her comment, "Flowers are better than bullets," has since become part of the rich set of meanings and narratives surrounding the shootings. It has been used since in various commemorative activities at Kent and elsewhere around the world as a statement against war and state oppression. It is also the epitaph on her gravestone.

For Ken Hammond and Mike Alewitz, the events took on more political significance. Both had been away at political meetings: Hammond in Buffalo with his wife and William (Bill) Arthrell, Alewitz at an antiwar conference in Columbus, Ohio. They each heard about the ROTC fire and returned to campus on Sunday. Noting that the situation ironically reflected the Weathermen's desire to "bring the war home," Hammond felt that "trashing downtown or burning the ROTC building, abnormal gestures as they might be . . . didn't really do much to advance a political agenda. And so the question was, where do we go from here? And my feeling was that something needed to be done to try to steer all that energy and all that anger into some kind of constructive, or some sort of forward dynamic."[60] Also looking at the larger picture—and regularly invoking the collective pronoun "we" when describing actions in which he participated—Alewitz emphasized the unusual spontaneity and lack of organization that distinguished the turn of events at Kent State and belied town fears that a carefully orchestrated radical plot was unfolding. "As I mentioned, I tried to—we tried to—we called a meeting and attempted to organize something and it didn't happen," Alewitz said.

> It really was the first time really . . . in any modern time in U.S. history—it didn't even occur really this way in the '30s except perhaps around like the sit-down strikes, the Minneapolis General Strike, Toledo, San Francisco, in a few instances like that where workers basically . . . where the upsurge of the working-class kind of swept aside all of their organizations and preconceptions and everything and just began to unfold in a very organic way.[61]

The dichotomies of experience, between calm and tension, between political and personal, between believability and "unreality" (as Catherine Delattre put it) all changed Sunday evening as students began to gather in violation of the ban on rallies—whether knowingly or unknowingly—and of the curfew in Kent. At 7:00 P.M., the Victory Bell began to toll and by 8:00 P.M. a crowd had gathered around the ROTC remains. Later surveys of those present indicated that they were there to protest the presence of the Guard on campus. The crowd grew larger, and at 8:45 P.M., campus police and the highway patrol recommended to the Guard that the 1:00 A.M. curfew be cancelled and that they impose an immediate one. One of the anonymous Guardsmen, who had been stationed around the remains of the ROTC building in the afternoon, described the start of the confrontation:

I recall our captain saying, "We're gonna look mean and green when we go down there," and "This is the big-time," and "We're gonna march, and we're gonna march in cadence. . . ." And then it became dark. Very quickly an officer came through and said to us, "OK, men, suit up. Get ready." And we got in line, we had the M1s, and we were asked to check our ammunition. And the officer said to each of us, "When the order is given to lock and load"—which in Army lingo is, you take the ammunition out of your belt and you put it into the weapon, and you lock it and you put it on "safe"—"That you are to lock and load, but you are not"—and he made it very clear, almost to each of us there going down the line—"Do not under any circumstances fire unless you are given the order. And do not lock and load until you are told to lock and load." I don't believe that evening we had locked and loaded.

The M1 was a World War II military semi-automatic weapon. It had eight rounds of a thirty-odd-six caliber. I'll tell you why it was best we had M1s and not M16s. Had we had M16s, I think the people who did the firing—we would have had ten times the number. It's a weapon that is not a wounding weapon; it's a killing weapon. The M1 was a still-jacketed 30-odd-six high-velocity straight-shot round. We all checked; we all had a clip of eight rounds with us. . . .

At that point it got dark, and we got the order to line up shoulder to shoulder and form a straight line somewhat behind the old Student Center and the ROTC building. We stood there about ten minutes and I was saying, "Why . . ." and people were running—and our officers running back and forth, lining us up. And I couldn't figure out what was the big deal. A helicopter came over, shown a light on the hill where the Architecture building was [Taylor Hall], and there were several thousand kids up there. They were very quietly massed there. They started moving and shouting, "Here we come!" And they did. I thought, "What are we gonna do now?" And a lot of thoughts ran through my mind: If we're told to lock and load, are we going to fire? are we gonna protect our lives? are we going to run? A lot of things go through your mind. They marched on over from Taylor Hill as we passed that bell—they were ringing that damn bell incessantly, I remember that.[62]

Just before 9:00 P.M., Major Jones read the Ohio Riot Act to the protesters and gave them five minutes to disperse. They refused, and at 9:15 P.M. campus police used tear gas. The demonstrators split into two: one group headed toward President White's house, the other toward Prentice Gate, entrance to the main campus at Lincoln and Main Streets. More tear gas drove away the crowd at President White's house. Some joined the group at Prentice Gate; others went back to the Commons. The protesters at the gate staged a sit-in at the intersection of Lincoln and Main. As they sang "Give Peace a Chance," helicopters flew overhead shining searchlights upon them, and they faced police, county officers, and National Guardsmen on the ground. Police gave a bullhorn to a student, who then relayed from protesters a call for Mayor Satrom and President White to meet with them to discuss six demands:

- abolition of ROTC;
- removal of the National Guard from campus by Monday night;
- the lifting of the curfew;
- amnesty for those arrested Saturday night;
- consideration of the demands from BUS; and
- a reduction in tuition.

Shortly after, a student announced to the crowd that Mayor Satrom would meet with them and that efforts were being made to contact White. The student told the crowd that if it would move off the street, the Guard would back away; both groups withdrew slightly. In the meantime, police met with Vice President Matson and Vice President Ronald Roskens in the KSU administration building. Both men refused to allow White to speak with the students and later said White concurred with their recommendation. They also refused to meet with demonstrators themselves. White later said he did not recall being contacted on this at the time. At 11:00 P.M., the police at the scene were informed that neither White nor Matson would come; the Guard again read the Riot Act to the protesters and announced that the curfew was in effect immediately. The mayor apparently tried to get to the intersection, but by the time he arrived, police and Guardsmen had begun to disperse the crowd.

"One of the student leaders came back and said, 'The mayor's coming, he's agreed to meet with us, and take our demands,'" said KSU undergrad Denny Benedict (1969–1973). "Everybody was happy. Next thing you know, the National Guard is putting on their helmets, putting on their gasmasks, fixing their bayonets. So, basically, they lied to us. They start clearing the area." Feeling betrayed, the crowd became violent; many cursed the Guard and police and threw rocks or other projectiles at them. Police and Guardsmen fired tear gas, and the crowd ran back onto campus as Guardsmen

On the evening of Sunday, May 3, students engaged in a sit-in at the intersection of Lincoln and Main, just off the main entrance to campus, to protest the Guard's presence on campus. (Photo copyright *Akron Beacon Journal*. Reprinted with permission.)

chased them with bayonets drawn. One group of about two hundred students was driven into Rockwell Hall, which contained the library, where police and Guardsmen held them for about forty-five minutes, followed by a grace period to leave. Guardsmen chased another group of about three hundred students toward the Tri-Tower dorms. At least two students were injured with bayonets, and three Guardsmen reported cuts and bruises from thrown rocks and a wrench. Many students were unable to return to their dorms because of the new curfews.[63] Guardsman Art Krummel described the experience of being in a situation that was stressful, with tear gas in the air, with trying to breathe through a gasmask and climb a hill was quite an effort.

> I just kind of was stumbling up the hill as best I could when suddenly the guy beside me fell, just knocked out completely cold. I discovered [after the fact] . . . that he had been hit by a rock and it was then that I realized that these rocks were a little more than just stones, that they were pretty dangerous things. And it increased my sense of the real danger.

Compared to the Teamsters in the truckers' strike, Krummel said, the KSU protesters were

far, far, far more scary because clearly there wasn't the same sort of respect given the uniform of the military that the Teamsters showed. The Teamsters were mostly vets from Korea or even probably some Second World War veterans or not far removed from them and still had a high degree of respect for the military uniform. The kids that were in school were a little more removed or were influenced a lot by various liberal groups. There were a lot of us who were in opposition to the Vietnam War and to the way these things were conducted. We understood entirely that our activation for Kent State and probably for the Teamster strike was a political move by Governor Rhodes to gain votes in the ongoing election that he was involved in at that time. So it was pretty commonly held that our involvement with Kent State was being motivated by politics.[64]

The anonymous Guardsman, who was a KSU student, believed that business owners and citizens in downtown Kent were heavily armed and would have shot students that night; the interviewer, Sandra Perlman Halem, agreed.

We were told to move the crowd; we were actually told that we were going to stop the crowd from going downtown. I knew some of the businessmen in town, and believe me, to this day I think it's just as well because, they were better armed than we were. I think the authorities knew that there were people sitting on rooftops on buildings and had those people moved on downtown to trash it again, there would have been gunfire, it was that simple.

[Interviewer]: I know many houses that had guns pointed in their windows those few days.

It was that simple. It was like saving someone from themselves. . . . At that point, when the gas was laid down and we started moving, you could see the group that was there for a party to see what was going on, quickly dispersed. They were outta there. . . . It's at that point that I saw the students again let go with the rocks, men standing there waving their genitals at us, and women shouting obscenities. I was no virgin, and I was used to a lot of things, but not on my campus. I looked at this and I said, "This gives me a whole different point of view on what's happening here again."

As with the ROTC building the night before, there is surprisingly little photographic evidence of the confrontations between protesters and the Guard. One undergraduate said he took a photo of a Guardsman bayoneting a student and took it to the *Kent Record-Courier* to be developed, only to see that photograph vanish from the *Record-Courier* offices by the following morning. (He claimed that after he left, Guardsmen came into the newspaper offices to develop their own film of the events, saw his, and confiscated the evidence.) Several narrators—including Dean Kahler, who would be paralyzed by a Guardsman's bullet on Monday, May 4—recall seeing or hearing about students getting bayoneted that evening. Kahler said he left his dorm to observe the protest and "see what was going on."

> I was hanging out there and I sat on the curb. . . . The police cruiser was sitting in the middle of the intersection and saying, "The mayor and the president of the university will be out in half an hour." Well, half an hour arrived and I didn't see any mayor or president. The only thing I saw was another helicopter flying around with a spotlight shining down. They brought in more troops and all of a sudden pop, pop, pop; tear gas again flying. So instead of running up the gauntlet of Lincoln Street I flew through the pine trees towards the east corner of the Rockwell Hall, which was our library, which is now the fashion museum. And apparently, I wasn't the only one, because about 15 or 20 come busting out of the trees. It took three or four National Guardsmen there by surprise. Apparently somebody behind us got stabbed by a bayonet right up against the Rockwell Hall, but it wasn't us. We must have been the first ones. I mean I was legging it out. I mean for some reason when I finally grew into my body, you know I was fast.[65]

Like Kahler, Eldon Fender observed Sunday night's action but was not an active participant.

> The Guard was trying to intimidate the kids off the street. There were probably 500 to 600 students, people that were sitting down in the middle of the road, blocking it, in all four lanes. The National Guard

had an armored carrier that they used to transport troops in, and what they would do is rev the engine up at the top of the hill—as you go down into downtown Kent there's like a rise there. This half-track carrier would actually charge like it was trying to scare the students off the road and at the last minute would turn right in front of DuBois Bookstore. And you can imagine if this man had misplaced his foot on the brake or the accelerator, he probably would have plowed right into the people.

Even when students returned to their dorm rooms, which were without air-conditioning on a hot night, the harassment did not let up. "The [Ohio] State Highway Patrol had a helicopter flying around with a big spotlight on it," Fender added.

And if they would see any number of students congregating on the ground they would throw tear gas out their doors of their helicopter. But mind you, this tear gas was going all over the place and that was my first experience with tear gas, so much so we had to escape our rooms into the interior hallway to get away from it. It was like a prison atmosphere in terms of how that was all being conducted.[66]

Rebecca Howe described the contrast between chaos and violence in one area of campus and what she described as Guardsmen coming up to her first-floor dorm window and "chatting with us, sharing hot chocolate." Nevertheless, Howe added, the helicopter floodlights that would suddenly fill her dorm room later in the evening were so traumatizing that "years later, when I lived in Kent, and some pranksters were flashing some spotlights, I fell on the floor and crawled to the door because it was so frightening and brought back so many memories."[67]

Janice Wascko, a freshman at Kent State in 1970 who lived a few blocks off campus, highlighted how the events featured equal parts comedy and violence for many of the participants.

We took a sheet and put a power fist on it, and [wrote] REMOVE YOUR ARMY OF OCCUPATION and put it on the front of our house. They put a staging area right across the street from of us. We were all really young. I was a very young nineteen-year-old. Cocky. We sat there going, "Hey, G.I.! You want my seester? You got chocolates?" We weren't real happy about them being there. At one point they came out with their guns and we heard them release their safeties, and we all decided to go in the house. It kind of shook us up. . . . Then later that night we had heard that things got real hectic downtown. The person on the phone said they were coming in, really beating people up and crap. So two men from my house decided they would go out and do a little diversionary work, and they went in our backyard and set off firecrackers, like I said, we were really young and naive. Well, for that, we got our very own helicopter, with floodlights hovering over our house. About seven or eight guys with arms from the National Guard marched through our yard, and they ripped the sheet off our front window. We never got our sheet back. And we had a Guard on the corners of our yard for the rest of the night.

Rick Byrum was not a political radical; today he calls himself a Republican. In 1970 he was, like many students, against the war and angry about having the National Guard on campus.

First of all, it was insulting to have the Guard on campus and telling you what to do. Hell, you know we're kids that have gotten our independence so to speak away from mom and dad, and now you're going to send the Army in to tell us what to do. Oh, you got a curfew on us? I can't go down and get a coolie at The Loft? I can't walk around at night? You're telling me this? What are you, nuts? . . . But we had—at least I had no animosity to the individual national guardsmen. I knew why they were there, a lot of them. They were there because they want to get out of Vietnam, too. So, by Sunday night, I had not taken any of this very seriously, that it was just another protest, because there were protests all the time. This is just another protest. This too will pass.[68]

An incident at a roadblock that involved Guardsman Art Krummel suggested a different outcome.

I believe that night, Saturday night, my unit, my squad, actually, was sent to man a couple of roadblocks. I was a squad leader, so we had two roadblocks set up on a couple of streets and our orders were to not let any cars enter that area. I noticed [at] one of the roadblocks there seemed to be a disturbance. I moved closer . . . to hear what was going on and I heard a man yelling out of his car window to get out of his way, he was going through this roadblock. And the National Guardsman who was blocking him by standing in front of his car said, "No, you aren't, sir. You have to turn your car around. We are not allowed to allow any cars through this roadblock." And this continued; the man insisted he was coming through, the National Guardsman—who also, incidentally, happened to be a very, very good friend who remains a very close friend of mine—was as adamant about not letting him through, when finally I yelled down to the Guardsman and said, "Bruce!"—his name is Bruce Mendelson—I said, "Bruce! Get out of the car's way. What do we care? Let the guy go about his business, no point in being killed." And I believe he either yelled back, or just simply said no, or just kept his position. The person in the car leaned out and said, "Come on, Bruce, get out of my way, I'm gonna come through if I have to run over you!" Well, when I saw this happening and the man was edging his car forward and bumping my friend who staggered back a couple steps each time. . . . I then unclicked the safety on my M1, which was loaded. One thing we were trained pretty well in the National Guard, and in the Army when we were trained in active duty, was to never click the safety off your weapon until you were ready to use it. And I was fully ready to use it. I can remember still the feeling on my finger of clicking that safety.

Following a long, emotional pause, Krummel finished the story: there was an auxiliary police station set up nearby; he flagged down a police officer who got the man—who was a drunk professor trying to get home—out of his car. Krummel then made a startling observation:

In my mind, that very incident could have changed the history of the world. If it had come to the point where I had to shoot the man, he'd run over my friend, the campus would have been closed then, there would have been no shootings on May 4, very likely the events in Vietnam would have unfolded differently. Although May 4 was only one of several events that were instrumental in changing the course of Vietnam, I feel like that event could have avoided at least four additional deaths, among other things.[69]

"What if?" scenarios are commonplace in oral history narratives, even the substitution of a "lesser" tragedy for a greater one. Instead of expressing relief for not shooting the professor, Krummel appeared to feel a near sense of guilt for showing too much restraint—that his inaction could have changed things not only at Kent State, but the Vietnam War. Yet this should be considered within the context of his remembrance of clicking the safety of his gun: that a peaceful man, who joined the Guard to avoid Vietnam, was still shaken by the feeling that he was ready to fire. If he had, it may have taken more than saving his friend's life to justify it in his reflective mind; it may have taken altering the course of history.

As Sunday segued into Monday, emotions—and lack of sleep—ran high on all sides. Midway through the above account Krummel observed, "I realized that this could be a very, very unhappy outcome at the least and very dangerous." On the opposite side of hostilities, Janice Wascko looked back at what she and many KSU students took to be a battle, certainly, and one in which they felt collectively in the right but also a conflict that emboldened them with what were, up to then, elements of farce. "We were mostly Ohio kids. We hadn't seen nothing."[70]

PART THREE

"A bullet is a drastic answer"

The university remained open and classes resumed on Monday, May 4. It was a sunny, mild, but breezy spring day as students, faculty, and staff tried to resume normal operations in the wake of the weekend's events and amid the continued presence of National Guard troops on campus and in Kent. Of course, Monday would be anything but normal. Confusion and uncertainty remained. Would the rally be held, and if so, would students attend in the presence of the Guard? Was it banned or not? What would President White and the other university leaders do? What would the Guard do? President White met with his cabinet at 7:00 A.M., and after an 8:00 A.M. meeting with the Executive Committee of the Faculty Senate, White agreed to attend the regular meeting of the senate and an afternoon meeting of the full faculty. While many classes remained in session, bomb threats cancelled some and professors cancelled others since many students planned to attend the rally. Banned or not, news of the rally spread by word of mouth and by signs across campus.

The Guard remained on campus and in town, and the Guardsmen's state of mind and physical condition would play a key role in the events of that day. According to the U.S. President's Commission's *Report*, the Guardsmen from the three units involved in the shootings had averaged about three hours of sleep the night before. Captain Ron Snyder's Company C of the 145th Infantry Regiment went off duty at 2:00 A.M. but was called back at 5:30 A.M. to patrol the city streets. Troop G of the 107th Armored Cavalry—the group that contained most of the Guardsmen who fired upon students on May 4—commanded by Captain Raymond J. Srp, had gone off duty at 6:00 P.M. Sunday night. Not long after, they were called back to duty again and served until sometime between midnight and 1:00 A.M. Monday. They were awakened between 4:00 A.M. and 4:30 A.M. in order to relieve the men of

Company A of the 145th Infantry at 6:00 A.M. According to the commander of Company A, Captain John E. Martin, his men did not get to rest until 9:00 A.M. since they had to move their bivouac area; Company A then got called to duty on campus at 11:30 A.M.[1]

The anonymous Guardsman who gave his oral history interview believed that after Sunday's events, the situation was winding down, but as the calls for moving out came in, his own frustration began to grow.

> We had our gear all lined up and our weapons laying down . . . and the old "Get it on" came and we went over and got our weapons . . . got in formation, and we marched up out of the stadium and marched up to the ROTC area. They said, "There's some kids forming again," and we said, "Oh, not this shit again." You know, we'd been through this, we're tired, why don't these kids go to school where they belong? And a lot of us started thinking, "Why aren't they in class?" "What's goin' on with these people?" You know, why aren't they there?[2]

At 10:00 A.M., leaders of the Guard, the city, and the university attended what would be their last official meeting together during these four days in May. General Canterbury called the meeting at the Kent Fire Station. President White attended, as did Vice President Matson; Mayor Satrom; Paul Hershey, the Kent city safety director; Major Donald E. Manly of the Ohio State Highway Patrol; and Major William R. Shimp, legal officer of the Ohio National Guard.[3] Controversy remains over what was said at this meeting, which is consistent with the general confusion over authority on campus and over whether the noon rally on May 4 had been banned or not.

The group decided to apply the 8:00 P.M. to 6:00 A.M. curfew to the campus. Then discussion turned to the planned rally at noon. When he testified to the Scranton Commission, General Canterbury stated that he first learned of the noon rally at this meeting and that when he asked President White if it should be permitted, White replied, "No, it would be highly dangerous." In his own testimony to the commission, White denied making this statement; he also claimed he played no role in banning the noon rally. White stated that had he been asked, from "past history, all know that my response would have been affirmative to a rally." Others in the room stated that they did not recall White asking that the rally be banned, but that there was a general consensus that the rally was banned under the declaration of emergency issued by Rhodes on Sunday.[4] In testimony given at the 1975 civil trial, President White and General Canterbury again gave different recollections of the discussion. Canterbury made similar statements to those he gave to the Scranton Commission. White, though, stated that there "was no general discussion that I recall concerning the status of assemblies in general." White also again denied that he told General Canterbury it would be dangerous to hold the rally. In addition, White claimed in 1975 that he did not know there was going to be a rally held that day at noon.[5] Legally, no one had sought the injunction required for a state of emergency, yet university, city, and Guard leaders all assumed one existed; hence, the acquiescence of university leaders to the ONG and the general assumption that any rally was banned. Some scholars have suggested that in asking White whether the rally should be banned or not, Canterbury and the Guard's legal officer, Major Shimp, knew that neither Rhodes's order nor Satrom's order from earlier in the weekend had the legal authority to ban all rallies.[6]

When the meeting ended at 11:15 A.M., students had already started gathering on the Commons as Canterbury returned to Guard headquarters in the Administration Building on campus; he reportedly informed those present that the noon rally had been banned. Major John Simons, chaplain of the 107th Armored Cavalry Regiment expressed concern that students might be unaware of the ban. Canterbury stated that a campus official would have the campus radio spread the word. President White and Vice President Matson returned to campus, held a brief meeting with other university officials, and then went to the Brown Derby restaurant for a luncheon gathering to discuss the upcoming meeting that afternoon with the Faculty Senate.[7] As Canterbury and White went about their business, political science professor Barclay McMillen broadcast his 11:00 A.M. class lecture to the entire Kent campus via the university radio station. After the 1969 protests, McMillen argued in a report to President White that the protests came from individual student disaffection with an impersonal university, and he recommended that White should implement a series of reforms including splitting the university into smaller units, having police wear professional attire and not military uniforms, and having teachers and administrators interact with students more on campus.[8] In his lecture, McMillen condemned the violence of the days before, dismissed the idea that those actions were a form of legitimate and effective protest to end the war in Vietnam, and argued that the presence of the National Guard was necessary to preserve order. He urged students to look to the state and national government and not the university to change the process of the war. McMillen argued that since the Guard had assumed control and prohibited rallies, students should not attend the one called for at noon.[9]

Like many students, Dean Kahler remained uncertain about the rules governing the situation on Monday. "You know, was there Martial Law? Was there no Martial Law? Was there an emergency declared on campus?" Kahler remains critical of President White in these moments. White, Kahler stated,

> washed his hands like Pontius Pilate of the whole issue because the governor was there the day before and toured the campus and did his little radical speech. And he just went to lunch on May 4th at the Brown Derby. He could care less about what was happening up there. So in reality, he had a lot of control but he didn't take it. He didn't—he didn't—he did not assume his responsibilities purposefully. He abdicated his power to the National Guard General.[10]

The bulk of the events that are the keystones to the various memory narratives occurred in the hour between 11:30 A.M. and 12:30 P.M. In this hour occurred not only the shootings, but also several matters directly related to the shootings that either justify or excuse them for some, while for others confirm they were unnecessary, and others tantamount to murder. We pose the issues in the form of several questions, answers to which emerge at various points in the oral histories and in the next chapter that covers the aftermath. How close were the students to the Guard? Were the students pelting Guardsmen with rocks and other items, and if so, were these rocks and other items hitting their targets and large enough to cause damage? Was the Guard surrounded, especially when they descended the hill onto the practice football field? Is it conceivable that Guardsmen were in danger, or that Guardsmen believed they were? When the Guardsmen stopped at the practice football field, did they make a plan at that point to fire upon students once walking back to the crest of the hill near the Pagoda sculpture? Was there a sniper, or did Guardsmen believe there was and fired in response? Was there a shot fired before the main volley of shots, and did Guardsmen respond by firing their own weapons? If there was a shot, who fired it? Was it a National Guardsman or was it student Terry Norman, who often acted as police informant and carried a nickel-plated .38 hidden under his sports jacket to the rally? Did one of the ONG commanders or some other Guardsmen give an order to fire once the Guard reached the crest of the hill near the Pagoda?

At about 11:00 A.M., students began ringing the Victory Bell, signaling the start of a rally. The Victory Bell is located at the base of Taylor Hall, which sits upon Blanket Hill. Taylor is between Johnson Hall, a dormitory to the northwest, and Prentice Hall to the southeast. The remains of the ROTC building sat some 170 yards away from the Victory Bell across the Commons, an open, grassy area. Canterbury and Lieutenant Colonel Charles Fassinger, commander of the Second Squadron of the 107th Armored Cavalry, arrived on the Commons at the ROTC remains between 11:30 A.M. and 11:40 A.M. Fassinger later estimated that the crowd that concentrated around the Bell to have numbered about five hundred at that time. A report from the Guard issued in the immediate aftermath states there "were several hundred students gathered there."[11] Later Justice Department findings estimated between two hundred and three hundred around the Bell.

By noon, in addition to the core around the Bell, assessments vary as to how many other students had gathered in the Commons area—between 1,000 to as many as 4,500. The Commons and Blanket Hill were at the heart of the campus, and the area swelled at noon as students moved between classes, went to lunch, or came out to observe the demonstration. Most reports and studies have concluded that beyond the several hundred students in the core group that was closest to the Guard during the demonstration, there were likely another 1,500 or so in the surrounding areas watching the events or navigating the area between classes, making the total number on the Commons and in the area around 2,000.[12]

Upon hearing the Victory Bell, Chuck Ayers made his way over to the Commons to what he correctly assumed was a rally. Like some students, he had heard that the rally had been banned "after the fact," while other students attended knowingly and willingly as a form of protest against the Guard. "[The] Victory Bell was ringing, the National Guard was around the remains of the ROTC building, and I could hear . . . footsteps marching," he said. "And the road that went down—it's now obliterated by the Art Building, but it came down around there, there was a ringed large contingent of National Guard marching down the middle of the street down to the ROTC Building. [I thought], Something's up here." Ayers then described removing his sweater-vest to reveal a Kent State T-shirt on underneath.

> It was a fairly warm day, but I don't think it had anything to do with being warm. I think I wanted to be identified as a Kent State student. Don't expect me to explain that, because I don't really know why. I think it was my protest, my somewhat show of solidarity with the students and what they were going through. But I stripped off the sweater-vest . . . took my camera and went back outside.[13]

In Taylor Hall, Dr. Bentley's advanced photography class took advantage of the beautiful day and went to the Commons with cameras ready. The number of student reporters taking photographs that day later reinforced what became a grim joke: if you want to stage a massacre, don't do it in front of the School of Journalism. "I remember that I thought that things were getting heated up, and that I decided beforehand that I'd let my class go about ten minutes early," Bentley said. "My class, as I recall, was from 10:00 to 12:00, and each student had at least one camera, so there were approximately twenty-four cameras, and all of them loaded."[14] The FBI used many of these photographs during its investigation of the shootings.

At about 11:45 A.M., a Kent State policeman, Harold Rice, stood by the ROTC ruins and using a bullhorn ordered the students to disperse. It is unlikely any heard him, given the distance, the wind, and the clamor from the crowd. The Guard brought up a jeep and Rice, his driver, and two other Guardsmen rode out toward the gathering. Rice again gave the order to disperse. Dean Kahler described "somebody with a bullhorn talking about the isms of the day." "I got a little bored," he recalled,

> wondering what the hell has this got to do with getting troops off campus and what our rights were, what our responsibilities were. You know: what can I do, what couldn't I do, and "Attention, students, you are gathered illegally. This is an illegal gathering. Please disperse." That was greeted with a lot of Bronx cheering [and] the anti-war slogans: "One, two, three, four we don't want your f-ing war"; "Pigs off campus"; "Green pigs . . ." something. I can't remember the rest of that, but that was the chant that was going on.[15]

Some protesters threw stones, and Rice claimed "the occupants [of the jeep] were hit several times."[16] Rice returned three times to issue the order to disperse, and on the last one Major Harry Jones ran out to bring the jeep back to the skirmish line. Captain Ron Snyder reverted to present tense as he recalled the experience: "With that, this thing rapidly deteriorates. We [had] seen certain individuals that we had seen before who seemed to be hyping everybody up."[17] Snyder did not elaborate on who these individuals were, but this suggests that for Snyder, outside agitators or at least a core of radicals were responsible for the events.

Also among the crowd was William Derry Heasley. He grew up in Kent, joined the Navy in 1963, and served in Vietnam. Heasley came to oppose the war, and as a Kent State student helped organize some of the "peaceful protests against the Vietnam War in '68, possibly '69." But he drifted out of the organized effort after seeing some of the more radical students become involved. As the Guard assumed control over the campus and the town, he mistakenly believed martial law had been declared. In his 1990 interview, he recalled his expectation that President White would address the students at noon on May 4.

"Encouraging communication was a key word," Heasley said.

I felt that in that direction lay any hope for peaceful change. And it really was with that concept in my mind that I walked out early to the Commons and sat down before there was anyone there. I felt lonely. I was in the middle of the grass before the bell, with no one around me. And to my back, tens of yards away, was the burnt-out hole of the ROTC building with—I thought, kind of in a ridiculous manner—a bunch of soldiers guarding it. I didn't understand what was left to guard.

He stayed there as the crowd grew larger. "I looked around and most people were simply students who placed themselves there to protest the war—maybe more specifically, the invasion of Cambodia after the President had promised not to do so. They were not there to, quote, attack the Guard, unquote."

Heasley heard the Guard read the riot act and walked across the line to tell the Guardsmen that the crowd could not hear them.

The only thing I succeeded in was having the jeep drive the man with the bullhorn around, which got the jeep pelted with some rocks, which ruffled feathers, got the men on the jeep irate and angry. I heard him say before driving off, "Okay, that's it. Let's go." And that's what led directly, as far as I know, to firing up tear gas.[18]

Kahler remained unconvinced of the Guard's justification in trying to disperse the crowd.

They actually performed their legal responsibility and read it to us and I'm looking around. I said [sarcastically], "Boy, I see a lot of rioting going on here." Windows being broken, people looting, people beating each other up, fires being set everywhere; I mean there wasn't any of that going on. It was just students. It was lunchtime, you know. Kent had a large commuter population. So where are these people supposed to go? A nice warm day. Student Union is right there. This is where we hang out anyway.

[Interviewer]: So there was a mixture of people who are there to protest. . . .

Ninety percent, 95 percent maybe more just out and about, wanting to see what's going on. Three to 5 percent actually maybe protesting until they read and started telling us we were gathered illegally on our own campus at noontime. Yeah, give me a break. There are 40 or 50 of them. There are . . . 2,000 or 3000 of us.[19]

Rick Byrum was among what he described as the "curiosity seekers" on the Commons on May 4,

not as a political radical or anything of that nature. I want[ed] to see what was going to happen, and there are many, many people that were like that. Let me say this though, I knew something was going to happen because I had a wet handkerchief in my pocket. And many of us carried wet handkerchiefs in our pockets because we knew we were—two days before that, we'd been gassed at some point in time, or the gas was in the air and it was pungent and it hurt.

Like many, he did not foresee the coming violence. "I . . . knew that something was going to happen, but I didn't think it was going to be that serious. They'd shoot some teargas, do what we've done on Sunday, play a little tag, chase the students off. [The students would] get tired of it and go to class."[20]

Ken Hammond had been among those involved in leftist and antiwar groups trying to organize and control the growing protest that Mike Alewitz had described as "organic." At the start of the rally, Hammond stood upon the brick structure housing the Victory Bell to call for a student strike. For him, the failure of antiwar groups to organize one helped contribute to the shootings.

And there was a meeting Monday morning over at the Sub-Hub to try to figure out what to do. By that point, things were just snowballing. We tried to call for a student strike on May 4th. I was the idiot that got up and made that little call. You can hear on that recording that they put out in the *Chestnut Burr,* you can just barely hear, some people in the crowd started going, "Strike, strike, strike!" And then that just gets swept away when the guard starts saying it's an illegal assembly and you have to disperse, and tear gas and all that stuff. So that, for me, sort

National Guard troops fired tear gas and began their movements against the crowd of students at approximately 12:05 P.M. (May 4 Collection. Kent State University Libraries. Special Collections and Archives.)

of—that moment on May 4th where it was just clearly, it was beyond control, that there was nothing that we could do . . . that was rough, because what happened then happened in part, happened because we didn't have the capacity to manage it, to manage the situation.[21]

According the Scranton Commission, ninety-six men and seven officers formed a skirmish line in front of the ROTC building. Other reports had 113 men and officers facing the crowd. Ten Ohio State Highway Patrol Officers were there as well.[22] Once Rice's jeep returned, Canterbury ordered the crowd dispersed and eight to ten grenadiers "with M79 grenade launchers fired two volleys of teargas canisters into the crowd."[23] Some students scattered, but the wind blew most of the gas harmlessly away. The general then ordered the line to march across the Commons area toward the crowd at the Victory Bell. The Guard had been ordered to "lock and load" their M1 rifles with an eight-round clip of .30 caliber ammunition and a bullet moved up into the chamber, ready to fire once the safety mechanism was released.

In his 2012 interview, Ron Snyder insisted on calling this demonstration a riot that, in terms of framing the memory narrative and interpretation of which happened and its meaning, helps to justify the Guard's response. "They did exactly what rioters do, you see. And the thing I want to emphasize here: anybody that says it wasn't a riot is wrong. It's a riot. It meets every legal and ethical definition of a riot."[24] Befitting his matter-of-fact tone and perspective, Captain Snyder in his earlier interview situates the events as just a mission to accomplish.

> [Interviewer]: What was going through your mind as you were leading your men?
>
> Only I was just waiting for a mission statement. What they wanted me to do, that was all. There wasn't anything that I'd seen that was insurmountable, anything like that. They proceeded to read the riot act, as it was known, that was the "cease and desist and remove yourself" kind of thing. It didn't appear to me that anybody was going to go anywhere, and it was just a foregone conclusion that eventually we were going to have to remove them, and probably with tear gas, which eventually we did. We moved everybody before us, tear gassed them, and moved on up the hill. Took our position where we'd been assigned, and then I just awaited on further orders.[25]

As Snyder describes, the Guardsmen advanced across the Commons with Company A on the right flank, Company C on the left, and Troop G in the middle. Canterbury stood behind them, still in his business suit that he wore earlier to avoid attracting attention to himself during his morning meetings. Reporters, photographers, and onlookers were nearby as the Guard fired tear gas and began to march. All but a few officers wore gas masks; most carried M1 rifles, some .45 caliber pistols, others had shotguns. As part of Canterbury's original plan, when the Guard reached the Victory Bell, the skirmish line split into two. Canterbury and Lieutenant Colonel Fassinger went with Company A and Troop G up to the crest of Blanket Hill between Taylor and Johnson Halls near the Pagoda sculpture. Major Harry Jones and Captain Ron Snyder followed Company C to the Guard's left to close the space between Taylor and Prentice Halls. This way, Canterbury could disperse the demonstration, clear the Commons, and prevent students from getting back through. "The plan was to drive them back toward the Tri-Towers, get them over the hill," Snyder remembers.[26] Indeed, students retreated as the Guard advanced. Most went up over the other side of Blanket Hill and down toward a practice football field or into the Prentice Hall parking lot. Others went inside nearby buildings.

According to Ayers, these early stages of the confrontation combined elements of fear ("It's impressive in that you are not, you will not fail to move when you see a line of soldiers with helmets and gas masks where you cannot see a face, M1 rifles with fixed bayonets") and farce ("And this lone jeep pulls out, and the guy on the P.A. was just not the right one to pick. Should have been somebody with this big bellowing deep voice. . . . But it was just a squeaky voice saying, 'This is an illegal gathering, you people have to leave and [imitates voice] rah rah rah.'").

The dark comedy continued with the Guard's indiscriminate use of tear gas. "They were shooting it everywhere," Ayers said. "If they saw somebody that looked like a student—I don't know what threat a student sitting in his dorm room posed to the National Guard at that moment. They weren't even chasing people at that time. They were standing there facing a group of yelling people."[27] An instructor in the Kent State University School of Technology, Lowell S. Zurbuch, was eating lunch with a colleague as they watched these events unfold. "And it was sort of a sense of frivolity that students were being chased around and throwing tear gas canisters and much of it looked to be in jest. I don't know that I really appreciated it. I was taken aback by the silliness of it all."[28] On the Commons, some students picked up tear gas canisters and tossed them back at the Guard. "As we were coming around back—I think it's called Engleman, the older dorm—this kid's running past me, and he's going, 'I've never been tear-gassed before!'," said Janice Wascko. "He was so eager. And I yelled back, 'Obviously!' This pathetic idiot," she laughed.

Joe Cullum was among the more politically engaged students: "I was there for the announced reason from the previous Friday that we were going to have a discussion, a vote to decide whether or not to join the national student strike or try to end the war by trying to shut down the universities." He tried to pick up a tear gas canister to throw it back. "I tried it and I burned my hand. There's a chemical reaction going on in that thing and it was hot. So I picked it up and dropped it. And then began to become overcome by the gas so I started moving up the hill and dispersing with the rest of the crowd."[29] Michael Erwin (like Cullum one of the Kent 25 later indicted by the Portage County Grand Jury) had purchased a gas mask at a military surplus store a few weeks before May 4; he had it in his car still and brought it with him to the noon rally.

They were using small grenade launchers—[they] looked like small shotguns—and the projectile that it fired had some sort of mechanism on the end that dispersed the gas but the rest of the projectile which was probably 4 inches or so was just a real soft rubber cylinder. I know this because I put the gas mask on and I ran out and started picking these things up and throwing them back towards the National Guardsmen.[30]

William Heasley recalled his own sense of anger as the Guard advanced and protesters countered.

You know, I wasn't an organizer, but I was angry enough when the tear gas landed in that crowd of so many innocent people. I found myself throwing the tear gas away. And . . . [one of] the outside agitators . . . thought I was joining the brotherhood or something and he began yelling encouragement. And I thought he was stupid.

"I went to it because I was pretty pissed off about all this army—it seemed like an army to me," recalled Carol Mirman. Many like her felt it was about a right to assemble.

Now they were stabbing people. Now there were tanks. And this time there was tear gas and awful things and it didn't seem to make any sense and we were not supposed to be in groups of more than two people at one time. "Excuse me, I've got my rights, I'm not dispersing." But in fact when they started coming at us with guns, I dispersed with the rest of them. And we ran up the hill with the Guard behind us marching in line. And that was . . . a scary sight.[31]

Mike Alewitz believed the protests at Kent were part of a mass movement: he uses the pronoun "we" to collectivize the experience of those on the Commons on May 4. He was there when the first shots of tear gas came from the Guard. He concurs that at the time, he (or "we") did not see the events as escalating the way they did; once the Guard had marched to the Pagoda and to the space between Taylor and Prentice Halls, he considered the demonstration over.

Like everyone else, I did not anticipate we were going to be gunned down that day. I did not have any particular insight that that was going to happen. If you had said, "Is there going to be a problem?" I'd have said, "It doesn't look like it." You know, they're over there, we're over here. They're not bothering us. They're gonna probably just let

us do what we're doing. People are gonna get up and talk. We're going to call something later on. That was my frame of mind. And even
when the gas . . . barrage took place, it was, "Okay, they broke it up.
This is going to be bad. Now we got to get our shit together. We gotta
have a meeting, we gotta organize this thing, but it's over for today.
Everybody go home." And everybody was going home. I mean, the
demonstration was over.[32]

Once he reached the crest of Blanket Hill, Canterbury decided to push the
students farther away. Snyder's men in Company C remained in position between Taylor and Prentice Halls and watched as Canterbury along with officers
and members of Company A and Troop G went down the hill, across a road,
and onto the football practice field. When the Guard reached the practice field,
the students split into clusters. Some remained in the Prentice Hall parking
lot in front of the Guardsmen. Others moved to the Guard's left and stood
along the balcony on Taylor Hall, others to the right of the Guard along the
hill near what is today the Gym Annex. Some filtered back behind the Guard
near the Pagoda. Chanting continued and some students threw rocks at the
Guardsmen as they stood on the field. (The most likely source for the rocks
was a construction site nearby at Dunbar Hall.) As before, some Guardsmen,
including General Del Corso, threw rocks back at students.[33] Guardsmen and
students also threw tear gas canisters back at one another. Included among
the Guard on the field was Terry Norman, the law enforcement major and
informant, who was taking pictures as he walked with the Guard. Reportedly,
Norman also threw rocks back at students. Chuck Ayers watched this spectacle
after ascending to the top of the hill adjacent to Taylor Hall:

We had the same routine. Somebody would come running up, usually
with a wet towel or something over their face, pick up the tear gas
canister and throw it right back into the middle of the Guardsmen,
who all had the gasmasks. So it would land in the middle of them,
they would pick up, throw it back. Sometimes these canisters, the same
canister, would go back three, four, six times. And there were some
rocks being thrown. I never saw anybody hit with a rock. Doesn't mean
it didn't happen. But every time I would watch someone throwing a
rock and could follow the trajectory of the rock, it would land some
distance away from the Guardsmen, and you could see them sort of
sidestep it. It rolled past. One of the Guardsmen would pick up the

During the demonstration, students and Guardsmen threw objects at one another; here, a student is throwing an object at the Guard. (May 4 Collection. Kent State University Libraries. Special Collections and Archives.)

same rock, throw it back into the parking lot of the students, who would see it coming and they would sidestep it. And so sometimes the same rock went back and forth several times. And so this was going on and I thought, this is really silly stuff. And it was exciting, but it still didn't feel any sense of it being serious at this time. It just didn't make sense to me.[34]

The Scranton Commission stated that as the Guard stood on the practice field, "The crowd on the parking lot was unruly and threw many missiles at the Guardsmen on the football field. It was at this point that the shower of stones apparently became heaviest."[35] James Best writes that the Guard faced "a heavy barrage of rocks" at this time.[36] Several narrators—Chuck Ayers among them—dispute or downplay the amount of rocks thrown and the damage they may have caused. They also state that there were not that many students in the parking lot or close to the fence surrounding the Guard. Alan Canfora, the closest demonstrator, who was waving a black flag at the Guard, was some fifty yards away. The rock throwing or lack thereof comes into play among the narrators as evidence for either overreaction by the Guard or justifiable fear and self-defense. According to later FBI investigations, it was at this point that the Guard reported the only soldier injured on May 4 was Lawrence Shafer, who suffered a bruise to his arm. According to the FBI investigation, he was treated after the shootings, and the injury did not prevent Shafer from being among the Guardsmen who opened fire—in Shafer's case, wounding student Joe Lewis.[37]

In addition, although the "sniper theory" has been roundly dismissed by most Kent State shootings experts,[38] and Ayers emphasized that he himself does not believe in any conspiracy theories, he nevertheless offers an intriguing remembrance in the middle of the protest as some of the Guardsmen on the practice field dropped to one knee and aimed their rifles at students in and near the Prentice Hall parking lot.

> At one point, I had my camera up. I remember panning across—a little 35mm camera—panning across the line of Guardsmen. Somewhere in the line, I can't even tell you where it was, although I think it was close to the front of the line facing the Prentice parking lot, I saw one of the guys pull his arm into the air—I can't tell you if it was right or left handed, because I've heard all the debates about that since then—and saw the arm recoil like that, and heard this pop. And I talked to several friends right after that and I said, "God, can you believe this guy is shooting in the air?" And they said, "What are you talking about?" These were people that were standing right next to me. It was in my viewfinder. That's why I saw it. If you weren't looking exactly there you probably wouldn't have noticed it, and there was so much noise that if I hadn't seen that, that pop probably would never have registered to me as a gunshot. There are rocks hitting pavement, there are people all around, there's yelling, there are people dropping books on the ground. Not like they're running or anything, but when people are standing there, you put your books down like that and stand and watch. There's a lot of noise. But I saw that and I just thought, That's even stupider. That just provokes people.
>
> It wasn't long after that that I noticed that this straight line suddenly turned like this, at a right angle, with several Guardsmen facing the parking lot. They knelt down on one knee, they took the rifles and aimed into the crowd.[39]

That an officer fired a pistol in the air while the Guard was on the practice field remains in dispute. The Scranton Commission noted that at least one other observer, Richard Schreiber, an assistant professor of journalism, saw what Ayers recalls he saw. One Guardsman (Barry Morris of Troop G) also claims he saw an officer fire a .45 caliber pistol; a spent .22 caliber casing was found the next day near the football field. Major Harry Jones carried a .22 Beretta, one he borrowed from Captain Snyder, but denied he fired at any point during May 4.

Ayers went on to dismiss arguments used to defend the Guard's actions.

> Here was this symbol of what everybody was angry about, kneeling, aiming rifles not just at protesters or rock throwers in a parking lot, but at a dormitory full of big glass windows filled with students. And I thought, That's really bad. Again, I'm thinking that all this is doing is, if they're trying to defuse the situation, they're doing the exact opposite.

Ayers stressed that even the most aggressive of the protesters retreated from the movements of the Guard.

> When you get a group of guys in full battle gear—helmets, gas masks and fixed bayonets—as they move it's like the parting of the Red Sea. The crowd goes this way and that way. Nobody stands their ground and confronts these people. They never had any difficulty moving anywhere they wanted to be, which is one of the reasons I was so surprised to see them stopped on the football field. I've heard all the stories about, oh, they were hemmed in, they were surrounded by students and this chain-link fence. Well, the chain-link fence is on two sides of a practice football field and it is wide open on the other two sides. Anywhere they wanted to walk they would have walked, and the crowd would have parted.[40]

Catherine Delattre was with her boyfriend, and together they were moving from the practice field to the Prentice Hall parking lot. She described the Guard's response as a cross between "scary" and "silly"—the latter, especially, when the Guard appeared to trap themselves on the practice football field. "If anybody really wanted to at that point, students could have thrown a million rocks because they were inside that chain-link area," she said.[41] Carol Mirman, who did throw rocks, said that she couldn't hit anything due to the distance between herself and the Guard. "I did see one rock hit a Guardsman," she said, adding that it bounced off the Guardsman's helmet. Next, Mirman said, each of the Guardsmen dropped to one knee and aimed their weapons at the protesters, like the Continental Army. "The Guard was not surrounded at that point. . . . Now that's not to deny that those people,

While on the practice football field, one group of Guardsmen kneeled and aimed their rifles at the students standing in the Prentice Hall parking lot. (May 4 Collection. Kent State University Libraries. Special Collections and Archives.)

those Guardsman that were down there, didn't feel surrounded, didn't feel threatened, weren't tired, weren't in all kinds of circumstances. But the reality, the physical reality was not that."[42]

While on the practice field, a group of Guard leaders gathered, leading many to speculate later that it was at this point these leaders made a plan to fire at the students once they reached the Pagoda. After being on the field for ten minutes, Canterbury ordered his troops back to the ROTC building. In order to get there, they had to retrace their steps back up Blanket Hill toward the Pagoda. This meant going through the larger crowd of students that was now standing there, perhaps hundreds. But as the Guard began to go back, the crowd parted, and the troops moved back up the hill. Again, how close students came to the Guard and how much rock throwing occurred are matters of difference among the narratives. In the oral history, in reading reports and transcripts of trials later, and in examining available photographs and film, the questions of distance have become malleable pieces of evidence deployed to construct meaning, as do beliefs about numbers of students, where they were, and what they were doing.

A grainy and very short 8mm film shot by Chris Abell showed that most students either remained away from the Guard at the base of the hill near the parking lot, in the Prentice Hall lot itself, or along either side of the

Guard as the troops moved back up the hill. Many students assumed the demonstration was over and had turned away from the Guard to leave. The majority of students in close proximity to the Guardsmen were not protesting but observing along the terrace of Taylor Hall or heading away or to classes along sidewalks near that building. Some were closer, like Joseph Lewis, who was about seventy feet away. He and other students near him were protesting the Guard, but they did not throw rocks or rush toward the soldiers. Lewis was standing still giving the Guard an obscene hand gesture as the troops reached the Pagoda. When the Guard reached the Pagoda, the film shows a loose group of perhaps twenty to fifty students begin to run from the bottom of the hill hear Taylor Hall and the parking lot, somewhere between two hundred to three hundred feet away, up the hill toward the Guard. In this group were some of the more avid protesters. The Scranton Commission report states that a few of them reached about twenty yards from the Guard as the soldiers reached the Pagoda, but most remained about sixty to seventy-five yards away. Later, many Guardsmen, including General Canterbury, claimed students were as close as four or five yards away as they charged. Watching the film, the longer distance for the loose group is more accurate; other reports and research suggest that the closest individuals in this group were about eighty-five to one hundred feet away and the bulk of them somewhere between two hundred to three hundred feet away.[43] Some individual students were standing closer in what became the line of fire. The larger group of twenty to fifty had begun to follow the Guard as they expected the soldiers to continue retreating toward the ROTC building.

In his oral history, Joe Cullum recalled being about twenty yards from the Guard as the troops reached the crest on their return. But then he remembered seeing John Cleary lying wounded across from him right after the shots. Cleary was 110 feet away. Cullum disputes much of what Guardsmen and their supporters later argued.

> When we got as far as the football practice field on the other side of the hill it's when I realized we were sort of walking into a trap. There was a big fence at that time that was on the east end of that field. So I was trying to encourage students to move away from the fence. I was kind of out in front of them trying to signal that we were going to get—that we were downwind from the gas and we were going to get stuck in there—and just gas us. And so I moved up—I actually went into Prentice Hall, tried to get some water in my eyes. . . . Then I left Prentice Hall; by that time the Guard had stopped. You know, students

had moved away from the fence so the Guard had stopped where they were. And when I got back out there that was about the point when they started to move back toward Taylor Hall and, ultimately, we assumed, back to the ROTC building. And they continued to move back up toward the crest of the hill by Taylor Hall and I was pretty close to them. I was way too close to them at that point.

[Interviewer]: You were following behind?

Yeah. But I was probably 20 yards behind them.

[Interviewer]: Were you the closest one that you could tell at that point? Or were there others near you?

No. There were others in front of me. A lot behind me. A lot beside me. But the crowd was really a lot smaller by that point. A lot of people really had left and also by that time as I was following the Guardsmen, there were people who had, you know, were not part of the demonstration, who were coming from the direction of the gym on their way to class. So, I was walking by people who were walking perpendicular to me on their way to music and speech or Taylor Hall or whatever. Or back to the dorms in that area around Prentice Hall for lunch. It was a little after noon.

So, there was sort of an atmosphere is that, you know, we were dispersed but, now they're going back. They're retreating. We won this skirmish. But as I said, the numbers were a lot smaller. They were actually walking behind the Guardsmen. By that point, I didn't see any more rocks being thrown. That was more down on the practice field but now they were going back up over the hill and there was this sort of . . . almost this circus atmosphere. We stood our ground. And so we were gonna walk back to the Commons. Maybe we're still gonna have this vote on the student strike.[44]

At about 12:24 P.M., as the Guard reached the crest of the hill at the Pagoda sculpture, soldiers on the right flank closest to Taylor Hall, most of whom were in Troop G, turned in unison about 135 degrees back toward the Prentice Hall parking lot, lowered their weapons and began firing. The soldiers fired sixty-seven rounds in thirteen seconds. The Guardsmen did not fire at the crowd of students closest to them along the terrace at Taylor

Howard Ruffner's photograph of the Guard as they opened fire near the Pagoda sculpture. (May 4 Collection. Kent State University Libraries. Special Collections and Archives. © 1970 Howard Ruffner. Used with permission of Howard Ruffner.)

Hall. Instead, they fired in a triangular field down toward the parking lot where the rock throwing had occurred: the left side of the triangle marked by Don Drumm's metal sculpture, *Solar Totem,* just next to the terrace of Taylor Hall and the right by a set of trees closer to Memorial Gym. Students in the line of fire turned and ran, some dove for cover behind trees or cars, some froze, others dropped to the ground. General Canterbury, who had marched ahead of the troops as they reached the crest of Blanket Hill and had begun descending toward the Commons, ran back and yelled at the troops to cease fire. Colonel Fassinger also yelled, as did Major Jones, who ran along the line of soldiers knocking rifles up with his baton and in some cases banging soldiers on their helmets to get them to stop firing.

After firing, the Guard continued its march down the hill, across the Commons back to the ROTC building. One student lay dead: Jeffrey Miller.

This image captures one scene moments after the shooting, with Jeff Miller's body in the foreground, and Dean Kahler lying in the grass just beyond and to the right, surrounded by a small group of students. (May 4 Collection. Kent State University Libraries. Special Collections and Archives.)

He was a twenty-year-old psychology major who had been protesting the Guard and at the time was facing them from the road near the practice field, 265 feet away. Three others lay dying: Allison Krause, a nineteen-year-old Honors College art major who also had been protesting, shot as she dove for cover behind a car in the Prentice Hall lot, 343 feet away; Sandra Scheuer, a twenty-year-old speech pathology and audiology major, shot as she walked to class 390 feet away; and William Schroeder, a nineteen-year-old psychology major and member of the ROTC, there to observe the protest, hit as he lay prone in the Prentice Hall lot, 390 feet away.[45]

Nine others were wounded: Joseph Lewis (70 feet away),[46] shot in the abdomen and left leg; John Cleary (110 feet away), shot through the left side of the chest; Thomas Grace (200 feet away), shot in the left ankle; Alan Canfora (225 feet away), shot through the right wrist; Dean Kahler (300 feet

Just after the shootings, students came to the aid of Joe Lewis, who lay injured 60 feet from the Guard. The Don Drumm sculpture is in the foreground. (May 4 Collection. Kent State University Libraries. Special Collections and Archives.)

away), shot in the lower back and permanently paralyzed from the waist down; Douglas Wrentmore (329 feet away), wounded in the right knee; James Russell (375 feet away), wounded as he stood near the Memorial Gymnasium off the main line of fire by birdshot fired from a shotgun; Robert Stamps (495 feet away), shot in the right buttock; and D. Scott MacKenzie (750 feet away), shot in the left rear of his neck.

Some of the most powerful oral history testimony comes from narrators who witnessed the shooting, including at least one wounded student. Carol Mirman is the individual in a white shirt walking behind Mary Ann Vecchio and the body of Jeff Miller in the famous John Filo photograph.

> I was with that group of people that followed them up the hill and said, "Yeah, get off the campus, get outta here, we don't want ya' here, what are ya' doin' here, get outta here," and was making lots of noise. And then I heard a single shot. And then there was a volley. I was very close to the Guard and the bullets whizzed past my ears. I was very much in the line of fire.
>
> I do recall . . . some of those things are sort of burned in my memory.

I remember thinking so clearly when that volley went by my ears, "This is not what it sounds like on TV. This is not what the sound of bullets sound like on cartoons." It was a very different sound, the bullets so close to one's head, to one's ears. Very different sound. And I jumped over bodies and ran down the hill. I also recall some students saying "Walk, don't run. They're only blanks." And I remember thinking "Huh? Why carry a weapon if you don't have something in it that's intended to work." I'm outta here. And I did. I ran over bodies two, three deep were hitting the ground. And so I ran down the hill to a place of safety, but by the time I was behind that yellow Volkswagen which was right near where Jeff Miller was shot, the volley had stopped. I got up when the volley had stopped to look to see what the heck had happened. And I did see Jeff Miller at that time . . . and . . . that's when the photograph of me was taken [with] Jeff Miller. I'd never seen blood like that. I'd never seen anything like that. It was a complete shock. I wanted to touch him. I remember wanting to hold him, but I was afraid of the blood. I did touch him, I did touch and hold his hand. 'Cause I didn't want him to feel alone.

And when I came back to the side of Jeff Miller that's when Mary Ann Vecchio was there. . . . I didn't know who she was. I knew she was a young person and she was freaked out and I put my arms around her shoulder and . . . I remember feeling her. She felt like a block of ice. She was frozen. She was stone. She couldn't move. . . . And I don't remember, I think it was before, when I was at Jeff first that there was a guy that had a flag and he dipped his flag in the blood, when I remember feeling—and then he jumped in the blood. His feet touched the blood and the blood smashed/splashed out. He was so angry. . . . It was all kind of shocking to me.

And then some of the National Guard came in the area, and this is all in the photographs. And I remember the Guard in that particular vicinity were as shocked as I was. I remember the looks on their faces. They didn't know what to do. And they didn't know what to say. But there were many students who had come from other areas that were gathered and they [the Guard] became afraid of what, of the emotion that was going on and they retreated. And more students gathered and then ambulances came and people took things away.[47]

Catherine Delattre was in the same area as Carol Mirman—the parking lot of Prentice Hall—when the shooting began.

Student Tom Miller (roommate to Tom Grace and Alan Canfora) jumping in the blood left where Jeff Miller (no relation) had been killed. (May 4 Collection. Kent State University Libraries. Special Collections and Archives.)

And my boyfriend said to me, "I think that's bullets." And I panicked. I turned around and I decided that I was going to run across the parking lot in the same direction from where I had just come, in the same path that I had followed, right along the cars, because there was a little dip in the land there where you can roll down a hill. In my mind—everybody was getting down—but I decided to run and that I was going to run there and roll down the hill and that I'd be safe. It's just, you know, I wasn't thinking. And my boyfriend was running after me, screaming, "Get down! Get down!" And I have a picture that I can show you. He just hit me in mid-air and knocked me down and threw himself on top of me. And at that point the shooting stopped. . . . And there was somebody—I think it was Bobby Stamps that had been shot in the buttock—was there and we walked over to the building, and he went in there was waiting for help. . . . Then we walked out of that and started back through the parking lot and saw each person who had been killed. It was just horrendous.[48]

Faculty marshal Jerry Lewis had moved into the Prentice Hall parking lot as the Guard began returning up the hill back toward the Pagoda. He was

Many students like these pictured here ran or dove for cover once the shooting began. Narrator Catherine Delattre was pushed to the ground by her boyfriend in right center of this photograph. (May 4 Collection. Kent State University Libraries. Special Collections and Archives.)

standing behind Sandra Scheuer as the shooting began. As he does often, Lewis reconstructs his thoughts and dialogue in this interview:

> Just as the Guard got to the Pagoda, the right rear echelon of the Guard turned together and fired. Now, I saw the smoke come out of the weapons, because light travels faster than sound, and having been in the Army, I knew those were real firings. And so I . . . and I never know why I did this, I've always puzzled, but for some reason I went to my right, who knows why, which took me out of the line of fire. If I had gone to my left, because I was standing right behind, of course, Sandy Scheuer. So if I had gone to my left, I would have been in the line of fire. But I took myself out of the line of fire, hid behind a bush, and was on the ground long enough that the firing continued. So the firing stopped, and there was this really hushed—Alan Canfora talks about this a lot—and I heard the hush as well.
>
> So I stood up, and I remember saying to myself, "What should I do?" And I describe this in other places as having a lifeguard mentality. . . . I realized my first responsibility was to the students, but I didn't know what to do. And a student who knew me rushed up, and said,

"Dr. Lewis, those were blanks, weren't they?" Now I realized that the students all thought that they were firing blanks. So I pointed . . . I didn't know it was Sandy Scheuer's body, but I pointed at the body . . . and said, "No, those were real bullets."[49]

Ellis Berns was also with Sandra Scheuer when she was shot and offers a powerful recollection of those moments.

So we were walking away, and you just didn't feel right. You just felt like there was something in the air. But I always believed that if people have guns they are going to use them. People don't have guns just to have guns. The concept of rubber bullets—no. That's why I was a little bit nervous about it, and that's why I thought, you know, this is getting to be too much of a game and somebody's going to get hurt and let's go. And that's what I had said to her: "Let's just go."

So we were walking away and we were over in the parking lot, and that's when we heard the—and I'll say the firing, but we didn't know what it was. I can say I didn't know what it was. All I knew was, instinctually, what I knew was this wasn't right. In a split second, I knew that I was going to grab her and we were going to go to some type of cover. And that's all I knew. I don't know why. Never fired a gun, never fired once. But I heard a volley of shots that I don't think I'll ever forget. It just seemed to last forever. We both hit the ground. I had my arm around her, my left arm around her. We both were kind of diving, if you will, towards cover. Not sure why, other than we just knew we didn't want to be standing. We dove for cover, and I remember waiting until I felt it was safe to get up. Until we felt like the shooting was over. You didn't know it was shooting. It felt like it was shooting. You knew it was some kind of shooting. So you waited, and I couldn't even begin to tell you how long we waited for. But we waited. Finally, you can kind of hear things in the background, kind of indicating that you're—you hear people screaming, and then you realize, okay.

I remember I had my arm around her, and she was laying on her stomach face down. I remember calling out to her, "Sandy, it's over. Let's go, let's go." I remember calling out to her, and there was no response. And then I looked. And then I realized that I believe she had been, she was hit, I think it was the left side or the right side? I think it was the right side. I could be a little off on this. [pause] It had to be the right side. The right side, because the bullet had not just grazed her but had severed a carotid artery. So there was a lot of blood . . . I don't know what to do. I remember trying to administer first aid. I remember trying to reach in, to try to stop the bleeding into her neck, because you could just see where the bullet had penetrated her carotid artery. I think it was her carotid artery, I'm not a doctor. But there was just blood all over. And she was totally unconscious.

I remember calling out for help, calling an ambulance, which seemed like an eternity. People came over to try to help out. We moved her. We tried to revive her. We tried some CPR. We just wanted to stop the bleeding. I remember trying to lift her feet so we could keep blood going to her brain. But it seemed totally unsuccessful. And then finally an ambulance arrived. I remember asking somebody in the ambulance, "I want to go with her." And they said, "No, absolutely not." So that was it. There are some accounts, I believe I have heard that she actually had a heartbeat to the hospital, but I can't attest to that at all. In my mind, she had died right there. Because to the best of my knowledge, she had never gained consciousness again. We did everything we could, but it was just a complete, it was just a really, you just couldn't believe it.[50]

Captain Ron Snyder recalled his experience as the shooting began and in the immediate aftermath. He and several of his men moved out and stood around the body of Jeff Miller. His matter-of-fact recollections contrast with those of other narrators.

Anyway, we see immediately that some students were hit. As I recall, I called for the ambulances at that time, because we had what we called a command post, I think it was down in front of the library or thereabouts, and we asked that they send the ambulances up. And then I kind of moved forward with a small squad or a couple men. In fact, if you look at the pictures, there was that young lady from Florida that was kneeling over one of the bodies.

[Interviewer]: Mary Ann Vecchio.

Yes. And I could see right away that that fellow was dead. And I recall, to my left, somebody was hit. And I think it was a girl, but I can't be certain as I sit here. I just know from what I've seen or read.

Immediately to my right, which I never really ever had anybody explain to me, seemed to be a meeting of some fellows with armbands

on, of three or four, that got right up in the corner of the one building and they're having this conversation. Which seemed odd to me.
Meantime there's all this other stuff going on, with regards to people
wounded, people running, people screaming, people crying. And it was
at that time that, I think about the time the first ambulance rolled in, I
think I decided at that time that I was going to pull back and see what
was going on, because there was too much confusion going on there
and they didn't need additional confusion. Some people asked to go
by our line and I could see that they were simply trying to escape the
area that they'd got caught in, and we let them go around the corner
of I think the architectural building.

And then we pulled back to our original position, back by the
burned-out ROTC building. I don't recall if I got an order to do that,
or one of my troopers may have said to me, "A Company's pulled back,"
and I just thought that was the right thing to do rather than get cut
off by a large group of people. You don't know those things, you have
to play it by ear on the ground.[51]

In his reports to legal authorities afterward, Snyder claimed he saw Miller
charging at the Guard with "his right hand raised and it looked like a small
weapon in his hand" and yelling "kill, kill"; Snyder also claimed he found a
gun on Jeff Miller's body when he walked over to investigate. In the subsequent
trials, Snyder admitted he had invented the story of finding a gun on Miller's
body as a possible defense for the Guardsmen should there be a trial.[52]

The anonymous member of the Ohio National Guard offered a dramatic
memory narrative in defense of the Guard and of his own thoughts as the
firing began.

We came back down over the hill, like, retreat, advance, retreat, advance. And things for a moment there got quiet, and I figured, well
they made enough advances, we got a show of force, the bayonets
were out. . . . And I was going back down over the hill, standing down
over the hill, and I heard pops. One pop, a couple pops, and [rapidly]
poppoppoppoppop poppoppoppoppop. And I said, "What the hell?"
I said to myself. And I'm sayin' to myself, "Should I shoot?" "Shouldn't
I shoot?" I couldn't shoot, there was someone in front of me.

[Interviewer]: Were you to the back?—

Captain Ron Snyder, holding the baton, as he and his Guard troops surround the body of Jeff Miller. (May 4 Collection. Kent State University Libraries. Special Collections and Archives. © 1970 Howard Ruffner. Used with permission of Howard Ruffner.)

I was down over the hill and I heard the shots going off, and I turned around, and it was a matter of a heartbeat, and the shooting was over. I didn't have my glasses on, I didn't see, but I saw men with the position with the rifles aiming, and some of the men I were with were starting to aim, but we didn't know when to shoot, what to shoot, or if we should shoot. Very quickly we got the order, "Cease fire! Cease fire!" I don't recall, it may have been our major going around with a baton, a night stick if you will, hitting the rifles, "Cease fire!" Oh, he was angry, he was pushin' and shovin'—"Cease"—knockin' the rifles down, "Cease fire! Cease fire! Cease fire!" Very quickly our order came to cease fire. An officer came and pushed our rifles up in the air—pushed mine up in the air. He said, "Stop! Halt! Don't move! Stay here! Don't move!" And he pushed our rifles up. Very quickly a line was drawn between those individuals that had fired and between the ones of us who were backup on the other side. We then very quickly were given the order to "About—" to form up in a formation—"About face," not look at what was going on. And we marched down—which the road is no longer there, it's blocked now—but where the one fella was shot that was laying—there was a road that went down behind campus, if I recall, somewhere. We marched down through there.

[Interviewer]: In your group.

Yeah. And we were a small group, thirty or forty. And we got down around, there was a group of students standing in the road, and I figured, "Boy, here it comes." And the sergeant said, "Keep moving. Keep marching. Do not, I say, do NOT again move your weapons!" And like the Red Sea, they parted. We went through and went back down to the bivouac area.

[Interviewer]: So you just knew that there had been a discharge of weapons and that you were moving away from the area. OK. I think that's important psychologically to know.

Quite truthfully, Sandy, had there not been our own soldiers in front of us, had we been a different group—I can speak for myself, I would have fired. I would have assumed that when others were firing, they were firing for a reason. I would have fired.

[Interviewer]: At anything that was there?

At anything that was there, because obviously the crowd was advancing. I remember we advanced, went back. I recall someone throwing—landing beside me—a, if you will, 2 x 2—there was some construction somewhere on campus going on, I'm not sure where, but there were reinforcement bars being thrown at that point—which is a reinforcement bar you put in concrete—landed beside me, was a 2 x 2 piece of wood, about two feet long, perhaps, with nails driven through it. If you will, about ten nails. That was not something you find laying around, that was made on purpose. Had it hit someone, it would have certainly caused a puncture wound, of sorts. And it just fell down beside—between several of us, and I sort of stepped over it. And there were all kind of missiles coming out of the air and things.

And I remember after the shooting, it got totally quiet . . . I heard air hissing out of a tire—that sound—bsssshhhoouu—the air hissing. It just got quiet. And then there were some screams. And then we again marched off, down to the side.[53]

While the FBI summary report stated that no "Guardsman claims he was hit with rocks immediately prior to the firing," it goes on to note that "one Guardsman stated that he had to move out of the way of a three inch 'log' just prior to the time that he heard shots."[54] It is possible that the Guardsman interviewed above by Halem is the same one as in the FBI report. Did the FBI report mean a three-foot (not inch) piece of wood? Did the size of the wood become larger with time in the memory of this Guardsman? Was the wood even thrown at all? So much remains in dispute among narrators, although in this particular case, it is doubtful, based on the evidence available, that anyone hurled an object like that described above. This narrator might be lying; he might be bringing in the statements and memories he heard from others then and in the intervening years or that he gathered from the news reports and trials. This version of events might also be "psychologically true," as oral historian Alessandro Portelli reminds us, something narrators deeply feel and believe although unsubstantiated or contradicted by investigations and other witnesses and narrators. This anonymous narrator also reveals something of the collective memory of the Guard—being under siege and fearful of attack by protesters on May 4.

Ron Sterlekar of the Mobrobius PIT was on the Commons; he was with James Russell when the firing commenced, and when it ended, Russell was laughing. "And he said, 'Ron, I've been hit.' [I said,] 'What are you talking about?' He said, 'Look.' And I looked down and he showed me his thigh, and there was blood coming from his thigh. Not much, it was like a trickle." Realizing Russell had been hit not only in his right thigh but also his head by birdshot from a shotgun, Sterlekar and other KSU students took him back to Stopher Hall. "And within twenty minutes"—or at least it seemed that way, he added—"the campus was shut down."

Dean Kahler had followed well behind the Guard as troops marched back over the hill. His knowledge of first aid and classes in zoology came to his mind the moment he was shot, giving him the immediate knowledge he had been paralyzed.

And I followed along and I got over almost to the edge of the practice football field and I saw them turn deliberately, lower their weapons, and started shooting. I mean I knew immediately just the way they turned, just the deliberate nature of what they were doing, that they were going to shoot. And I thought, "Geez, I have no place to hide." So I jumped on the ground, covered my head, and I keep hearing bullets hitting the ground around me. I said, "What the hell did I do? I never got close to these guys," you know. And suddenly I got hit. It felt like a bee sting and I thought, "Oh my god. They shot me."

And you know my brain kicked in because I—I did a lot of first aid work as a Boy Scout. So I told myself to slow down my breathing, relax, check myself out. Well, meanwhile, there are still bullets hitting the ground around me. So I checked my ribcage and felt a little something weird here. But I knew that I had a spinal cord injury to my legs because I told you earlier I was in Zoology class. We'd pith frogs. So I knew from that the reaction I had was just the exact same as pithing a frog. And then—then all of a sudden, bullets were still hitting around me and then it all got quiet when they quit. And then the screaming and howling started up again but this time there was more—there was more of an edge to it. People were seeing Jeffrey Miller bleeding to death and Allison Krause on the ground and you know various other people; Joe Lewis, John Cleary. You know, it's a wonder the three of us are still alive with the wounds that we sustained at that point, yeah.

After the shots, Rob Fox recalls "pandemonium," confusion, and a sense of powerlessness among those in the line of fire and the observers along the sides. "People were saying, 'Where are the ambulances?' It seemed like eternity 'til an ambulance finally got there."[55] Joe Cullum was photographed along with two other students giving first aid to John Cleary, an image that became the cover of *Life* magazine days later. Before the ambulances came to take the dead and wounded away, Cullum said, the Guard shot another tear gas canister into the crowd. This was likely a member of Captain Snyder's unit who had come out to investigate the condition of Jeff Miller; when the crowd around these Guardsmen began shouting obscenities at them, one of them threw a tear gas pellet at them in response.[56] "I thought maybe they would have had first aid training and after the shooting the National Guard might help the people who were wounded. That shows you how naive I was. . . . Then they went down the hill and back and I assumed where they had been originally by the ROTC building. So, when an ambulance finally came, that's when I realized how many there were that were hit." After helping Cleary, Cullum rode in an ambulance with another wounded student he realized later was Joe Lewis.

Ellen Mann, a senior at Kent State University School, established as part of Kent's early focus as a teacher training, or normal, college, administered first aid to Joe Lewis.[57] A polio survivor and self-described "hippie sympathizer," Mann saw Lewis flipping off the Guard right before he was shot.

> The next thing I know, he falls, he screams, "Oh my God, they shot me!" . . . I mean, he was . . . probably about four feet, five feet. And I rushed right over to him. He was kind of wriggling around. He was in pain. A couple of other guys came up, and we took his pants down . . . because there was a lot of blood. So we unzipped his jeans, pulled it down, and there was a hole blown out of him. It was really gory and really bloody.

After getting Joe Lewis to an ambulance, she began to walk back toward her school and by some Guardsmen who were smirking and laughing.[58]

Also in the line of fire was Ken Hammond, who had seen Sergeant Myron Pryor on the practice football field say something to each Guardsman in Company D.

> I was . . . twenty, thirty feet from Jeff Miller when he got hit. And I just went flat. But I remember dirt kicking up, and realizing that they were actually shooting at us, being a little creeped out, to say the least. . . . My wife and I had a policy that we always split up when things got hairy. . . . But at that point, I immediately started looking for her, and I found her very quickly. Then we just had to figure out what we were going to do.

As a prominent campus radical and the only visible speaker at the Victory Bell, Hammond, along with his wife, were "a little concerned that there might be some immediate repercussions. . . . So we got off campus, and got out of the area later on that afternoon."[59] Julio Fanjul, a Cuban American student, recounted the belief that one of the commanders with a .45 pistol, in this case most likely Sergeant Myron Pryor, fired first or gave a signal to the troops to begin firing.

> As I was looking, I could see that they were all up the hill except the one, what would be the platoon leader, with the .45 and the baton. And as I, I don't know what his name was, I don't know which one he was, I just know that he was that. And as he got up to the hill, he turned around, he dropped the baton and the rest is history.[60]

Believing, as many did, that the confrontation was over, Chuck Ayers had gone inside Taylor Hall and never heard the shots.

And just about that time it was like this bang like the doors, and there was screaming and yelling. . . . And this surge of people just came through the hallways, past the *Stater* office. I remember going to the door, and the first words I heard were, "They just killed four kids." I don't know how this person determined this in seconds. They must have seen four people down. . . . But this mass of screaming people and people crying kept coming in, and there was one guy who I recall was a freshman, who had been somewhere and saw most of the shootings, came into the *Stater* office crying, had a puppy with him, and he crawled under a desk and just sat there and cried. [pause] That is emotional.[61]

With broken glasses, Janice Wascko searched dazedly for her friends.

And I walked up to Jeff Miller. I didn't know who he was then. I'd never seen a dead person outside of a funeral home. I started to bend down to help him, but I knew he was dead. And it dawned on me they had really killed people.

And then I got really frantic, because I didn't know where my people were. I didn't know this guy lying there, but there was a lot of shots, and I started getting really mad. . . . I went back to my friend, and I was really mad that I couldn't see. I went back, and my friend was standing there crying. I was mad. I just patted his hand, but I was really angry at him. . . . And I said, "John, go look for them, okay? I can't see." And by this time, I could tell that there [were] people helping hurt people, and I didn't want to get in the way. But I had to know. So I sent him out, and I said, "I'll wait right here. You come back." And he went. And he saw them all. He saw them all.

What we didn't know, because somebody had already carried her away, was one of our friends had ducked behind the same car as Allison Krause and had seen her die. But we didn't know because they'd gotten her out of there already. Another friend of ours had ducked behind a tree that had a bullet-hole chest-height when he came back out. Another man that lived at our house. I didn't even know there [were] people hurt back by the cars. I didn't know bullets could go through cars; that's how naive I was. Or trees. Lethally go through a tree.

Finally John came back, and said that he had found one man from our house up on the porch at Taylor. He was fine, and he had spotted almost everybody else. One of our friends had got a graze over the knuckles. He said he had heard the bullet and he felt it, but it was just like a scratch. He came that close. I tell you, to this day, May 4th is like Passover for me, because everybody I loved survived.[62]

Tim Moore of BUS was shocked when he heard about the shootings.

[Interviewer]: What do you remember your personal reaction being when you heard about the shootings?

Surprise. How could this happen? But again, I was not into politics per se, except that I got woven into being involved in politics by virtue of my— well, at this time I wasn't even president of BUS, I was still a freshman.

[Interviewer]: Minister of Culture.

Right. Or previous Minister of Culture at that point. So I knew of everything, but it did not really affect me directly. It was more an observation of the events going on that led to us being shut down for the year, because of the closing of the university and et cetera. But unexpected. Who would ever have thought that anybody would shoot some students, even if they had bricks and bottles? A bullet is a drastic answer.[63]

Eldon Fender offers a unique account of the events on that day. Fender was an undergraduate at Kent State and is in the background of the famous John Filo photograph. On the day of his oral history interview, Fender and coauthor Simpson went out to the site of the shootings, which has changed somewhat over the years: fewer trees and the presence of the Gym Annex, to name a couple of examples. As he walked the site, Fender recounted seeing Jeffrey Miller taunt the Guard. This episode provides an example of how the geolocation of memory and the use of the walking interview can be powerful but also somewhat misleading as well.[64]

[Interviewer]: You've drawn a map here, and is this where you are?

This is a map, and I can put everything in front of you and point out what I observed. I watched Jeffrey Miller exclusively. I was all by my-self. Most of the other students were probably about 80 to 90 yards to my right in front. I observed Jeffrey Miller throwing many, many rocks at the Guard. Probably more than ten. Unfortunately, the last rock he threw cost him his life. What I saw happen, I saw the second he got shot. He had basically run up behind the Guard, and they were in a platoon formation which was just near Taylor Hall, and they were kind of grouped together there. And when he threw the last rock, the Guards were retreating down into the commons area which is where most of the company was bivouacked. As Jeffrey Miller threw the rock he started to turn, and that's when a shot ran[g] out. I saw him literally stumble into the road of the Pulitzer Prize–winning photo of the girl bending over his body—and she was screaming her head off and I couldn't figure out why—but basically I saw him, the second he got shot stumbling into the road and finally falling. At that point I couldn't see him because there was a little bit of a rise in front of me going up to this access road. . . .

The interesting thing is, Jeffrey Miller couldn't have been more than fifteen feet away from the Guard. He took a head shot. I would probably say human nature being what it is, he probably nailed somebody in the back of the head with a rock. And they knew where he was because he'd been throwing many rocks up to that point. And he took a shot [at] very close range. I can tell you, quite frankly, having observed his body sprawled out in the street that an M1 [rifle] up close can do a lot of damage. And his whole neck was twisted almost 360 degrees and the blood was flowing down the access road. . . .

[Interviewer]: Did you know Jeff Miller prior to that?

No, I did not know him.

[Interviewer]: But you focused on him precisely because—

I focused on him because I thought it was kind of—he had a very bright, kind of red or red-orange shirt on. A long sleeved shirt I might add, which when you consider the temperature and everything else, I thought that was kind of strange in itself. This young man was literally picking up rock after rock. He'd throw a rock and look for another one to throw. Basically, that was the action on that hill, was watching him. Now, granted, there were other students off on Taylor Hall itself, around the balcony of Taylor Hall, screaming and stuff, but my focus was strictly on him because of what he was doing. I was in a direct line from him, but some hundred yards back. Luckily for me I was at a safe distance so I wasn't affected by the fire. As I said, I would have possibly been in the field of fire had the fire gone out straight ahead as opposed to going off at an angle. On the map I'm showing here, if you take Metcalf Hall—which I believe is a girl's dorm—is where the shots primarily ran[g] out into that area. If you see where Jeffrey Miller was standing the moment he got shot, it is totally different from the angle of fire where most of the shots were placed.

[Interviewer]: From your position, did you see him hit any of the Guardsmen?

I have to assume he had to have hit them. Either that or he was an awfully poor thrower. When I say he was probably no more than fifteen or twenty feet away, I'm not exaggerating. He would actually get up close to them when he would throw a rock. The intent, in my opinion, based on that observation, was that he was definitely trying to hurt somebody with whatever he was throwing. He made a very conscientious effort to try to find any material on the ground to throw, which in hindsight I kind of wonder how all those rocks got there in the first place. Perhaps other things had happened, maybe the rocks were placed there from other demonstrations, who knows what? But it was quite a sobering experience seeing someone shot like this. It's just amazing to—it's almost like someone said, I want you to watch this. You're going to see something that you'll always remember the rest of your life. And I certainly have done that.[65]

Fender's sincerity shows how events can be psychologically true, even as it is in this case where these recollections contain several inaccuracies. The most glaring is his claim that Miller was shot several hundred yards away from the official marker. It is highly unlikely that after getting shot in the face, anyone could stagger back that far. Fender also claimed that Miller wore a red or red-orange shirt, when actually he wore a blue and white cowboy shirt. What Fender's interview may show is how changing the geography of a site can influence's one recollections of a particular event. The construction of the Gym Annex in 1977 (discussed in Part Five) would be a source of this very controversy.

News of what was happening on campus began to reach the Kent community. A mixture of reactions surfaced in the immediate time frame of the shootings. The woman interviewed in 2000, whose father was a police officer and who wished to remain anonymous, recounted several rumors: the students (or radicals, or protesters, or outside agitators) were going to drop LSD in the town's water supply; they were going to bomb business establishments; they were going to blow up the mill, which "would have leveled the downtown and killed a great deal of people."[66] John Panagos, then a new member of the Kent faculty in the Speech and Hearing program, was eating lunch at a nearby restaurant when he heard about the shootings and a familiar name among the victims:

> Sandra Scheuer. . . . [I] had to sort through my class list in my mind to pin down who she was exactly. . . . Now probably one of the most heart-wrenching—gut-wrenching—aspects of that particular event was that Sandy was such a lovely young woman, and just the way she has been characterized since then—kind of a naive, friendly, optimistic young woman. And then the rumors flew very quickly that there were insurrectionists on campus, and outsiders were coming in to stir up trouble. There was so much media anger expressed at that point. Some came from faculty, surprisingly. Some came from the University employees, custodians. But the key idea that these four young people, who were all radicals—including Sandy—was so ironic and seemed to characterize the unreality of the time; that so much was being said that was or was not accurate. And so much of it was being projected on students who were involved in protests at that time.[67]

Another townie, Rosann Rissland, first heard news of the shootings from a neighbor, who, like many in the community, had heard it on the radio.

> That morning I took my son, who was going to be two in June, to our neighbors, the Kingsleys. We would go to them every morning during the week, and the kids would all play together. . . . There was a roofer on the house next door to the Kingsleys, and he had his radio on. All of a sudden he called down to us, and he said, "Oh, my God! My God, they've killed the Guardsmen!" And then he said, "Everyone's being told to stay in their houses. No one's allowed to be on the street at all." So we separated and I went home, which was just across the street. . . .
>
> And I would have to say this is the only time I think I've ever done anything that I would have to feel took courage. I was terrified. And I took my son by the hand, and we walked the two blocks to her house.

On the way a man came out and started asking me questions, and I said to him, "We're not allowed to be congregating on the street! I can't talk to you." [laughs] I kept walking. There weren't any police or any Guardsmen going up and down the streets in my area, but the fear was so great. And the sense that things had gotten so totally out of hand and that the students would come over the rise and attack. We were very close to the university. Thinking about it now, I think how irrational that was. But I was scared. I was really scared. And I walked up to her house, and I stayed with her until her husband got home. Then he drove me back to my home. I was really scared.

Afterwards, we didn't hear anything good about the students. It was terrible the things that were said about the students who were killed. We were told that the coroner said that they had venereal disease and that they were drug addicts and everything. We did not know who they were. We didn't know one was from ROTC [Bill Schroeder], or another one was an honors student [Allison Krause]. Truly, I believe it was Governor Rhodes' fault. Of course, President White was not on campus. My mother had had him as an instructor, so she knew him and thought he was a wonderful man. He was a very nice person. But he was not on campus, and he had to rely on what the people on campus were telling him—[the] Provost, et cetera. And I really could not understand why, when they had martial law in the town, they didn't close the university for a weekend. For a week! It would have made all the difference in the world if they had just done that. I truly believe that Rhodes was terribly at fault here; and the Provost at the time should have taken steps.

The community itself became very embittered. We really thought kids were going to come down and burn us out. Not just the downtown. The people who owned businesses downtown really hated the students; there was a real issue about that for a long, long time. Anybody who had anything to do with the university was a little bit suspect. I don't think it's that way so much now. I don't hear it as much. We all feel the students drink too much and all that stuff, but other than that I don't feel the animosity that I did. At that point in time, you became aware that there really was a gap. It was not just something that people might talk about once in a while and complain about a little bit. It was a real gap. We had been attacked. As far as anybody in town was concerned, it was the university, the students, who did it. Even though most of the people involved weren't even students at the university.

[Interviewer]: I was going to ask about that. Did people make a distinction between the students and "outsiders" in town?

I don't think so because—[pause] the downtown stuff really was probably mostly outsiders. But, in [the townspeople's] minds, they're all the age of the students. How are they going to know who they are? They really don't know who they are. And there was a lot—*a lot*—of anxiety people had over that. I can't imagine what it would be like for some of those houses—they're right near the downtown area—how you would have felt, how frightening it would have been. I just know that, as a mom with a little kid, being alone in the house through that was—you were so isolated. I don't think I've ever, ever felt that way before, and I've never felt that way since. There was nobody I could reach. There was no one I could talk to. No one I could be near. I wasn't supposed to go anywhere. I couldn't leave. And that was really very upsetting.

[Interviewer]: The gentleman from whom you first heard the news, who said that the Guardsmen had been shot, did he say where he got his information?

He heard it on the radio. And I understand that's the first report that went out was that a Guardsman had gotten shot. And, of course, anybody in the town hearing that a Guardsman was shot would immediately—and for a long time, I really feel they felt the students had fired shots. So they really did blame them. They really did blame them. But the kids that got killed, they weren't even the ones who were doing anything. That's the ironic part of it. In a way, maybe that's a good thing, in a sense. Because as people, when we realized how we jumped to the conclusion that these were the deadbeats, the rotten people, the "whatevers" of the community—as we jumped to that conclusion, we didn't have that turned away as reality for years. Decades. We had that as the reality. Unless you went in and researched it and stuff, you really didn't know. And no one released the information, no one made it really available until much, much later.[68]

The myriad of detail in Rissland's recollections—the impact of the inaccurate initial reports that Guardsmen had been shot, her criticisms of the governor and university administration, her sympathy for the victims, her ability to simultaneously share how the fears of the community had

ALLISON B. KRAUSE

WILLIAM K. SCHROEDER

JEFFREY G. MILLER

SANDRA L. SCHEUER

The often-used composite image of the four students killed on May 4. (May 4 Collection. Kent State University Libraries. Special Collections and Archives.)

consequences while also suggesting that they learned from their mistakes—shows the complexity involved in the "sensemaking" of why the Kent community, generally speaking, reacted favorably to the actions of the Guard.

Tension remained on campus just after the shootings, and more controversy erupted. Immediately after the shootings, Terry Norman was spotted holding his .38 revolver and several people then chased him from Taylor Hall back to the Guard line, where the soldiers had resumed their position in front of the ROTC building. As they chased him, some were yelling that they had seen Norman firing his weapon. Once there, Norman surrendered his gun to campus police, who checked it; they reported then and later that it had not been fired; other witnesses claimed that Norman himself stated "I had to shoot" and that the first police officer to handle Norman's gun exclaimed that it had been fired.[69]

With the Guard in position near the burned-out remains of the ROTC building, between two hundred and three hundred protesters and onlookers alike gathered into an impromptu sit-down on the Commons just northwest of the Victory Bell. Tensions mounted again as the crowd faced the Guard across the Commons with the likelihood of another deadly confrontation looming. Faculty marshals Glenn Frank, Jerry Lewis, Seymour Baron, and Mike Lunine and history graduate student Steve Sharoff (who had been among those to call for the noon rally that day) tried to persuade the students to leave and convince the Guard not to fire or march again. At this point, Canterbury remained determined to remove the students. In *Kent State: What Happened and Why*, James Michener reported the tense dialogue that occurred between the faculty, the students, and the Guard. Using a bullhorn borrowed from the Guard, faculty marshal Dr. Seymour H. Baron convinced the crowd to sit down and warned that the Guard might shoot unless they dispersed.[70]

Jerry Lewis again used reconstructed dialogue as he recalled his actions as he made his way toward the Commons again, witnessing the gathering of students there as they faced the Guard across the Commons.

So I was in front of the crowd, going back and forth, telling people what was going on, what the Marshals were saying. Can I use dirty words?

[Interviewer]: Absolutely.

While I was going back and forth telling students what was going on, particularly [Glenn] Frank was negotiating with [General Robert] Canterbury. And, of course, that's when he said, "You must leave, or we'll come again." And you could see them forming up, getting ready to come again.

So, Glenn Frank gave us a sixty-words speech, which everybody knows, was very emotional, convincing students to leave. And students got up, and started to leave. Just as we were heading towards the tennis courts, we were all going in one direction, this rather large student, who had an American flag upside down—which was a protest symbol in those days—was giving the finger to the Guard, and saying, "Motherfuckers! Killers!" He was a big guy too, and I said, "Shut up. There are women in the crowd." Very sexist. But he did, he quit, and we eventually got off.[71]

This is what Frank said, his voice choked with emotion. "I don't care whether you've never listened to anyone before in your lives. I am begging you right now. If you don't disperse right now, they're going to move in and it can only be a slaughter. Would you please listen to me? Jesus Christ I don't want to be a part of this."[72] William Brauning, an undergrad in 1970, described Frank's expression:

as part hysteria, it looked part disbelief, it looked part . . . of that look after there's a tragedy of some kind and the people's eyes are as wide as they could be. . . . And he said something along the line of, "My God, they've killed people. I plead with you, I beg of you, leave now or they're gonna . . . we're all going to get shot. They're gonna kill us all."[73]

Undergraduate Naomi Goelman Etzkin said she watched from her dorm window after running back there following the shots.

People began coming back into the dorm, having walked over bleeding bodies. We then went to another window in the dorm, and we watched Dr. Frank address the students who were still on the hill. Everybody sat down in shock, and he said . . . to the best of my recollection, "They had already committed murder and they can do it again. Now I want you to follow me off this hill." And miraculously everyone followed.[74]

Janice Wascko had gathered with the crowd; she remembers having a different reaction to Glenn Frank's plea.

And they had us all . . . they kind of us herded us to go sit on the grass, and this prof [Glenn Frank] was talking. And he's kind of a hero today, but at the time, like I said, I was in a real vile mood myself. And at one point, and I realize now this man was blithering to save our lives, but at one point he said something about, "Well, it's a beautiful day, sit down in the sunshine, we'll get some sandwiches and things." And I lost it. I just came unhinged and I jumped up and started screaming, "What is this, a fucking picnic?" And people tried to pull me back down, and I just went stomping off. I went back to the Student Center. I just fumed. And my friend followed me, because he didn't know what I was going to do. I didn't either. And then we realized that we had to get out of here. It suddenly kind of dawned on us that the reason this guy was herding us in is because they were closing the campus and the noose was getting tighter. And we had to get out of there, because for all we knew they were going to kill us all just to silence the witness[es]. And he's going, "We've got to get out of here." [I said,] "You're right, we've got to get out of here."[75]

Eventually, it was Glenn Frank's pleading that finally convinced the students to leave; for many, Frank was a hero for preventing further bloodshed. By 1:30 P.M., the Commons and surrounding area were clear. Guard officers had been checking weapons to see who had fired, but some officers only made mental notes as to who fired and wrote down the information later. Major Simons, chaplain of the 107th, reported that Guardsmen were tired, angry, and disgusted. Some were crying. Those that did fire were instructed to fill out incident reports.

After the campus closed, Ellis Berns went to his girlfriend's house in town and noticed he still had bloodstains and tissue from Sandy Scheuer on his green fatigue jacket and his arms. Later that afternoon, his girlfriend's father, an impeccably dressed president of the local Citibank, entered the house looking completely disheveled.

He apparently had gotten into a fight, because after this whole thing had happened on May 4th, the whole town went crazy. I remember protesters walked down the street and they started ripping American flags down. Well, David—that's his name—David apparently got into a fight with one of the protesters and got thrown into jail, because a protester tore the American flag down in front of the bank. He was conservative, but a very respectable gentleman. I really mean that. He was a true gentleman. And he got into a fight with a protester and got thrown in jail!

Fortunately, they . . . I have to do some conjecture here . . . but I think they realized who he was and released him. I don't know what the terms were. The only reason I say this, it was kind of the irony. I'm over at my friend's house, my girlfriend's house, and then her father shows up. Here I am, having just been in the war at home, and he had just gotten taken out of jail for fighting the protesters. Like I say, he was a gentleman. We seemed to deal with it okay. But I think we were both in shock and in awe of what was going on, and not really had ever had an opportunity to talk about what happened and why and what his perspective was or anything.

Naomi Goleman Etzkin was one of last students to leave the university. Initially, she had hitchhiked to her boyfriend's house off campus when her parents, on the phone, told her to return to her dorm room at Olson Hall where they would pick her up.

The National Guardsmen were having dinner in our cafeteria. And I sat down at dinner, and a couple of them came and joined me. The guys who I was having dinner with were not the people who had shot, because it was my understanding that they were whisked away. The guys that I had dinner with were people my age who went into the National Guard so they didn't have to go to Vietnam, and they felt a deep sense of horror over what had happened. My parents came to get me at approximately 8:00 p.m. It took them four hours to drive from Cleveland to Kent. They had to go through Streetsboro [a small but growing suburban city in Portage County] where shop owners were boarding up their windows with giant sheets of wood because they were terrified that the students were going to come and destroy their city, too. And two weeks later we were told to come back and pack up our bags, in a matter of four hours. And then we finished our courses by correspondence. The campus was never the same.[76]

PART FOUR

"The divide in this country"

I n this part, we examine the aftermath of the shootings and begin shifting our time frame from seconds to hours, days, months, and years. Chronologically we move from thirteen seconds at 12:24 P.M. on Monday, May 4, 1970, to the end of the 1970s. Simultaneously, we broaden our focus to include not only the physical site of the shootings and first efforts to memorialize them on the Kent State campus, but also other events and settings that played a role in the narrators' oral histories and in crafting the social memory of the events. These include governmental and journalistic investigations, reports and books, and legal procedures and court cases. In putting oral history together with these other forms for memory, we follow the ideas of Michael Schudson. Writing about Watergate, Schudson argued that memory is not only "a psychic event associated with individual minds," but also something social, located in cultural forms, institutions, and institutional practices "in the form of rules, laws, standardized procedures, and records." People recognize "a debt to the past" whether it be financial or practices such as "punishment, retribution, restitution, restoration, reform, inheritance, and promise and its enforcement through contract."[1]

As we explore the ways in which oral history of the immediate events intermingles with memory and memorialization in the aftermath of the shootings, Schudson's points about how memory is constructed, contained, and utilized in cultural and institutional forms provide useful tools to examine the reports, investigations, and trials that created and housed for the future the struggle over the memory of the shootings at Kent State. Through practices of reports, investigations, and trials in the 1970s, individuals and groups assigned or removed responsibility, found meaning, and sought a cause for the deaths. Sensemaking of the events now moved from the immediate experience into formal functions of the state and other institutional mechanisms. Oral history testimony reveals how narrators participated in or remembered these events and their meaning.

Immediate Aftermath

The experience of traveling to and being in the hospital immediately after the shootings became a critical part of the memory for several narrators. These events also served functions in shaping the meaning of the shootings. Most of the wounded went to Robinson Memorial Hospital in Ravenna, about seven miles away. Ambulances transported there the four students who were killed as well. William Schroeder died while in surgery; Allison Krause died just as she reached the hospital; Sandra Scheuer died a few minutes after being shot; and Jeffrey Miller died instantly.

Mike Brock was a football player and a rebel who had gone to the rally. Nearly shot when the Guard opened fire, he carried the wounded Tom Grace to safety. Brock initially wrote of this experience in 1970 as his final assignment to finish his freshman English class with instructor Barbara Becker Agte over the summer, as many students were doing. Also in the class in May 1970 were Allison Krause and Barry Levine. Agte kept Brock's writing and the other responses "in the back of a filing cabinet drawer" until she decided to publish them more than four decades later as *Kent Letters: Students' Responses to May 1970 Massacre* (2012). When they were published, Agte identified each writer only by his or her initials; Brock was M.B. In his June 1970 letter, Brock expressed shock and anger. "The horrors and the tragedies of the afternoon of Monday, May 4, 1970, will remain with me for the rest of my life. The senseless massacre, of harmless students, begging for their rights, by a group of bloodthirsty national Guardsmen still haunts me." Brock "hit the dirt" when the shooting started. "After the volley of shots, which seemed to last forever, I heard the boy next to me shout 'They shot my foot off.'" Brock picked Grace up and carried him across the parking lot into Prentice Hall, where "a girl began to administer first aid to him."[2] In a 1987 interview published that year in *From Camelot to Kent State*, Grace remembered, "So I was lying there, and all of a sudden this real husky, well-built guy ran to me, picked me up like I was a sack of potatoes, and threw me over his shoulder." In a later interview for Christian Appy's book *Patriots* (2004), Grace named Brock as the husky guy who carried him.[3]

In both interviews, Grace recalled being carried out of Prentice Hall to an awaiting ambulance, but his later interview is more detailed in focusing on his own sense of anger and defiance. Grace declined to be interviewed for our book, but his descriptions here are a reminder of how oral histories can evolve over time; how the context, setting, purpose of the interview, and the relationship between narrator and interviewer may all have an effect. Looking back after nearly another twenty years, Grace's later interview is also more reflective about his own frame of mind then and the meaning he gave to being shot. Here is Grace in 1987:

> The ambulances came. Some attendants came in, put me on a stretcher, and carried me outside. The blood loss had lessened because of the tourniquet that was on my leg. I remember having my fist up in the air as a sign of defiance.[4]

Here is Grace describing the same scene some years later in *Patriots:*

> When the ambulances arrived I was carried outside, there were hundreds of people standing around. I remember putting my fist into the air. It wasn't pride, it was just raw anger. The worst thing that can happen to you is to be in a situation where you're being fired upon and not have any way of returning fire. We had no way of stopping them from doing what they were doing. If I'd had a gun, I definitely would have fired back. Without question. For me, it just would have been self-defense and survival. Of course that would just have unleashed more killing.[5]

From the first interview, Grace also recalled being loaded into the top tier of an ambulance: "I looked down and saw Sandy Scheuer. I had met Sandy about a week or two beforehand for the first and only time." Grace recalled that Scheuer "had a gaping bullet wound in the neck, and the ambulance attendants were tearing away the top two buttons of her blouse and then doing heart massage. I remember their saying, 'It's no use, she's dead.' And then they just pulled up the sheet over her head." Grace arrived at the hospital and after waiting to be examined, he was wheeled into an operating room where surgeons managed to save his foot.[6]

Joe Cullum was in another ambulance that transported Joe Lewis and John Cleary to Robinson Memorial. Ambulance workers put John Cleary in the back of the ambulance. Because there were not enough ambulances,

> they loaded Joe in and he was just laying on this seat, on this simple canvas stretcher. So myself and one other guy rode along to hold him on. And we rode into Ravenna and the ambulance driver I guess

thought that speed was the most important thing so he's swerving all over the place. Both of these guys, every bump in the road, every swerve caused them a lot of pain so they were screaming back there.[7]

As he connected the experience at the hospital with his larger sense of how the shootings revealed deep divisions in the nation, Cullum continued:

It was also at the hospital that I saw them bring Jeff Miller's body in. He lived in the same apartment building . . . it's an old house and he actually played on a softball team with me. There was this one team of hippies and I was on it. So was he. So when I saw him being brought in I knew that he was dead. But I didn't know what the toll was until quite a bit later.

[Interviewer]: When you are at the hospital, what were you doing? Did you hear people talking?

Well, you know, Portage County can be two very different places and Kent's one place and Ravenna's a real different place. And so, we felt animosity. We felt some tension there. They were gonna treat these people, but maybe they didn't really deserve to be treated. So that was . . . the beginning of my experience of the divide in this country over the shootings at Kent.

I could vote, even though the 26th Amendment hadn't yet been ratified. Ohio had lowered the voting age. So I voted in the primary and I went to the polling station back in Canton, where I registered and a woman that was working in the polls who was a mother of a friend of mine from grade school said, "I heard you were up at Kent." I said, "Yeah, I was. I saw all this happen." She said, "Well they should have had machine guns."[8]

John Cleary did not remember Cullum's help or the ambulance ride, but he did remember some details of being in the hospital:

kind of being in a corridor and being afraid that someone was going to leave me there, that they were going to forget about me. It was very chaotic. There were a lot of people running around. I was sitting on a stretcher and I was kind of stuck out on a corner somewhere, but then eventually I must have been taken in to an operating room or whatever. I don't remember too much after that.[9]

Timothy DeFrange was in Robinson Memorial with his dying father as ambulances began bringing dead, dying, and wounded students in from the Kent State campus.

So May 4th was a very upsetting thing for us as a family, but mostly on a personal level. My father was dying, at the time. He'd been in intensive care at Robinson Memorial Hospital that whole month. He had come there with a problem with gall stones that turned out to be pancreatitis, and he was dying. There was no way to save him. My mother had been practically living there, sleeping on the couch outside the ICU unit, and going in every, you know, couple hours, for fifteen minutes, to hold his hand.

My brother Mark had been killed in Vietnam in '69, and my mom had been against the war, and my father had been for the war, and suddenly, the whole war just didn't matter anymore, with Dad dying, and Mom at his side. And . . . the pain of Vietnam was . . . nothing compared with what we were going through as a family.

Now I had at the time, in my wallet, a critical patient pass, because the Guard had been stationed all around Kent, so that you couldn't just drive through. But I needed to go that way to get to Robinson Memorial Hospital from Field High School. So I needed to get through the Guard, and I had this critical patient pass, which got me through.

As I drove through Kent, I raced to the hospital, hurrying as fast as I could, and flashing my critical patient pass to the guards that were stationed on [Route] 59. When I got there, my mom was already downstairs. She said, "He's gone." I said, "Well, how did it happen? How did he die?" She says, "You just won't believe," she says, "I was upstairs, and . . . all of a sudden there was all this noise and commotion. Then all these young people were wheeled into the ICU, from the shootings. And the doctors and the nurses were just crying. One doctor went over and he held an x-ray up, and he was holding it, showing it to another doctor. He said, 'Look where this bullet is lodged. This bullet is lodged in this boy's spine. He's never going to walk again. In all my years of medicine, this is the most senseless thing I've ever seen.'" So my mom, who had been there for a whole month, she walked to the window, and said, "Lord, Nick has had 55 good years. All this time, all this month, I've been praying that you would spare him. But how can I ask for that when these kids haven't even had twenty years? From now on, it's whatever you want." She turned around and went back into the ICU, and he had died.[10]

The boy with the bullet in his spine was Dean Kahler. In his oral history interview, Kahler recalled the ride to the hospital and the immediate reactions and discussion when he arrived.

When I was riding into the hospital, it was early May. So everything was just coming out in bud and leafing. Maybe it was because my body was in a state. But the color just seemed so magnificent. I've never taken any hallucinogenics [hallucinogens], but I mean the colors were almost hallucinogenic in my brain just the way they were. I couldn't believe the colors that were out. I mean the differentiations between trees and the bushes that were coming out and the daffodils that were blooming and yeah. I remember sitting there looking at them just thinking, "Wow. So this is what it's like."

I get to the hospital and they get me off the ambulance on some table somewhere. I hear somebody hollering, "Get blood types on all these people." I didn't know how many people were shot. I knew that there were other people who were shot who were there. And I said to myself, "Okay. I know what to do." So I got out my wallet, got my driver's license, my student ID, and I got my blood donor's card and my insurance card. I saw somebody walking by with one of those little blood things, you know, the little cart or the little tray that they carry with all the vials and everything. I said, "Would you like to have this?" She goes, "What?" I said, "Here." She was actually a nurse. She looked at it and said, "Oh my god. That's great." She just ran back to the desk. I've run into her several times at the various May 4th functions too.

But then eventually they get me into the prep room. They gave me some shot and I was starting to go deliriously out. And the next thing I know they're starting to wake me up Thursday sometime. They put me into an induced coma. Apparently, they told my parents that if he makes it an hour we'll pray for another. I mean that's how much they gave me a chance to live, an hour. After 24 hours, they upped that to every four hours.

But I talked to the abdominal surgeon that actually did the work. He says, "I worked on a lot of hearts. But I've never seen one that looked so strong and mean as yours was." He says, "Mean in a good sense because it was fighting like hell." He said, "You had a perfect heart. You had a perfect heart. So obviously you're lucky. You're extremely lucky."[11]

Kahler also remembered cards he received as he was recovering from the wound that paralyzed him.

> Well, the first one [I] opened up was a really nice-looking card. I opened it up and on the inside on the side there was a lot of handwriting and on this side was your normal get-well greeting that sort of stuff. So I started reading them on left of the inside. "Dear Communist Hippie Radical, I hope by the time you get this you are dead. We don't need people like you. I hope you're dead." That was the first thing I opened up. I got a few of those, probably more than a few. But I got ten times more, maybe 100 times more that were just the opposite: very friendly, very understanding, very concerned about my welfare. Many of them had political diatribes in them as well talking about the stupidity of this war and all that sort of thing, so that was good.[12]

While DeFrange, Cullum, Kahler, and others were in the hospital, the town and the university remained under military control. Authorities controlled traffic into and out of Kent with roadblocks, and Kent Bell telephone shut down phone service to the dormitories. A dusk-to-dawn curfew remained in place. President White returned to campus from his lunch and ordered the university shut down for the remainder of the week, but Portage County prosecutor Ronald Kane went further and obtained a court injunction to close the university until "conditions merit the reopening."[13] The order was modified on May 13 to allow some students, faculty, and staff on campus, and students completed coursework for the spring quarter via correspondence or locally in homes and other spaces. The National Guard remained in Kent until May 8.

"I remember seeing something I'll never forget as long as I live," recalled Bruce Dzeda, who arrived in Kent about an hour after the shootings,

> and that is cars of Portage County redneck toughs driving up and down the street. I remember one car in particular, a white car, with four men riding it with rifles sticking out of all the windows. Quite literally, they were looking for students to shoot, they were looking for people who were just gonna act up or demonstrate. . . . I think what people have to remember, there was a great deal of jealousy and distrust of students. After all, we had an easy life, you know, all we did was party and get laid and we didn't have to work hard, we didn't have to go to Vietnam, and I think a lot of people who did work hard, did have to go to Vietnam, felt that way.[14]

On campus, Catherine Delattre was among those allowed in to do research. She worked on a book project, *Violence at Kent State* (1971), authored by Stuart Taylor, Richard Shuntlich, Patrick McGovern, and Robert Genther. The authors sent questionnaires to all students to gauge their perceptions and feelings on the shootings and received seven thousand responses. For Delattre, working on the book "meant everything to me, to not leave school," to feel like she "was doing something" because "of the feeling of helplessness." To get to campus, she had to drive through Ravenna, the county seat with a generally more conservative mindset, where she remembered "vigilantes" and "people on the roofs of buildings, and pointing guns," because "if you looked like a student, they would threaten us."[15]

While most of the town took a conservative stance, John Carson, the former Democratic mayor and then proprietor of a local pharmacy, had earned a reputation for being sympathetic to the students in particular and an inveterate contrarian in general. He "wore a black armband I know during that period of time and I lost a bunch of customers, the conservative group."[16] Chuck Ayers, who, like many, tried to resume some semblance of day-to-day life just after the shootings, attended a wedding in Kent where he noticed armed guards at a visible distance from the premises. "'Course everybody is joking with these folks about it being a shotgun wedding and stuff," Ayers said. "We had a great time with it."[17]

Away from official actions, along the periphery of events, James Mueller took an unorthodox approach to deal with the aftermath of the shootings.

I didn't used to tell this story because I thought it was kind of nuts. And in a way it was nuts, but in a way it was probably very sane too. The next morning I got up and I just wanted to get away from things, and I went to Columbus to visit my brother on Tuesday May 5th, and—I tried to make a citizen's arrest of Governor Rhodes.

I was just roaming around downtown. And the thought possessed me that I should try to arrest Governor Rhodes for criminal misconduct, as I referred to it. And in a way it was kind of nuts, people don't usually do those kind of things, and obviously I even felt after the fact that it was a bit off the chart because I didn't share it with anybody for years. When I finally did, this girl I was dating, who I still know, she says, "That wouldn't surprise me," [laughs] is what she said.

So anyhow I went in his office and I can still see this lady was maybe 25, and very striking kind of person. And she said, "May I help you?" And I said, "I'm here to make a citizen's arrest of Governor Rhodes for criminal misconduct in regard to the Kent State shootings of two days ago." And she gave me this look—I'm still not sure I could put it into words—I could probably describe it to an artist. I really felt guilty about it for years, it's a wonder this woman didn't have a heart attack. I'm sure she never ever anticipated this was going to be part of her daily activity. So she was very calm, cool, and collected and I was amazed.

This gentleman came out, had a suit on, it turned out he was an undercover guy from chief of security, I think, for the governor's detail at the State House. And we talked for about an hour, and he had a lot of people skills. I said, "You can make citizen's arrests, can't you?" And he said, "Well, yeah, but that's only in the case if you observe a felony." He said even though there would be people who would question Governor Rhodes' handling or mishandling of this depending on the kind of spin you wanted to put on it—that wasn't his words, that wasn't the phraseology of the time—he said this isn't kind of like the situation that you could describe. He said, for example, you can't go make a citizen's arrest of President Nixon and accuse him of being a war criminal. He said our society just isn't set up to doing that. And he said people of an idealistic bent might think it is. And he said he really respected the fact that I cared enough to put myself out there. That was kind of the thrust of the conversation. He was just the most cordial, likeable person you would have ever wanted to meet, which surprised me because my stereotype was that all these people were set in their ways and inflexible. He was even talking about Jefferson, and protest, and he was really quite a unique individual.

So, after about an hour he said, "Thanks for stopping down," [laughs] and it was kind of like I had applied for a job. And he said, "You understand now why you can't make a citizen's arrest of the governor?" and I said, "I do, and I thank you for your time." I almost felt guilty that I'd intruded on his time, but of course he was getting paid.[18]

While campus leaders and civil authorities shut down Kent's campus, the nation witnessed an unprecedented wave of student strikes at colleges and universities. According to a report by the Urban Research Corporation published in May 1970, the shootings at Kent prompted strike activity at one hundred new campuses per day for four days afterward. Combined with the protests that began on April 30, the report found that "at least 760 campuses, or 30 percent of all the colleges and universities in the country, participated in some way in the first national student strike in U.S. history."[19] The report also found that confrontations between police and National Guardsmen occurred at only 2 percent of these protests, about fourteen campuses.

During these strikes and protests, two African American students, Phillip Gibbs and James Green, were killed at Jackson State College (now Jackson State University) just after midnight, May 15. (In the annual commemoration at Kent State, the ceremony pays homage to these two students as well.) Violent conflict occurred during the Hard Hat Riot on May 8, 1970, in New York City. Hundreds of construction workers—organized by Peter Brennan, president of the Building and Construction Trades Council of New York and vice president of the New York AFL-CIO—arrived on Wall Street to attack antiwar demonstrators who had gathered to protest the Kent State shootings and the Vietnam War. The next day witnessed a massive demonstration of some one hundred thousand in Washington, D.C. Mike Alewitz traveled to the nation's capital after the shootings to be part of the May 9 demonstration. He appeared in a story published by the *Cleveland Plain Dealer* in which the newspaper quoted him speaking at a news conference organized by the Student Mobilization Committee in Cleveland before he and others left: "We cannot allow the government to use the killings [at Kent] as a pretext for closing the campuses in order to defuse the antiwar movement. Instead, we must use the campuses to stop the war against which the four students [killed by gunfire at Kent] were fighting."[20] He was part of the Committee of the Kent State Massacre Eyewitnesses, who then traveled across the nation to encourage protests.

In his oral history interview, Alewitz, still a dedicated leftist, reflected on that experience. What inspired Alewitz were the events of 1968 in France, when students and workers united in a massive protest that nearly toppled the conservative government of Charles de Gaulle. He and other student leftists in the antiwar movement in the United States worked with soldiers and workers in their effort to build the antiwar movement. He was also involved in union activity, as he references a strike by GE workers in 1970 (which is likely the major GE strike in 1969 that lasted into early 1970). Alewitz in his interview moved back and forth between the experience of the 1960s and today.

I think people who are really being a little clear in their thinking, it was pretty clear May, June '68 shows that the working class is not dead, and it inspired the world. And directly at Kent, for example, when I was running for student body president at the time of the shootings as a socialist and it was the program for the red university. It was really the program of the French students. The idea that we were going to do in the United States what the French students had done. The French students shut down the universities and marched to the factory gates and called out the workers. Of course, we weren't quite at the point where we could march to the factory gates and call out the workers. But we did go to the Army bases and call out the soldiers. And they came [laughs]; you know, those were just workers in uniform. And we did go to the picket lines. There was an important General Electric strike in 1970. We went to the picket lines and we leafleted the workers and union meetings. We did these things and the workers were not ready yet, but they were getting there. Within a couple of years, they were there. And today, they're there. Today they're there. They haven't been called out yet, but they're there and they're ready.[21]

Public forms of support for the Kent students occurred outside the United States as well. Demonstrations occurred across Canada after the shootings, including the largest Canadian antiwar demonstration, on May 8 in Toronto, attended by upwards of fifteen thousand people.[22] Kent State history professor Lawrence Kaplan was a visiting research scholar and lecturer at the University of London in May 1970. In his essay for Scott Bills's *Kent State/ May 4: Echoes Through A Decade,* Kaplan recalled the hostility he faced from many students as he lectured in London and then later in Germany. Compared to 1968, the reaction in Europe among students to the shootings was more subdued. Still, there were large demonstrations in London (5,000), West Berlin (10,000), and Paris (between 50,000 and 200,000), and there remained widespread opposition to the war in Vietnam.

While protests spread, for many Kent students, perhaps most, the main issue was finishing classes; for seniors it was graduation, which the university held on June 13. "There was a meeting for Kent students at a church in Lakewood, to talk about what to do, and I remember being thoroughly unhappy with my own classmates," Dzeda said.

Some of whom, their sole worry was: "How am I gonna graduate? What about my credits?" I remember a bunch of us thinking, "Jesus Christ, don't you realize that four of us are dead? A bunch of us were wounded, they were shooting at us, for God's sake, and you worry about your goddamned grade." But grades are important to people, and me too.

A senior, Dzeda opted to take the pass/fail option, and he attended the graduation ceremony held in the Memorial Gym. Less successful was his intention to go to graduation without wearing a cap and gown—a form of protest. "I guess I've always knuckled under my parents ultimately, because I loved them and didn't want them to be unhappy and college graduation was a big thing, so what the hell, I wore the goddamned robe, you know," he reflected. "They gave us our folders and later on we got our diplomas and teaching certificates and I shook the dust of Kent State University off of my sandals and, and went on."[23]

The local newspaper coverage in Kent remained staunchly on the side of the National Guard, while editorials outside the city varied in their response. The editors of the *Chattanooga Times,* for example, echoed President Nixon's response to the shootings, calling it a "tragic outgrowth of campus disorders coast to coast." The editors, though, went further and stated that "every disaffected protester on the campus must now know that reckless reactions, destruction of property or other violence can cost his or her life."[24] The *Lorain Journal,* William Schroeder's hometown paper, called him and the others killed "innocent victims of the student riots and National Guard shootings." The paper largely blamed Nixon and Rhodes for escalating the tension with their rhetoric and urged civil authorities to separate the radicals, who the paper assumed were violent, from the majority of other student protesters.[25]

The early news stories further constructed the memory and meaning of the shootings and in some cases contributed to the rumors and misinformation that emerged. The first newspaper reports coming out from Kent were, like those on the radio, inaccurate. The local paper, the *Kent-Ravenna Record-Courier,* ran an afternoon edition on May 4 with the headline "2 Guardsmen, 1 Student dead in KSU violence." The *Cleveland Press* ran a similar headline for its afternoon paper. Both cited reports from Robinson Memorial Hospital and police radio as their sources. UPI and radio broadcasts then picked up the headline and spread it nationally. In the same afternoon edition with the erroneous headline, the *Record-Courier* published an editorial, "Universities must oust hooligans." The editorial—written before the events on May 4— came in the wake of the disturbances in downtown and the burning of the ROTC building. The piece supported the statements made on Sunday, May 3, by Governor Rhodes, adding that "Kent in the past three days has had its fill of these violence-prone toughs who use legitimate causes, such as a drive for peace, as vehicles to allow them to riot and disrupt." The paper supported peaceful protests, but not violence, destruction, and rioting.[26] Robert Dix, a conservative and president of the Kent State University Board of Trustees, owned the *Record-Courier.* Dix also owned the local radio station, WKNT.

On Tuesday, newspapers in Kent and elsewhere published comments from Ohio National Guard adjutant general Del Corso that abetted the dissemination of misinformation regarding the shootings. He argued that the Guard was out of tear gas, which it was not, and that "a sniper opened fire against the guardsmen" as the "mob" started to move forward "to encircle the guardsmen" once the tear gas ran out. He added, "Guardsmen facing almost certain injury and death were forced to open fire on the attackers." A second story reported on comments made by Colonel John Simmons in the Ohio National Guard adjutant general's office to the effect that the situation was a riot and that therefore troops were ordered to carry loaded weapons. "Every man has the right to defend himself," Simmons argued.[27] Here began the basic legal and historical defense of the National Guard, reinforcing the calls for law and order that President Nixon and other conservatives would deploy effectively to gain greater power and influence.

Support for the Guard grew stronger in Kent in the days and weeks that followed. On Thursday, May 7, prominent business leaders in Kent purchased an advertisement in the *Record-Courier* that read, "Thank You General Del Corso and the National Guard."[28] The same day, Mayor Satrom issued his first statement since the shootings: "I cannot speak with enough praise when I speak of the protection of the City of Kent offered by the Ohio National Guard while they were on our streets. All of these men deserve a great deal of credit for preventing further damage and injury."[29] On Friday, May 8, the *Record-Courier* ran a story that noted "Kent area citizens by the hundreds today were signing declarations of support and appreciation for National Guardsmen, all law enforcement agencies and city officials in the aftermath of the past week's violence."[30]

Letters that poured into the *Kent Record-Courier* recorded the deeply felt local reaction. These letters serve as efforts by the men and women of Kent and vicinity to interpret and shape the memory of the events. Most writers expressed support for the Guardsmen. As James Michener noted, the newspaper "was being forced to find space for what will be remembered as one of the most virulent outpourings of community hatred in recent decades. It seemed as if everybody in the Kent area suddenly wanted to unburden himself of resentments against young people, colleges and education which had been festering for years."[31] The letters also express in a powerful way the divided nature of American political culture, showing in this case those drawn to conservative appeals to law and order. Here we offer a few samples.[32]

A woman wrote, "I am not happy that anyone is dead—not at all! However, it appears ridiculous to blame the National Guard. Maybe, if they had shot a few rioters in their antics Saturday night when they prevented a fire from being extinguished, the rioting would have ended there." She expressed a number of other views common to many letters sent in. "Why are parents, faculty and even the law coddling these disrespectful destructive radicals? It's time to clamp down. It's time for the administration to demand of stu dents 'shape up or ship out!'" She also expressed a common sense of fear among many Kent residents at the end of her letter: "If you have to use my name please don't use my letter. My husband travels and I'm alone with two small children. To be honest with you, these radical students frighten me!"[33] Another female defended the Guard: "It is a terrible tragedy that there was anyone killed but the Guard did not create the atmosphere that resulted in the tragedy; this was created by the radical movement in our colleges. So put the blame where it should be and not on the National Guard."[34]

For these writers and many residents of Kent, the Guard represented what Michael Flamm has described as the conservative vision of order and decency. The majority of residents in Kent and the surrounding area viewed the National Guard as coming to defend local institutions and neighborhoods, to protect, like the "neighborhood policeman" "local values—political, moral, and property" and keep "the civil peace despite outside interference." Many Kent residents supported the conservative contention that "the community's right to order—to public safety as they saw it—took precedence over the in- dividual's right to freedom." They rejected the claim made by many radicals that "public space was where demonstrators could assert such rights as free speech and free assembly." For conservatives, and for many Kent residents and newspapers who defended the Guard, public space "was where citizens with a legitimate stake in the community could enjoy themselves if they complied with the legitimate demands of legitimate authority."[35]

National Guard captain Ron Snyder kept many letters sent to him after the shootings. All, he says, were positive in their support for him and other Guardsmen.

I'll read this to you. This was from Riverside, California. The day is May 6, 1970. "Dear Members of Charlie Company. I was just watch- ing some members of your outfit being interviewed on the news.

One of the men said, "Nobody cares about us. All they care about is those four kids who were shot," I just want you to know that's not everyone in this country. Everyone in this country has lost their sense of perspective in this matter. Of course it is too bad anyone had to be shot. However, when people engage in violent activities they should be prepared to accept the consequences. Your men were in a difficult position. Rocks can be deadly weapons and no one can expect you to stand around meekly and allow them to harm you." And it goes on and on and talks about "You deserve to be heard" and so on. It goes on for several pages.[36]

However, not all letter writers defended the Guard. One writer to the *Record-Courier* recommended sending the National Guard to Vietnam. "Since these immature, undertrained National Guards enjoy shooting those rifles so much—send them to Vietnam and let them point those rifles at the Viet Cong—who are pointing rifles at them, instead of at students who are armed only with rocks, sticks and slanderous words." Another asked this question: "If each of the four KSU students really were guilty of every crime committed in the Kent riots—the looting, the vandalism, the throwing of bricks—would any jury prescribe as drastic a penalty as death?"[37]

Catherine Delattre was one of the few students permitted to stay on campus that summer, working as an assistant on a study about the shootings. A questionnaire was sent to KSU students, the results of which appeared in *Violence at Kent State, May 1 to 4, 1970: The Students' Perspective* (1971). According to the study,

- 83 percent of participants in the rally believed the Guard was guilty of murder, while only 49 percent of nonparticipants believed that.
- To a question about whether the demonstrators were provoking the Guard: 46 percent of participants believed there was "Slight provocation," 28 percent "Moderate," 19 percent "No provocation," 6 percent "Intense," and one percent "Extreme." Among observers, there was more variation. Of this group, 30 percent thought there was "Moderate provocation," 25 percent answered "Slight," 22 percent answered "Intense," 15 percent thought "Extreme," and 8 percent answered "No provocation."
- To the question "How justified do you think the Guard was in firing at the demonstrators?," there was more consensus among participants and observers. Fully 96 percent of participants answered, "Not at all justified," and 73 percent of observers agreed.

- Answers also varied depending on the respondent's self-stated political views. To the question: "How justified do you think the Guard was in firing at the demonstrators?" among the observers of the events on May 4, all nineteen radicals responded "Not at all justified." Of the 457 liberals, 88 percent said the same; 60 percent of the 563 moderates and only 28 percent of the 207 conservatives agreed that there was no justification for the Guard to shoot.

- Among observers, a plurality of 45 percent of the twenty-nine conservatives said that the Guard was under "Extreme provocation" by demonstrators at the time of the shootings, and none thought there was "No provocation." Among the 19 radicals who responded, none thought the Guard was under "Extreme provocation"; they split between answering "Intense provocation" (16%), "Moderate" (21%), "Slight" (37%) and "No provocation" (26%). Among liberals, a plurality of 37 percent thought there was "Slight provocation," and 31 percent believed there was "Moderate provocation" of the Guard. For moderates, they split between "Moderate provocation" (31%), "Slight" (25%), Extreme (24%), and "Intense" (16%).

- As to whether or not the Guard was justified in shooting, all nineteen radicals who were observers answered, "Not at all justified." Among liberal observers, 88 percent responded that the Guard was not justified. For moderates the figure was 60 percent and conservatives 28 percent.[38]

Additional responses came in the writings collected in Barbara Agte's work *Kent Letters*. One student, M.H., blamed outside agitators: "If Kent State students had been allowed to carry on these demonstrations without the intrusion of professional agitators and radial instigators, this sad and tragic event may have never occurred." Students, this writer argued, "were warned time and again" and then disobeyed the Guard. "What can we expect?" Like Mike Brock, many students expressed shock and outrage. One student, C.G., was a witness to the shootings. "I don't care what anyone says, throwing stones is no provocation for murder."[39]

The immediate faculty response echoed these latter sentiments. On May 5, about half the faculty met in the Akron Unitarian Church and issued a resolution that condemned the shootings. It read, in part, "We hold the Guardsmen, acting under orders and under severe psychological pressures, less responsible for the massacre than are Governor Rhodes and Adjutant General Sylvester Del Corso, whose inflammatory indoctrination produced those pressures." The resolution went on to "deplore the prolonged and

Members of the Ohio National Guard and others examine the bullet hole made by a Guardsman's M1 rifle during the shootings in the Don Drumm sculpture *Solar Totem #1*. (May 4 Collection. Kent State University Libraries. Special Collections and Archives.)

unduly provocative military presence on campus" and to "regard student protest against this rule of force as their moral prerogative."[40]

Investigations and Reports

Official investigations began as press reports and letters to editors swirled with their own various accusations, rumors, and conclusions about responsibility and guilt. Three major governmental bodies conducted separate investigations in the immediate time frame following the shootings: the Federal Bureau of Investigation (FBI), the Scranton Commission, and the Ohio State Highway Patrol. These ended up having the most impact on the subsequent legal cases, covered later. The Ohio National Guard also conducted its own investigation. Along with these were several other investigations and reports. The *Akron Beacon Journal* earned national recognition and its first Pulitzer Prize for its coverage and investigation of the shootings. In addition, the Ohio Civil Liberties Union, the Ohio Council of Churches, the American Association of University Professors (AAUP), and the Ohio Bureau of Investigation engaged in their own investigations and reports.

President White led the university response. White preferred to work with a low profile but placed now in a very high-profile position, he operated with a high degree of sensitivity to Kent State's public image. He sought to avoid more negative publicity and also had to navigate the political realities of being a state-supported school whose funding lay in the hands of a state legislature decidedly in favor of the law-and-order viewpoint. As to his own beliefs about the causes for the shootings, White seemed to support the idea that outside agitators were largely to blame. At a May 22 meeting of the Kent State External Communications Advisory Board, chaired by *Kent Record-Courier* editor Loris Troyer, President White maintained that a small group of outsiders was largely responsible for the unrest that set up the situation on May 4. White told the Board that "there was a clear cut and classic instance of outsiders planning and manipulating a series of events. Outsiders who cared nothing at all about Cambodia. Outsiders who were and are dedicated only to an out-and-out revolutionary purpose."[41] In a publication directed to alumni, the Office of Alumni Relations made the same argument. Many press reports continued to cite outside agitators, SDS activists, and the Weathermen as being involved and causing the shootings. Yet as wounded Kent demonstrator and historian Tom Grace has written, the reverse was true; rather than imported, the protests at Kent were homegrown, and, indeed, many Kent students were active in leading and organizing protests elsewhere.[42]

Although he deflected direct blame upon the Guard, President White seized on the desire to promote nonviolence as a way of directing the lessons learned from the shootings. White's administration "established several university commissions to determine the nature of the antagonisms that had made Kent State an instant symbol of death and dissent."[43] One of these was the Commission on KSU Violence (CKSUV), a special commission made up of students, staff, and faculty charged with collecting statements about the shootings and investigating causes and with beginning the process of institutionalizing the commitment to nonviolence. No governmental agency or police cooperated with this group; the evidence consists mainly of statements collected from students and others on campus. Kathy Stafford, who at the time of her interview was vice president for university relations, recalled her experience as one of the student representatives on the CKSUV:

[Interviewer]: Why were you selected to this committee?

Well, I had been active in student government. I was in the Student Senate and I had been on an advisory committee to the vice president. I was fairly well known because of the involvement that I had had. I assume that's the reason that I was invited to be a member.

Well, of course, it was an unbelievable experience. We spent every day for six weeks taking testimony and going through whatever materials, documents there were, but trying to just learn what had happened. So it was a very intense time, and interesting.

[Interviewer]: Who did you file the report to?

I think it was supposed to be filed to the president, but I don't believe there was ever a report formally given to anybody. We had, as a committee, some problems coming to a consensus on what should be in the written report. We actually had a minority report that was developed, and I have a copy of it. I don't have a copy of any of the—of a full report, which is one reason I don't think there was one. But I do have a copy of the minority report that was written by the author . . . [who] was one of the professors on the committee, Doris Franklin, but several of us participated as a part of that minority group that had some different feelings.

[Interviewer]: And you were one of the people who was on the minority report?

Mm-hmm.[44]

White, seeking to avoid any further negative publicity, withheld publication of the CKSUV report since it was not unanimous. When asked, Stafford stated that she "could not give you any of the specifics now" about the report. The minority report, signed by Stafford and three other members of the CKSUV, alluded to outside agitators. It is not clear why Stafford refused to discuss this in her interview.

Our work on the present Commission together with evidence alluded to by the President's Commission on Campus Unrest as having been supplied by the FBI has nevertheless led us to conclude that without "outside agitation" and preplanning, the weekend of May 1 would not have taken the ugly shape it did. Indignation, dismay, and wrath, expressed in meetings, rallies, and perhaps even in some kinds of disruption, there probably would have been; for not only had long-existing student disaffection been little ministered to during the preceding year, but students and faculty in large numbers were deeply disturbed by what looked to them like an unscrupulous invasion cloaked in high-sounding phrases and like a dangerous broadening of the war. Yet on no reasonable supposition would there have been the irresponsible and criminal violence that brought the National Guard to the campus and that on Monday culminated in death.[45]

Albert Van Kirk, who witnessed the shootings, maintained a similar belief and was quite willing to share it. Not unlike those who see the FBI, or possibly Nixon, behind the shootings, Van Kirk saw larger (in this case leftist) networks responsible.

I had a working relationship with several fellas that were involved in the intelligence agencies that were on campus. So I heard bits and pieces of information through them. It's amazing what sitting down after the fact and buying a guy a beer will do. . . . And what was clear to me even as a young student was that what took place was very well-planned, it was very well-financed, and it was very well-executed. According to one of the guys, by the FBI count there were twelve-hundred license plates in Kent the night the ROTC building burned that had no—quote—"business being in Kent."[46]

Later in his interview, Van Kirk criticized Michener's book for not mentioning "the original gunshots." Believing that the bullet hole in the Don Drumm *Solar Totem* sculpture came not from the Guard but from someone else firing at the Guard, Van Kirk's interview is another instance of reviving the sniper theory.

You don't have to be a ballistics expert to tell which way the bullet holes came from. As I—walking across campus—you know, things get blurry, but it seems to me I remembered one or two shots before a volley of shots. . . . Who knows what the facts are, but that piece seemed to make a great deal of sense to me at the time. But it was completely discounted. I suspect because it didn't fit the story that they wanted to tell.

Investigations by the FBI and a test firing by the *Akron Beacon Journal* conducted within the first two weeks after the shootings confirmed that only a bullet from the National Guard side of the sculpture, and consistent with those fired by the M1 rifles the Guard used, could have made the hole.[47]

Van Kirk elaborated more as he moved from his suspicions about a sniper, to rumors about guns found in the river, and larger concerns about the investigations and causation for the shootings.

> From a factual standpoint, I don't believe the whole story was ever told. There was supposedly a couple of guns, two or three, I'm not sure which fished out of the river within an hour of the shooting with witnesses that that was sort of just deleted from evidence. They discounted or discredited the people that claimed they saw it. That was the end of it. It ended that day. So it led me to believe that maybe there was something more at stake than just people's reputations. I think it was a complete error in judgment on the part of the president [White] to have Jerry Rubin here. That added credibility and credence to the radical agenda that he was putting forth and as a result of that four young people lost their lives. Several others are hurt badly for the rest of their life. And I look at that and I say "For what?" I mean, what was gained from that? They were protesting liquid crystals. Do you know what liquid crystals do?

> [Interviewer]: Not really.

> OK. Liquid crystals give you the ability to see at night. Your night vision goggles? That's liquid crystals technology. Came right from Kent State University. It was being used in Vietnam to save American infantry soldiers' lives. And that offended people on this campus. And the radical element of the Weathermen were the vocal ones at the forefront complaining about this. I was deeply indebted to it because as a function of that I'm probably here today. They used the liquid crystals in an archaic form relative to today, but it was put on the belly of a helicopter. They would fly around bases looking for North Vietnamese trying to overrun them. It was very effective, at least one time for me. So, as I said, I fully agree with the idea that if people don't like what the government's doing they have an absolute, in my opinion, responsibility to protest, but that protest I also believe needs to be within the confines of the law. You

can't take the law into your own hands and call it civil disobedience. I have very strong feelings about that.[48]

Over the years, some rumors have evolved into more formal allegations, a belief stronger than hearsay, which for some has approached psychological truth. These have only added to the many other allegations, hearsay, rumors, and conflicting claims that make up the history and memory surrounding the Kent State shootings. One is the belief that a sniper on a nearby rooftop either took aim at, or fired upon, the Guardsmen, prompting the shooting. A second is that a KSU student, Terry Norman, has been accused of firing his gun during the demonstration that prompted the volley from the Guard. That Norman gathered evidence for campus police—and recent evidence shows he worked briefly for the FBI a month before the shootings—added suspicion to his activities at the time and since. No doubt there were FBI informants on campus during the events in April and May; their precise involvement in any of the demonstrations, the ROTC fire, or in setting up the shootings resides mostly in the realm of speculation.

A recent news story from the *Cleveland Plain Dealer* reports on the evidence gleaned from the tape recording made at the time of the shootings by Terry Strubbe that suggests it may have been Norman firing his gun seventy seconds before the Guard fired. However, the writer is careful to conclude, "It is not clear how or if the altercation, pistol shots and firing order are related."[49] This has overlapped, somewhat confusingly, with the rumor that a sniper on a nearby rooftop took aim at the Guardsmen, prompting their decision to open fire. In the testimony of the Guardsmen and others who state they heard a shot before the volley, both Norman and the sniper have figured in explanations to support these statements.[50] The Kent community developed its own version of this rumor as well—that SDS-sponsored snipers were perched atop Reiker's Market, ready to take aim at townspeople as a form of "radical revenge" for the shootings.

That the "Terry Norman theory" has persisted is likely due to just enough circumstantial evidence to lend it a degree of credibility. Joseph Sima was a key source in the news report from the *Plain Dealer* cited above. In his interview, Sima, a Kent State student in 1970, began with a prepared statement in which he distinguishes between a "100 percent verifiable" fact (from a friend of Sima's who briefly dated Norman, and who said that Norman told her he was an FBI informant) and his own conjecture (about an elaborate connection between the Kent State shootings to J. Edgar Hoover and to Hoover's death leading to the Watergate break-in). Blending fact and opinion is Sima's claim that on the night of May 4, he saw Terry Norman on the Cleveland evening news admitting guilt: "I had to shoot, I had to shoot, they would've killed me," Sima remembers Norman saying. Sima then states that he relayed this information to the FBI during their investigation and that, to this day, the video footage of Terry Norman's admission has disappeared. In likelihood, Sima's belief about the video footage comes from statements made later by WKYC television reporters Fred DeBrine and Joe Butano, who claimed that when Norman surrendered his gun after the shootings, the Kent police officer who first took it exclaimed, "My God, it's been fired four times!" Two Guardsmen who were there also claimed to have heard this.[51]

These details remain in dispute, and the absence of firm evidence to either prove or deny all or parts of the story of Terry Norman's role leaves public cultural space for the allegations to persist. In "How Idle Is Idle Talk? One Hundred Years of Rumor Research," Pamela Donovan suggests that rumors persist, and even strengthen, from opposition, and that the adversarial relationship between rumors and their denial is an essential part of their development. From Donavan's research on Internet crime legends, debunkers "inadvertently helped promulgators and believers refine their ideas, reinterpret the contextual meaning of the stories they valued, and relaunch a more 'bulletproof' story."[52] The collective memory of the Kent State shootings contains numerous examples—the "Terry Norman theory" being among the most prominent—of how the cycle of attest-and-denial plays a vital role in the evolution of some rumors into more formal allegations. Returning to the work of Fine and Ellis, the study of rumor "uncovers the concerns—some hidden, some explicit—of citizens."[53] The oral history in this case, combined with news reports, further reveals the different perspectives on the shootings and their meaning. The continued suspicion surrounding Terry Norman serves to perpetuate ideas that there may have been a cover-up to protect the Guard. We suggest as well that these differences, revealed in rumor and in other details found in the oral history testimony, help explain the divergence in our political culture over not simply Kent, but over the meaning and memory of the 1960s and more generally over democracy and citizenship.

Further reports in the immediate period of the shootings followed these and other rumors and allegations that fed into conclusions about cause and responsibility. On May 24, the *Akron Beacon Journal* published findings conducted after an investigation by some of the paper's writers and others from the Knight Newspaper chain. The report's main conclusions were:

The four victims did nothing that justified their deaths. They threw no rocks nor were they politically radical.

No sniper fired at the National Guard. No investigative agency has yet found any evidence sufficient to support such a theory.

The Guardsmen fired without orders to do so. Some aimed deliberately at students; others fired in panic or in follow-the-leader style.

It was not necessary to kill or wound any students. The Guardsmen had several other options which they did not exercise, including firing warning shots or marching safely away.

There is no evidence to support suggestions by university and city officials that four members of the Students for a Democratic Society [SDS] planned and directed the trouble.

No reasonable excuse could be found for three violent and illegal acts by the students—breaking downtown store windows, burning the university ROTC building and throwing rocks at the Guardsmen before the shooting. All these created turmoil and ill feeling.

The prime and immediate cause of the trouble was President Nixon's decision to invade Cambodia. Kent State, a basically conservative campus, has not generally been violent in the past.[54]

The Ohio State Patrol and the FBI also began their investigations immediately after the shootings. Each completed a report by July; neither complete report was made public, but newspapers did publish a summary of the findings of each. In the meantime, President Nixon did not authorize the Scranton Commission until June 13, and the members of that body came to Kent for public hearings from August 19 to August 21. Their report was made public in September 1970. The Department of Justice used the FBI report as a basis later to create a federal grand jury that led to the first of three federal trials. The Ohio State Highway Patrol report played a role as the basis of the indictment of twenty-four students and one faculty member (the Kent 25) issued by a special state grand jury empaneled in Portage County. This led to a 1971 state criminal trial against these twenty-five defendants.

Catherine Delattre was one of those interviewed by the FBI.

I remember that the FBI came. I was picked out from photographs like many people were, and I came home from school one day—or not from school but from, school was closed but we were doing the research, and I came home and there was a sign, an official sign from the FBI and it said—I forget his name, and I wish I still had that piece of paper, but somehow it got lost—

[Interviewer]: It was on your door?

It was on my door. "Agent So-and-So would like to speak to you." [laughs] "You must report at this time and at this building on campus for this interview." And it was kind of weird. Nobody came and got me. He had put it on a nail on my door. I was so nervous, I asked some people who had been interviewed what happened. "Oh, they're just going to show you like a zillion photographs and they want you to identify people." So I went in there to this interview and literally, I swear, he had a stack, there were more than 350 photographs to go through. And he sat there while I looked at every single picture, and he said, "I want you to tell me, point out people you know." And I didn't know anybody. I probably did and I think I did, but I'm not going to say anything. He really didn't talk, he just sat there, and I was very uncomfortable but I think that was his intention, was to make me very uncomfortable. Then he did ask me questions. He did ask me very specific questions about the four days and if I had been involved in anything other than in these photos from Monday, and what, any groups that I had been involved with. And he wanted to know about outside agitators, if I knew anybody who had come on campus. That was it. I never heard from him again.[55]

Chuck Ayers reported a similar experience with a pair of FBI agents who had requested an interview:

Finally they said, "We have some photographs here. . . . We want to know if you wouldn't mind looking at them and seeing if you can identify some people?" And I said, "I'll look at them." Looked at all these photos, and again, I didn't really know any of the protesters that were really involved with it, and the photos they showed me I could pick out a couple of people, because they were all people who were standing around with me watching. And I knew they weren't involved, So I thought, Sure, I can identify them and it's not going to hurt anything, because I know we were just standing there. And we went through it, and that was kind of the end of it.

When school started up again in the fall, I saw some of these people. I'd walk up to them and say, "Hey, I identified you to the FBI!" And these same people, every time, would say, "Oh, yeah? Well I identified you to the FBI!" We started talking, and we all realized at the same time that from the shootings on Monday until Sunday afternoon, they had time to collect all these photos and determine who most of the people were, and track down these people to see if they could identify other people. We all realized that as we were identifying each other in these photos, none of us ever saw ourselves in any of the photos. I was not in any of the pictures, but people that I was identifying, who I know were standing very near me, were in the pictures. And the pictures that they were identifying where I was, and I was standing near them, they were not in the pictures when they saw them.[56]

The FBI submitted its nearly eight-thousand-page report to the Justice Department; the report also served as a foundation for the Scranton Commission's report. On July 23, 1970, the *Akron Beacon Journal* printed highlights of the Justice Department's summary of the FBI report; other newspapers around the nation did so as well. Here are some of the more significant findings that served then and now as evidence in the battle over responsibility and causation. The summary of the FBI report did not go so far as to blame the Guard, but it pointed strongly toward that conclusion. The Justice Department summary of the FBI investigation issued to the public found that "six Guardsmen, including two sergeants and Captain Srp of Troop G stated pointedly that the lives of the members of the Guard were not in danger and that it was not a shooting situation." Moreover, the report noted that "many Guardsmen do not mention the students or that the crowd or any part of it was 'advancing' or 'charging.'"

"The Guardsmen"—the report stated—"were not surrounded. No guardsman claimed rocks hit him just before the firing began." Even more troubling is the statement, "We have some reason to believe that the claim by the Guard that their lives were endangered by the students was fabricated subsequent to the event." There was no sniper. The summary also reported an earlier finding by the *Akron Beacon Journal* of one Guardsman who stated that "the Guardsmen had gotten together after the shooting and decided to fabricate the story that they were in danger of serious bodily harm or death from the students."[57]

On July 23, the Ohio State Highway Patrol submitted its report to Ronald Kane, Portage County prosecutor. The Highway Patrol supported the FBI's report in dismissing the idea of a sniper. Yet its general conclusions put responsibility upon the students, not the Guard. The Highway Patrol report, like the FBI one, covered events beginning on May 1, putting the shootings into the larger series of events that began with the unrest downtown Friday evening and included the burning of the ROTC building and the sit-in and encounters on Sunday night.

Much of the report included testimony from members of the Guard. Without access to a large amount of oral histories from the members of the Ohio National Guard, it is impossible to place their memories and narratives in direct comparison with those of the students and faculty. Nevertheless, by using documents such as after-action reports and statements to the Ohio State Highway Patrol and investigators, we can get a good sense of how some of these men were feeling and what their impressions were of the events. Again, these testimonies reveal what many Guardsmen believed was true, or felt, or, if the FBI report is accurate, created after the fact. We can also see elements of difference regarding the circumstances surrounding the shootings emerging at this point in the narratives of May 4. The narratives that would emerge during the trials—of blame on students or the Guard—began here in these immediate hours and days after the shootings.

The central question is why the Guardsmen turned and fired. Some wrote that once they reached the crest of the hill at the Pagoda, they heard a command to fire, whether over the students' heads or at the students. Sergeant William James Case, who carried the CB radio for Captain Raymond Srp, commander of Troop G, signed a statement replete with exaggeration, fear, remorse, and confusion. Case's account is similar to that of many Guardsmen in framing the event in dramatic, desperate ways with an unwavering conviction that the Guard faced great danger: "We were under attack by around 800 people. For force, they were using bricks, stones, sticks and bottles. They had hate in them and I feel they were trying to kill us." Later in this statement, Case wrote,

> When the real trouble started, I was separated from Cpt. Srp. God, I don't know where he was. It was hard to protect ourselves because items being thrown were coming in three directions. I noticed that our left flank to their firing position. During this period everything happened real fast. I do honestly, but I'm not sure, heard one or two shots fired. I don't think they were ours because the sound wasn't loud to be that close. I noticed that we were being rushed again from

the rear. I did not hear the order fire given, but I did hear someone say "not at them, over their heads." Then the left flank started firing. He then looked for Captain Srp. He did fire one round into the air. "I know where I shot because I know only God can take lives and only by his order. I didn't get the order from him to aim at any human, no matter how hard they threw the rocks, I just couldn't shoot at them."[58]

James McGee of Troop G indicates in his typed statement that he heard an order to turn around once he reached the crest of Blanket Hill as the men were on their way back to the ROTC building.

I was hit many times by rocks, once by a brick. When we got the crest of the hill I was running. The students were very close. The order was given to turn around, I turned, the students were approx. 30 feet away still moving ahead fast. The rocks were really bad. I was hit many times. At this time, I was very frighten. The only thing I could think of was being shot with my own rifle. I wondered what supiorers [sic] were going to do next. That was when the fire started. I fired 2 shots in the air and one at the left leg of a student.[59]

The statements of other Guardsmen are equally dramatic. Barry Morris seems to support the idea that Sergeant Pryor may have indeed fired his pistol as part of the barrage against the students:

Upon reaching the hill most of the men were looking back and saw how close they were and how fast they were coming. At that point, I heard gunfire to my left, looked . . . saw an officer firing and I drew my pistol, dropped to cover and fired two shots into the mob where the most of the rocks were coming from.[60]

James Edward Pierce did not hear an order but assumed one had been given as the men around him began to fire.

After the firing I felt no remorse because it seemed to be the only to defend myself. I feel that if we wouldn't have shot at them, we would have been overrun and killed. I don't feel they were people but "savage animals." I am sorry it came to this but I don't feel there was any alternate.[61]

Howard Fallon had been a platoon leader in the Akron riots of 1968 and the truckers' strike. He received "numerous hours of riot training." He did not fire and did not hear an order to do so. "In my mind the volume of objects being thrown reached its greatest volume at that point." Fallon claimed that just prior to the shootings, "I heard what I feel was small arms fire, 2 to 3 rounds, distinct rounds. Prior to that time I was in fear of great bodily harm when I saw my men struck with large rocks. I saw one grown Guardsman knocked completely off his feet by a thrown rock." He believed the students were intent on overrunning the Guard.[62] James Farriss fired his weapon on Blanket Hill; he also was among those who aimed at the students when down on the practice field. Once the firing began, he did not aim at a particular person: "I just fired in the air for a warning shot." He did not feel it was necessary to shoot the students. He also stated that while on the practice field, "I saw someone with a .45 caliber automatic fire one shot into the air."[63] Lieutenant Colonel Charles Fassinger thought the Guardsmen who fired were provoked by "a steady barrage of both verbal and physical abuse." He stated he was hit by a large rock just prior to the shootings. When asked what caused the firing, Fassinger stated, "I, in all honesty cannot answer that question."[64]

Major Harry Jones gave vivid testimony to the Ohio State police that crafted a narrative of the Guard being under attack by an assortment of objects. He noted that he was carrying a .22 caliber Beretta given to him by Ron Snyder.[65] He claims he did not fire the weapon and that he did not hear an order to fire. He also stated that he did not give an order to fire. "No verbal order or no gesture which could be interpreted as an order to fire." Jones was on the practice field with the troops. After they stopped Jones stated: "Rocks, bricks, iron spikes, golf balls with nails in them, etc., started flying from the students were coming from the front and both flanks, especially from the left flank. They were hitting the troops." He determined they were out of tear gas and then decided to withdraw back to the ROTC building. "We started withdrawing up Blanket Hill. The intensity of the missiles increased. The students began to close in. At times the students were 10 to 12 feet from the troops." Jones claimed he was hit in the stomach with a brick about halfway up the hill so hard that it knocked him to his knees. "I believe the person who hit me was Jeffrey Miller."[66] He heard explosions like firecrackers just prior to the shootings. "I saw students 4 or 5 steps from the Guardsmen and moving in. Just seconds later the firing started." He then moved along telling soldiers to stop firing. Jones felt he and the men were in danger. "I felt that [the students] were going to attempt to wrestle the weapons from the Guardsmen and possibly use them on the Guardsmen." Jones also thought that many persons in the crowd "were on narcotics of some form." And he also testified that when the firing was going on, "I saw people in the crowd jumping up and down cheering. . . . It would take a person who is insane, intoxicated or under the influence of drugs to react in such a manner."[67]

Lawrence Shafer fired at and severely injured Joe Lewis, who was at the time seventy feet away. Shafer offered an explanation during the investigation afterward:

The person on my right fired a couple of times, so I opened fire. At first I thought it was warning shots. When I saw the person who I shot coming toward us I could see his one hand up giving the finger, he was also yelling something I couldn't hear. I couldn't see his other hand. Since he was approaching swiftly and I couldn't see his other hand I assumed that he was going to do me harm so I turned and fired. At that time we were being barraged with rocks.

When asked about his personal motivation, Shafer replied: "Due to this person's actions, I felt that he was intending to try to overpower one of us. I felt at this time that my life was going to be in danger if he took another step forward. I decided that the only way to stop him was to shoot him."[68]

Ed Grant and Mike Hill, two Guardsmen who were on campus that day but not involved in the shootings, published their own account in 1974, *I Was There: What Really Went on at Kent State*.[69] In it, they recalled their own sense of fear and placed the cloak of inevitability on the events: "We were now, I believe, in an untenable situation from which there was no turning back. For the first time in the many riots in which I participated, I believed there was a possibility that the demonstrators could attack us and be successful in overrunning our position, with little or no effort." The feeling was not his alone, he wrote. "Many of the Guardsmen shared it."[70]

Much recent debate over whether there was an order to fire—either verbally or implicitly—stems from a study publicized in 2010 by wounded student and researcher Alan Canfora. As the story on the tape from the *Cleveland Plain Dealer* noted in May 2010, "The original 30-minute reel-to-reel tape was made by Terry Strubbe, a Kent State communications student in 1970 who turned on his recorder and put its microphone in his dorm window overlooking the campus Commons, hoping to document the protest

The President's Commission on Campus Unrest, the Scranton Commission, hears testimony at Kent from student activist Robert Picket. Left to right: General Benjamin O. Davis, Martha A. Derthick, Scranton, Bayless Manning, Revius O. Ortique Jr., Joseph Rhodes Jr., William M. Byrne, J. J. Kirby. (Kent State University Libraries. Special Collections and Archives.)

unfolding below. It is the only known recording to capture the events leading up to the shootings." Two forensic audio experts reviewed the tape at the request of Alan Canfora and concluded that there was an order to fire.[71]

Ron Snyder related in his 2013 interview that he asked both Lawrence Shafer (who later became the fire chief of Ravenna) and Harry Jones about what had happened. One thing is certain for Snyder: there was no such order.

Now when Major Jones was dying of cancer in Tennessee, I asked him, I said, "Harry. . . . What the hell happened up there? Tell me the truth." Because . . . if you listened to the protesters' side it was a big conspiracy or something. But let me assure you once you tell anybody, one person, the cat's out of the bag. I have never ever heard anything and I know, besides Harry Jones, I know one of the guys that did shoot and was charged and then of course it was dismissed who later become the Fire Chief of the City of Ravenna [Lawrence Shafer]. I asked him and he said, "I don't have a clue." But they thought they were being fired on or something like that. But Harry told me, he said, "Snyder, I wish to hell I knew." He said, "I wish the hell I knew what happened up there. . . . All I did was try to stop it."

[Interviewer]: No idea what prompted it then, still?

Snyder: Not a clue, not a clue. And, again, you know, he was an experienced officer. He had been all of his life and I think that bothered him a whole lot. You know I mean these things happen.

[Interviewer]: That's one of the things people are always confused about is how could this have occurred. Was it ordered, were they just scared, were they thinking they were being rushed?

Well, I can tell you that nobody in charge ordered that. I can say that. I can't say it with a 100 percent idea. But everybody that could have given that order had better sense than that. . . . I have to think—and again this is speculation—I have to think that it was an accident caused by perhaps maybe one individual thinking that he was getting run over or something and fired.[72]

The Ohio State Highway Patrol report concurred for the most part with the narrative offered above by Major Jones, in that it concluded the Guard was under assault with large rocks and concrete and the "assault continued with greater intensity with radicals and rock throwers advancing as close to 30 feet" from the Guard. It noted that more witnesses reported hearing a gunshot or firecracker shot before the volley than did not. As to the members of the Guard who fired, the report concluded that the "physical and verbal assaults were more than enough to push them to the breaking point and forced severe defensive action, according to some witnesses." The report went on to connect the events on May 4 and days before with radical activity and supported the idea of outside agitators as behind much of the violence. "Several left wing and radical groups are represented in the demonstrations rioting. Evidence indicates that their members played active roles in the planning and carrying out of these disturbances." The report also summarized what police found when they searched the dormitories after the shootings and then displayed for the press on May 15. It included "a rifle, shotgun, several revolvers, baseball bats, knives, bows and arrows, syringes and needles."[73] They also found marijuana and pipes and various pills. The idea was to paint a picture not only of the violence but of the lifestyles of the students, which would come up often in the narratives, letters, and trial testimony that supported the Guard.[74]

The last of the three major reports to be made public was the Scranton Commission's, issued on September 26, 1970. The Commission first found fault with the students.

> The conduct of many students and nonstudent protesters at Kent State on the first four days of May 1970 was plainly intolerable. We have said in our report, and we repeat: Violence by students on or off the campus can never be justified by any grievance, philosophy, or political idea. There can be no sanctuary or immunity from prosecution on the campus. Criminal acts by students must be treated as such wherever they occur and whatever their purpose. Those who wrought havoc on the town of Kent, those who burned the ROTC building, those who attacked and stoned National Guardsmen, and all those who urged them on and applauded their deeds share the responsibility for the deaths and injuries of May 4.[75]

However, the commission also put responsibility on the Guard. Its report had some sympathy for the individual Guardsmen but less for the leadership.

> The May 4 rally began as a peaceful assembly on the Commons—the traditional site of student assemblies. Even if the Guard had authority to prohibit a peaceful gathering—a question that is at least debatable—the decision to disperse the noon rally was a serious error. The timing and manner of the dispersal were disastrous. Many students were legitimately in the area as they went to and from class. The rally was held during the crowded noontime luncheon period. The rally was peaceful, and there was no apparent impending violence. Only when the Guard attempted to disperse the rally did some students react violently.

The commission report included its famous line often quoted in narratives critical of the Guard: "The indiscriminate firing of rifles into a crowd of students and the deaths that followed were unnecessary, unwarranted, and inexcusable." The report then shifted back to the issuing of live ammunition to the troops.

> The Guard fired amidst great turmoil and confusion, engendered in part by their own activities. But the guardsmen should not have been able to kill so easily in the first place. The general issuance of loaded weapons to law enforcement officers engaged in controlling disorders is never justified except in the case of armed resistance that trained sniper teams are unable to handle. This was not the case at Kent State, yet each guardsman carried a loaded M-1 rifle.

Furthermore, the commission argued that even

> if the guardsmen faced danger, it was not a danger that called for lethal force. The 61 shots by 28 guardsmen certainly cannot be justified. Apparently, no order to fire was given, and there was inadequate fire control discipline on Blanket Hill. The Kent State tragedy must mark the last time that, as a matter of course, loaded rifles are issued to guardsmen confronting student demonstrators.[76]

Legal Proceedings

As the official reports began to reveal the struggle over the facts, as well as the memory and meaning of the shootings, so too did the legal proceedings that emerged in the wake of May 4. It was not a federal probe, but rather a special state grand jury, impaneled in Ravenna by order of Governor Rhodes, that moved first. After conducting an investigation and calling witnesses, the grand jury issued indictments against twenty-five people, twenty-four Kent State students and one Kent State faculty member. No Guardsmen were indicted. It also issued a report that reflected the dominant view in Kent and the surrounding area that was supportive of the Guard and calls for law and order. The grand jury report, issued in October 1970, used the Ohio State Patrol's findings as its main source. As expected, the grand jury exonerated the Guardsmen. In doing so, these men and women upheld the growing call in the United States then for "law and order" and put into writing the fear and frustration many in the Kent area felt with protesters, the counterculture, and the KSU administration for its perceived failures in controlling them.

It should be made clear that we do not condone all of the activities of the National Guard on the Kent State University campus on May 4, 1970. We find, however, that those members of the National Guard who were present on the hill adjacent to Taylor Hall on May 4, 1970, fired their weapons in the honest and sincere belief and under circumstances which would have logically caused them to believe that they would suffer serious bodily injury had they not done so. They are not, therefore, subject to criminal prosecution under the law of this state for any death or injury resulting therefrom.

The report cited the obscenities used by students as a defense of the Guard's actions; the language, the report claimed, reached

a level of obscenity and vulgarity which we have never before witnessed! The epithets directed at the Guardsmen and members of their families by male and female rioters alike would have been unbelievable had they not been confirmed by the testimony from every quarter and by audiotapes made available to the Grand Jury. It is hard to accept the fact that the language of the gutter has become the common vernacular of many persons posing as students in search of a higher education.

Members of the grand jury were also disgusted at the university administration; indeed, most of the report focuses on this area and not the actions of the Guard. "The administration at Kent State University has fostered an attitude of laxity, over-indulgence, and permissiveness with its students and faculty to the extent that it can no longer regulate the activities of either and is particularly vulnerable to any pressure applied from radical elements within the body or faculty." The university had "allowed a vocal minority to seize control of the university campus. This will continue until such time as the citizens, university administration, faculty and students take a strong stand against the radical element bent on violence."[77]

The report and indictments led to a 1971 state criminal trial of the Kent 25. Lawyers for the Kent 25 filed appeals as soon as the indictments were handed down; the courts ultimately ordered the report expunged but let stand the indictments. Trials began in November 1971, but obtaining guilty verdicts for the accused proved difficult. One student was convicted of interfering with a fireman on May 2; two pled guilty to first-degree riot. But after the fifth trial, on December 7, all charges were dropped against the remaining defendants.

Michael Erwin participated in the rally on May 4 and was one of the Kent 25.

> I got a phone call on a Friday night—a man identified himself as a detective from the Portage County Sheriff's, and he said, "I can't tell you why I'm calling you, but if you would like to take a guess, I can tell you 'yes' or 'no.'" I said, "I've been indicted." He said "Yes. I'm making this call to give you and your family the opportunity to make arrangements for counsel and a bond to make bail. We would like you to turn yourself in sometime on Monday."

The legal proceedings related to the indictments continued through the end of 1971; meanwhile, Erwin tried to continue living a regular life.

> I couldn't drive through that town without the local police stopping me. "Oh, your tail light is out." "It looks fine now." "Well it was out when I stopped you." One night, I remember being stopped and my best friend was in the car with me who did work with the Police Department. The guy looks down and sees that Mark is in the car and says "Mark, you know you really need to pick your friends better."[78]

Joe Cullum was also indicted.

> I was probably subpoenaed because my picture was on the cover of *Life* magazine right after the shooting. So I was clearly identifiable in student records. They knew who I was. I felt that I should testify as honestly as I could in the hope that there would be some sort of attempt to achieve some justice and find some responsibility. . . . I went over to the courthouse with a couple of friends and went in asked them if I was indicted. The guy said, "Well, just wait here a second." And he walked around outside the cage and got behind me and told me to put my hands up on the wall. He felt the need to handcuff me, take me back around and fingerprint me and stuff. They threw me in the bullpen that night. I made the mistake of not lining up a lawyer first.

Ultimately, Cullum avoided conviction like most of the 25: "They never got to my trial. They dropped all the charges. So there was a sense of relief but also a sense of vindication that these were all trumped up anyway. There's nothing here." Of the grand jury report, Cullum saw in it the tenor "that the university was being besieged by these radicals and outside agitators and the students were out of control. I saw it as insane and not really reflective of the reality.[79]

Ken Hammond was among the more high-profile members of the Kent 25. After the shootings, Hammond fled Kent and lived in Cleveland, Buffalo, and finally a camp in central New Hampshire used as a refuge by antiwar protesters and other activists. Finally, he turned himself in to Ravenna authorities in October.

> They booked me and all that stuff, and we posted bail, and I got right back out. But it was a really weird process, because they didn't send out a dragnet or anything. They weren't going out and actually arresting people. They sort of waited for people to come to them. It was strange, but so many things were.
>
> Then I was one of the Kent 25. Got involved very quickly organizing the Kent Legal Defense Fund. We had some meetings down at JB's, up on Water Street. That's when Bill Kunstler was here. We had wonderful attorneys. David Scribner from National Council on Civil Rights came out, saved us all in many ways. That got all that started. Of course that went on for the next fourteen months until the December of '71.[80]

Like Ken Hammond, Carl Moore played a key role in organizing the Kent Legal Defense Fund to assist those indicted by the special state grand jury. This interview is from 1973:

> [Interviewer]: What was your role in the Kent Legal Defense Fund?
>
> Well, I was a member of the Board of Trustees, and I attended most of the meetings and participated in the decision-making of that organization. I'm sure they wanted me to be a member because I was also the Chairman of the ACLU and they wanted to interface with the ACLU because they didn't have much money or anything at that time, and they needed the legal resources of the ACLU as well as they wanted to coordinate.

No one expected it to go as well as it did and ultimately, we raised a lot of money and it did a lot of good, I think. But there were some hairy times. Even later on when decisions were to be made as to how money should be spent and what have you, there were terrible conflicts between the lawyers, who would see the need to spend money some ways, and the lay people, who couldn't understand why the money had to be spent that way.[81]

While the special state grand jury indicted students and faculty, the Ohio General Assembly used its power to defuse future protests and reinforce the position of Rhodes and the grand jury. On September 16, 1970, House Bill 1219 became law; it established "hearing procedures for persons arrested on campus for any alleged violations," made "suspension mandatory for students, faculty, and staff arrested," and provided "for their dismissal upon conviction." The bill also provided for "expedited trials for persons accused of such offenses."[82]

Additional litigation also began in the fall of 1970 that would extend until 1979. The cases were a mix of both criminal and civil law and proceeded simultaneously along these two tracks. Initially, and unknown to the public, in 1970 President Nixon pressured his then attorney general John Mitchell not to seek a federal grand jury investigation—this despite Mitchell's public view that the FBI and Justice Department findings indicated possible violations of federal law by the Ohio National Guard. In August 1971, Mitchell announced there would be no federal grand jury. Two years later, however, the Justice Department announced it would reopen the case as a civil rights issue. The change stemmed from several factors. One was the unfolding Watergate scandal that implicated Mitchell and others in the Justice Department. New attorney general Elliot Richardson sought to revamp the image of his agency. J. Stanley Pottinger became the new assistant attorney general and chief of the Civil Rights Division. He made the official announcement and seems to have acted both on the basis of his own curiosity and because of continued pressure from the families of the killed and wounded students (the Kent Families), who filed lawsuits to open the case.

Additionally, the various publications and news stories about cover-ups raised many questions about the shootings, as did congressional inquiries. On December 12, 1973, Pottinger announced that a federal grand jury would investigate the shootings, and on March 29, 1974, the jury handed down indictments against eight Ohio National Guardsmen for depriving the wounded and killed students their due process of law. Five Guardsmen—

James D. McGee, William E. Perkins, James E. Pierce, Lawrence A. Shafer, and Ralph Zoller—faced possible life sentences. Three—Matthew McManus, Barry W. Morris, and Leon H. Smith—faced lesser charges that could have meant one year in prison and a $1,000 fine. Yet in another blow for the families of the dead students, and vindication for the Guard, after only ten days federal judge Frank Battisti on November 8, 1974, dismissed the federal criminal case on the grounds that the federal government had failed to prove specific intent on the part of the Guardsmen to deprive students of their civil rights.

Another round of litigation proceeded along federal civil law. The effort to sue the state of Ohio and its officers under *Krause v. Ohio* in state courts failed. However, in a separate suit, *Scheuer v. Rhodes,* the U.S. Supreme Court ruled that state officials and members of the Guard can be sued in their individual capacities. The Supreme Court's unanimous ruling—coming on April 17, 1974, a month after the federal grand jury indictment on criminal charges—allowed the civil lawsuits to go forward.[83] The individual suits were collected together under *Krause v. Rhodes,* and the trial began in May 1975, with U.S. District Court judge Donald Young presiding. The Kent Families, led by attorney Joseph Kelner, sought $46 million in damages from Rhodes, former Kent president Robert White (who had resigned in 1971), and twenty-seven individual Guardsmen. The trial lasted fifteen weeks, with 101 witnesses and twelve thousand pages of trial transcripts and involved a series of complex legal issues included in a seventy-six-page set of instructions to the jury. In the end, the jury voted 9–3 in favor of the Guardsmen, Rhodes, and White.

Reactions were more heated than for earlier trials. Inside the courtroom as the verdicts were read, student plaintiffs cried "Murderers!" and "This is an outrage! There's no justice!" Mrs. Scheuer cried, "They're still murderers!" For the Guard, there was joy and relief. Lawrence Shafer remarked, "I hope it's the end." General Del Corso called the verdicts "a great day for justice and law enforcement in this country." The *Record-Courier* asserted that the public in Portage County approved of the verdict. However, a daily opinion poll by the *Akron Beacon Journal* found that 51 percent of callers disagreed.[84]

The trials generated tensions not only among those involved but for those observing as well. In her 1990 oral history, Linda Fifer related a vivid memory from that time. She began her studies at Kent in the fall of 1970:

> During the five years that I was here—I graduated in August of '75 with my master's in speech pathology—the message that I kept receiving from

Ohioans was that students were at fault for the shootings; and that was something I never believed. That was something that I couldn't believe. I never felt that students were at fault for any of the incidents there. I was angry with the sense of blame that students were expected to carry.

I was in Montana—where I live now—two days or so [after] the Guardsmen were acquitted, and for the next three years or so, I would have recurring dreams about the shootings even though I was not here. It was the same dream, where I was a member of a jury, I guess, and Guardsmen were called in to re-enact the shootings so that we, the jury, would get an idea of what was happening; except that it happened again, and people were being shot again. And I would wake up from this dream not ever knowing why I was having this sensation since I wasn't here at the time of the shootings. And I really do believe it was a lot of the blame that we were told to carry for this.[85]

The legal drama continued as the Kent Families appealed. Sanford Rosen, a lawyer from San Francisco with ties to the ACLU, joined as the lead counsel for the appeals process. In September 1977, a three-judge panel in Cincinnati agreed to a new trial, citing the fact that in the 1975 trial, someone had threatened one of the jurors to side with the Guard and that Judge Young did not question or remove the juror. In December 1978, the federal retrial resulted in an out-of-court settlement made public in January 1979. No one was found legally responsible for any of the events on May 4; the civil cases that ended in 1979 produced a $675,000 settlement with the families of those students killed and wounded and a statement of regret signed by indicted members of the Ohio National Guard and Governor Rhodes. The distribution of the settlement was as follows:

- Dean Kahler, $350,000
- Joseph Lewis, $42,500
- Thomas Grace, $37,500
- Donald MacKenzie, $27,500
- John Cleary, $22,500
- Alan Canfora, Douglas Wrentmore, Robert Stamps, James Russell, $15,000 each
- Families of the four students slain, $15,000 each
- Attorneys fees and expenses, $75,000.
  The statement of regret read:

In retrospect, the tragedy of May 4, 1970 should not have occurred. The students may have believed that they were right in continuing their mass protest in response to the Cambodian invasion, even though this protest followed the posting and reading by the University of an order to ban rallies and an order to disperse. These orders have since been determined by the Sixth Circuit Court of Appeals to have been lawful.

Some of the Guardsmen on Blanket Hill, fearful and anxious from prior events, may have believed in their own minds that their lives were in danger. Hindsight suggests that another method would have resolved the confrontation. Better ways must be found to deal with such confrontations.

We devoutly wish that a means had been found to avoid the May 4 events culminating in the Guard shootings and the irreversible deaths and injuries. We deeply regret those events and are profoundly saddened by the deaths of four students and wounding of nine others which resulted. We hope that the agreement to end this litigation will help to assuage the tragic memories regarding that sad day.[86]

Ron Snyder, in a second interview, this one on May 3, 2013, believed the litigation provided justice under the law for those killed and wounded.

I think it was obvious that although the May 4th Coalition doesn't think they got justice, they got justice within the full extent of the law. Some, not necessarily all, have used the fact that the State of Ohio turned loose of some cash money to put this thing to rest finally. Now the only reason for that, this is what we were told by our lawyers. They said, "Look, the State of Ohio has decided to throw some money just to get rid of it because the cost of the trials is so excessive that they want to save some money up and make this go away." I think it was $7-$800,000 dollars. You know that would in no way compensate for those lives and those students. But it made it go away because I think the lawyers on the side of the aggrieved parties; they understood that this was a loser, okay. Things happen like this and it's unfortunate. But I don't think that there was any justice that didn't come their way. And I think the case, the court cases bear that out.

I would hope that . . . the parents of the dead students and the severely wounded people would understand that at some point in their life that this thing occurred. It's more like a mysterious occurrence to them, I'm sure, because when that young person left home, they thought they'd see him next week, next month, or next semester, you know? And here we are, we're down the road 43 years tomorrow thinking about this and there is no other solution. Sometime you've got to draw the line and say, "There is no more." I mean they've turned every stone there is to turn. I've never seen anything that's had so many stones turned over.[87]

Dean Kahler sees the trials and the results differently.

We could tell right off the bat that we were going to get screwed. Oh, they were crazy. I mean they were absolutely nuts. When we get there we find out that we got a judge on retirement status who'd never tried any kind of case like this and only worked on juvenile cases before and never on the big trials that related to murder and all that sort of thing. He was related to the U.S. Senator, Steven Young. Then we get there and we find out that they didn't even give us a real courtroom. He'd stuck us in an overflow unused courtroom. The place was cramped and small and it really didn't fit the circumstances.

Do you know the Chicago Eight Trial in Chicago after the 1968 conventions? I would have made it look like Little Orphan Annie coming to visit. I mean if I had been a little more mature, they would have me bound and gagged into my wheelchair and I would have found ways to fall out of it to flop around and make a mess in the courtroom just to disrupt the proceedings because that's exactly what the defendants' attorneys were doing. Charlie Brown is this guy about 62 or 63 years old, tall, balding hair. And he always wore really cheap-looking suits. I think he was just trying to garner sympathy from the jury. He would suck snot out of his nose into his mouth, pull out his handkerchief [sound effects]. You know just the whole thing of sucking the snot out of his nose and into his mouth and then blowing and spitting it into his handkerchief and then he would clear his throat. He was just disgusting. Then you had Burt Fulton, the other lawyer, who was pinstripe right on. The juxtaposition between two of them—one was the greasy slime ball and the other guy was the consummate professional. They did everything they could to disrupt our lawyers all the time. And they got away with stuff. A normal judge . . . would have thrown them into jail.

I think the U.S. Federal Court, just reading the transcripts, the Supreme Court was just appalled by what happened in that trial. You know they remanded it back for a brand new trial, totally new judge. They said, "Put them in a damn real courtroom and get a real judge." So we got Judge Thomas. Who in 1979 was a great judge. He read the transcripts. He knew what was all there. He went to both attorneys and said, "There isn't much more you're getting out of this." We had a few things we wanted to get out and we were able to get those into the record. He said, "How about if we settle this thing?" We said, "We're only going to settle until they apologize for shooting us." We never got an, exactly an apology, but they took responsibility for shooting us. They said they shot us. They were wrong for shooting us. So we settled out of court basically. We were idealistic people. We weren't after millions of dollars like you get in jury verdicts now.

First time in American history that any state let people who normally would have been protected by sovereign immunity off—they were taken out of that sovereign immunity protection. Today now because of our case, if you do something stupid as a state official, you can be sued and the state doesn't even have to defend you. So that was *Krause v. State of Ohio.*

[Interviewer]: So with that apology and the settlement—do you feel there's some closure there?

Do I trust them to actually tell the truth? No, I don't trust them to tell the truth. Even if we got the exact same thing that they're doing in South Africa or in Ireland or in Croatia or Bosnia with the truth and justice systems that were going on over there, truth and justice things, I don't think they would tell the truth, to tell you the truth. Who would want to be known as the people who deliberately shot students? I don't think they would.[88]

The gathering of testimony by the Guard, the Ohio State Police, and the Scranton Commission relied upon witness memory from the immediate aftermath of the shootings. The oral history interviews done years later—and in a different setting, context, and with different interlocutors—are also testimony. Together, they are valuable not only for critical analysis to detect truth, but also for their value as an "interpretation of experience, and as an intervention into the field of historical discourse."[89] To paraphrase James Young, the value of these statements and interviews comes, like Holocaust testimony, not so much from their neutrality but as records of "'telling history.'"[90] Furthermore, "memory," according to Dominick LaCapra, "poses questions to history in that it points to problems that are still alive or invested with emotion and value."[91]

As testimony just after the shootings, and as oral history in recent years, these statements and interviews reveal the efforts by individuals, whether on their own or acting as part of a group or institution, to "work through a past that has not passed away."[92] Kent remains, like the 1960s remain, alive in the minds of those who made the history, witnessed it, and sought to shape its meaning and significance. Gleaning the facts from the fiction is critical; so, too, is documenting and understanding that "there are divergences, inconsistencies, different versions at different times"[93] to see how memory was and remains a site of struggle. We will now turn to the issue of memorialization.

PART FIVE

"The beginning of an ending"

The opening of the May 4 Visitors Center (M4VC) in 2012 in Taylor Hall came after decades of efforts to memorialize the shootings of May 4, 1970, and the events preceding them. It signaled greater acceptance of the events as part of the institution's history. Given that the M4VC received funding from the National Endowment for the Humanities and gained listing in the National Register of Historic Places in 2010, the opening also signaled greater acceptance on the part of the federal government of the events as a significant moment in American history. Slowly, there was acceptance of some sort on the part of the state of Ohio. In 1990, then-Governor Richard Celeste apologized to the families of the dead and wounded on behalf of the state of Ohio. In 2007, a historical marker was placed near Taylor Hall. Its text ended with the conclusions of the President's Commission that the shootings were "unnecessary, unwarranted, and inexcusable." Markers for a walking tour of the site, funded by the Ohio Humanities Council, came in 2010. The oral history project upon which this book is based also came into being in 1990 and has continued since. But as with the oral histories, there may be acceptance of the events, but just how and what is remembered, interpreted, and forgotten are open questions. And in the case of the M4VC, the fact that it took four decades to create and that it followed several other contentious efforts at memorialization only adds to the long and difficult history and memory of the shootings.

The transformation of the site of violence at Kent embodies the set of ideas put forward by geographer Kenneth E. Foote. In his work *Shadowed Ground,* Foote analyzes the relationship between landscape and violence. He notes that sites of violence can move through or be considered to be in one of four stages: sanctification, designation, rectification, and obliteration. According to Foote, *sanctification* occurs "when events are seen to hold some lasting positive meaning that people wish to remember." *Obliteration,* on the opposite end of the continuum, "results from particularly shameful events people would prefer to forget—for example, a mass murder or gangster killing." *Designation* is "the marking of a site" that "simply denotes that something "important" happened there. *Rectification* "involves removing the signs of violence and tragedy and returning a site to use."[1] Designation at Kent of the site of the shootings came with the first marker placed by a group of students from Kent's Hillel chapter, a Jewish campus organization, in 1971. A small, aluminum plaque listed the names of the four students killed with the words "In living memory." Foote notes that designation "is sometimes best viewed as a transitional phase in the history of a tragedy site."[2] Indeed, the marker served in some ways as a holding effort, lying between the desire of some to forget, or obliterate, the site of the shootings and efforts to sanctify it. Sanctification usually involves the creation of a marker and is made sacred through a public ritual dedication. This category demonstrates "most clearly the relationship of landscape and memory." These sites are then transformed into "a symbol intended to remind future generations of a virtue or sacrifice or to warn them of events to be avoided."[3] At Kent State, the annual walk and vigil and the commemorative activities were early efforts to sanctify the site; later, the memorial by Bruno Ast, the walking tour, marker, and Visitors Center added to this. As we discuss below, in the 1970s the university constructed an annex to the Memorial Gym on part of the landscape where the confrontation between students and Guardsmen occurred on May 4. Here, drawing on Foote, we can see this battle over the Gym Annex—dubbed Tent City from the demonstrators' occupation of the proposed construction site—as a struggle between efforts to sanctify the site of the shootings and those who sought either obliteration or rectification—to repurpose the land for the gym.

Since the 1970s, as John O'Hara has noted, "the university's concessions to public demands for official recognition of May 4 were ameliorated by ambivalence." This came because in the 1970s, the shootings had a negative impact on enrollment. The university was "immobilized by its conflicted role in accounting for the event without favoring one ideological position or another." Caught between the state government that funded it and that ordered the National Guard to campus and the "political and emotional needs of various constituencies among whom disagreements about the shootings flourished," university officials "refrained from providing a narrative of the shootings and contributed to the power of the event to fester in the community."[4] Yet the events and the controversy surrounding them were woven into the fabric of the university; like the narrators themselves who witnessed the shootings, KSU could neither deny nor escape the events, and over time and with a great deal of struggle, crafted a narrative about the four days in May. The various forms of memorialization on campus, including the Visitor's Center, paired with our narrators' memories, reveal further divisions and fracturing over the shootings and their ultimate significance. They also demonstrate that the memory of the 1960s and its political and cultural clashes remain contentious. The battles over memory on campus and the oral histories that speak to those battles are together testaments to the tension between remembering and forgetting.

First Anniversary and Annual Commemoration

The abrupt closing of the university after the shootings denied many in the campus community a chance to grieve. Yet as Scott Bills noted in *Kent State/ May 4,* when classes resumed in the fall of 1970 and on the first anniversary of the shootings, "there were already disparate attitudes concerning an 'appropriate' memorial ceremony, reflecting opposing analyses of the shootings themselves." "From the beginning," Bills writes, "there was a struggle over who 'owned' May 4 and who should control its potent symbolism."[5] Two main institutional vehicles of annual remembrance emerged: a candlelight walk on the evening of May 3 followed by a vigil at the sites where the four students were killed and a commemoration program on May 4. In addition, in 1971 KSU created the Center for Peaceful Change as a "living memorial" to May 4. The Center changed its name to the Center for Applied Conflict Management in 1994. In the library, KSU also opened the May 4 Resource Center to house materials related to the events. In 1971, B'nai B'rith Hillel placed a small cast aluminum plaque in the Prentice Hall parking lot in memory of the four slain students, three of whom were Jewish: Allison Krause, Jeffrey Miller, and Sandra Scheuer. The plaque was stolen in 1974 and replaced the following year with a pink granite marker that was also later damaged and then replaced with the current granite marker. Each year, the stone marks the end of the candlelight march. And the first memorial sculpture was installed in 1971 as well: Kent faculty artist Alastair Granville-Jackson's piece *The Kent Four.*

The struggles over memory and memorialization added to the tension as classes reopened in the fall of 1970. The political divisiveness of May had not dissipated. The investigations that began in the summer morphed into the legal proceedings that started with the Special State Grand Jury indicting the Kent 25 in October. In her 1990 oral history, Linda Fifer recalls the tension on campus and her personal anxiety during first anniversary of the shootings in May 1971. "There were rumors that students were buying guns and it was going to happen again. And I was very scared." She tried to get off campus before the anniversary, but her parents initially refused to come and get her.

> I remember my father asking me if Kent State was going to give him a refund for the two days that classes would be cancelled. That was the kind of mentality a lot of parents and adults had. He was angry and they refused to come and get me. The rumors were so strong that this would happen again that it reached my hometown north of Dayton, and a friend of mine's dad who used to work for the government had also heard that things were going to be rather uneasy here, and happened to run into my mother and convinced her that yes, I should come home. So that first anniversary, I was not here, but I remember coming back and it was still as a pin dropping on a carpet. You could not hear even the rustle of the breeze. It was just so quiet, so respectful and so, almost, repressive with the silence when I did come back that Tuesday afternoon.[6]

Peter Jedick recalled "it was strange" coming back to campus. "All of a sudden Kent was in the national news, international news, as you know it was on *Newsweek, Life* magazine. They still had rallies," he remembered, "and people went. But everything was different. Just somber."[7] In his 1990 recorded remembrance, William (Bill) Wilen recalled coming to KSU as a new faculty member responsible for training student teachers by placing them in local schools. "Teachers were confronting students with their very strong negative feelings about Kent State and the happenings there. My major problems were trying to diffuse situations that had occurred between my student teachers and faculty in the schools in which they were doing their student teaching experience."[8] Tom Grace has written that in the fall of 1970, "Two thousand students held an unplanned candlelight vigil at the site of the killings, beginning a tradition that continues to this day on the anniversary of the fatal shootings."[9] Racial tension also continued on campus as members of BUS were arrested for assault. There was another series of antiwar activities, especially after February 1971, when U.S. forces invaded Laos. Activists organized a noon rally on February 5 "at the scene of last Mays massacre to show our *Outrage* with the Nixon administration and the war in S.E. Asia." This invasion created "the very same conditions that led to the murders of 4 students and the wounding of 9 others last May at Kent State University. We will not let the atrocities of last may intimidate us in any way, we will still continue the fight against American aggression, whether it be in S.E. Asia, or in Kent, Ohio."[10] Students were arrested for flag desecration. There were bomb threats throughout the 1970–1971 year and one real explosion at BUS headquarters in October 1970.

President White and the KSU administration did not advance the idea of a commemoration but responded to the growing desire among many on campus for some kind of memorialization or recognition. White responded in February 1971 by creating the May 4 Commemorative Committee (M4CC). Led by Craig Morgan, student body president (and one of the Kent 25), graduate student Steve Sharoff (who played a role in the May 1 rally), and KSU vice president Richard Bredemeier, the M4CC sought input from all students as it developed a plan for the first commemoration. But as Tom Grace has written, the antiwar Left refused, seeing the committee as a reflection of the university's effort to coopt and dilute the meaning of the shootings. This alternative group became the May 4 Coalition, organized by Ken Hammond and Vietnam veteran Ken Johnson.[11] In the end, separate observances went on. Perhaps the continued political and emotional strain was too much for President White, as he announced his retirement in February 1971.

The university-sponsored event in 1971 was a Memorial Observance from May 1 through May 4 and included the candlelight walk and vigil that is now part of the organized remembrance. Following the impromptu one in the fall of 1970, professor and former faculty marshal Jerry Lewis and sociology student Michelle Klein, along with Jeff Auld, organized a walk and a vigil, despite an initially negative reaction to the idea from President White and other administrators. The first commemoration also included a blood drive, concerts, and speakers who included Jesse Jackson, Julian Bond, Dick Gregory, and James Ahern. From 11:00 A.M. to 12:30 P.M., there was a memorial service on the Commons. President White was adamant in making this only for "members of the University family" and not open to the public. He and the university committee in charge of the events assured others that the group wanted to present a "balanced program."[12]

Meanwhile, the alternate May 4 Coalition commemoration went on as well. Combined, anywhere between seven thousand and ten thousand people attended one or both. After the May 4 event, activists occupied the new ROTC building for several hours, but none were arrested. However, some students

Dean Kahler on stage in his wheelchair at the first commemoration in May 1971. To Kahler's immediate left is Ken Johnson, president of the Kent chapter of Vietnam Veterans Against the War. President White is seated at far right. (May 4 Collection. Kent State University Libraries. Special Collections and Archives.)

from Kent State, included wounded student James Russell, were arrested in Washington, D.C., as part of a rally to close down the nation's capital in protest of the Laos invasion.[13] Some more radical students saw the early institutional efforts inside KSU to create and manage a commemoration as "an effort to sanitize the imagery of the shootings, to 'isolate' them in the past and deny a continuing political relevancy." As a result, an alternative effort emerged. In her 1982 essay, "The Kent State Legacy and the 'Business at Hand,'" which appeared in Bills's book, Miriam R. Jackson—a freshman at KSU in 1970, an antiwar activist, and a witness to the shootings—argued that

> Kent State University would have preferred us to make May 4 simply a day of mourning. How much easier for successive Kent State administrations to classify the shootings as a "tragedy" and concentrate their annual blessings on the May 3 vigil, an event, according to former Kent State president Glenn Olds, "in which all concerned persons may participate, reflect and silently commemorate the meaning of these events without distractions of any alien, partisan, or political interpretation."[14]

She believed that the Center for Peaceful Change (CPC) was a compromise "between two groups: campus radicals who wished May 4 to be memorialized in an entirely political manner and conservatives from both campus and community outraged at the idea of May 4 being memorialized at all."[15] Such radical efforts continued into 1973. That year, Tobie Fixler wrote a letter to the *Daily Kent Stater* in support of the alternative programming sponsored by the May 4 United Front, Vietnam Veterans Against the War, and the Joe Hill Organization. Fixler argued that the use of peaceful change was an insult to the students killed. "By naming the CPC, the university has implied that the students should have changed their tactics. What was needed was a peaceful change school for the Ohio National Guard, not the students who were engaged in legal assembly." The radical students preferred to "openly discuss a system which must quell free speech and people's rights in order to maintain power."[16]

Ken Hammond remembered his beliefs on these divisions in his 2012 interview.

> But in those early years, that was really a question. Some of us didn't want to just be sort of a grieving thing. I mean, obviously, that's a major aspect of it all and especially in those early years. The pain was still very, very, fresh and raw and personal and that was perfectly understandable.
>
> A lot of people want to relate to those events and the killings on May 4th as a tragedy, as something that, "Oh it just happened, it wasn't really anybody's fault, it's a terrible thing, but, you know, we should all learn lessons about how we can avoid this sort of thing in the future" and all that. My feeling has been tragedy isn't the right word. It was a massacre or whatever you want to call it. I don't know if this meets the statistical threshold for that, but it was certainly a case of the violent repression of legitimate protest.[17]

Such sentiments appeared again in May 1974 when, at the alternate commemoration, speaker Jane Fonda said that the 1970 shootings "happened in the context of repression and terror that was aimed at crushing the antiwar movement." Wounded Vietnam veteran and activist Ron Kovic put his wheelchair next to Dean Kahler's and told the crowd, "Our bodies were destroyed by the same administration."[18] Another skirmish in the 1970s memory wars erupted in 1975. That year, the university leadership announced it would cease university-sponsored commemoration events. Student government responded by calling for the creation of a student-led organization, the May 4 Task Force, which received official recognition in October 1975.

Amid the battles over which groups should control the commemorations, the walk and vigil became a central part of the memorial activities surrounding May 4. Jerry Lewis recalls in this 2010 interview the creation of the walk and vigil. He compares the vigil at Kent to the one that occurred after the shootings that killed thirty-two people at Virginia Tech in 2007. The event begins when those participating in the walk gather at 11:00 P.M. on May 3 to take part in the procession around campus. Following the walk, a vigil begins with one person standing in each of the spots where one of the four students was killed. Individuals rotate every half hour through the night. The vigil continues until about 12:15 P.M. on May 4, when the last group of four walks from the Prentice Hall lot down the hillside and across the Commons to signal the transition to the next set of events.

> What was so sad, and this is going to sound terrible—and I apologize ahead of time—but we never had a chance to mourn as a community, because we were, and I'm going to use this, and it's unfortunate words, but I think it communicates—I felt envious of Virginia Tech, because they had a memorial service that evening. I started crying. I said, "We never had that." And that was one of the reasons I developed a vigil, with a couple of students, which remarkably has lasted. It gave us a chance to mourn as a community, which as a sociologist I know is very important. [Émile] Durkheim taught us that.[19]

In his study of religion, Durkheim emphasized rituals such as funeral rites "involve a *collective obligation* to mourn; a mourning that is not generally 'the spontaneous expression of individual emotions,' but results from the moral pressure on individuals to 'bring their feelings into harmony with the situation.'"[20] These rites "show the continued strength of the group in moments of weakness—that is, the death of its members."[21]

Linda Fifer's 1990 remembrance illustrates how this collective need to mourn comes into being by revealing how, as a student arriving after the shootings, she felt a connection to the victims.

> I was in Prentice Hall and we watched the Candlelight Vigil from my room, and I was amazed that so many people could be so quiet. It was a carpet of lights on the parking lot. It was all these flickering candles and lights. And I never saw so much respect for people that they didn't even know. And part of me started to understand the impact of these shootings.

The march as part of the first campus vigil, May 3, 1971. Professor Jerry Lewis is in the front row, wearing a cap at the extreme left of the picture. (Kent State University Libraries. Special Collections and Archives.)

The next day it really hit me. I opened my curtain to look out, and here it had started raining; and I looked out and there standing in the four marked places were four people standing in the rain holding candles. And it was kind of like a zoom lens on a camera; my mind just zeroed in on those four people. And at that point was when I realized that my life had been forever changed by this, that I would never be the same. I cannot describe it but it is as if I have lost something here, too. I cannot describe the sadness I feel on this day. And yet the anger I have toward this state and towards the government and towards the national government, because I do believe they were involved in making such a disastrous decision just shooting down innocent people. I don't understand that. In light of Tiananmen Square last year when people were shot down and Americans everywhere said, "What a horrible thing that is!" And yet, still to this day, people say, "Those kids at Kent got what they deserved." I do not see the difference. To me it is the same thing.[22]

Though brief, her remembrance contains deep levels of importance. Geoffrey Cubitt has written that the ways in which divisive or traumatic events transition from event to memory is often shaped "by the strategies which public bodies" use in the afterlife of the event.[23] In the case of the vigil, this ceremony of remembrance served as one of the first rituals to craft a collective memory that fused public and private needs to remember, to grieve, to ascribe meaning to the deaths of four students. Students like Linda Fifer who came to campus in the fall of 1970 arrived at an important moment in the transition to memory and began building a collective meaning to the shootings for the campus community. A witness to the vigil, Fifer grasped the meaning that the vigil intended to impart and accepted it, thereby transforming her life. As she notes, the meanings she gave to the shootings in 1970 stayed with her and gave her a structure to connect them directly to the Chinese government's 1989 repression of the student-led pro-democracy demonstrations, centered in Tiananmen Square in Beijing.

The vigil emerged independently from the Kent State administration, adding to the initial tension between limited and often reluctant administrative participation in and sanctioning of memorialization and remembrance of the shootings on the one hand and on the other the desire among others on campus to never forget them. There were still those on campus and in the immediate surrounding area who reacted violently to any effort to memorialize the students. In her 1990 remembrance, Shirley Ohles reveals these tensions as she recounts the story of the placement of the granite memorial marker in the Prentice Hall parking lot that replaced the initial one placed by Hillel in 1971. Her husband, education professor John Ohles, was involved. In 1974 the aluminum marker was stolen, and John Ohles initiated a faculty campaign to replace the marker with something more permanent. They succeeded in getting a granite marker; on the morning of May 4, 1975 as the vigil ended and the group prepared to dedicate the new granite marker, Ohles and others discovered the original metal plaque had been returned "full of bullet holes." The granite marker stood until 1979, when it was damaged by fire caused by candles from the vigil left in the wood chips surrounding the marker. Repairs were made in 1980. But Shirley Ohles read her husband's comments in a 1984 letter to the *Kent Stater* that related the history of the marker and her husband's frustration at the lack of cooperation from the leaders of KSU:

> "It should be emphasized that the marker was intended solely as a permanent replacement for the cast aluminum plaque dedicated by Hillel on May 4th, 1971, and stolen in 1974. My greatest concern from

the first efforts to provide the marker, to the present, has been the apparent lack of interest and concern on the part of the administration, where there should have been the original plaque or the replacement marker. The actions I initiated were taken only when it seemed obvious that the University would not replace the stolen plaque, and later, would not repair the fire-damaged marker. I'm not aware of any commitment by the University to assure security and maintenance of the marker. I would hope that there will be a formal assignment for the responsibility of the marker, as well as the steel sculpture and May 4th room in the library, to the administrative office." This was really in response to being asked if he thought that marker was adequate as a university memorial. And his feeling was that it was not. Because it was not a university memorial, it was originally a Hillel, and then it was a faculty replacement for the Hillel memorial.[24]

Tent City

The tensions building in the early 1970s over ownership of the memory erupted over the university's decision to build an annex to the Memorial Gymnasium over part of the ground that witnessed the shootings. Using Foote's language, as the protesters saw it, they were fighting against the obliteration of a site that in their minds ought to be sanctified. The university solidified plans for the annex in April 1974. Originally, KSU president Glenn Olds opposed the site, but he revised his position after hearing from Carl Erickson, then dean of the School of Health, Physical Education, and Recreation. The Ohio Board of Regents approved the money for the Gym Annex—$6 million—in March 1975.

The first concerns raised by students came in November 1976, once the State Architects' Office approved preliminary plans. In November, some trustees expressed their own concern about building on the site; the group nonetheless approved the first report to allow plans to be completed. At the May 4 commemoration in 1977, the some 3,000 attendees heard speakers Dick Gregory, William Kunstler (the self-described "radical lawyer" who had helped organize the Kent Legal Defense Fund for the Kent 25), and Vietnam veteran Ron Kovic call for a protest against the Gym Annex. Following the program, about 1,500 marched in protest; about 250 continued on to Rockwell Hall, where the KSU trustees were meeting to consider a possible successor to President Olds, who had announced his resignation,

A proposed layout for the Gym Annex that led to controversy and a protest against the construction. (May 4 Collection. Kent State University Libraries. Special Collections and Archives.)

and to award the contract for the annex. The group occupied the building until about 1 A.M., and at this point the May 4 Coalition was formed.

Nathan Sooy became acquainted with Dean Kahler when Kahler returned to campus as a student. It was through Kahler that Sooy became active in the CPC and then the Gym Annex protests. Sooy was one of the first to lead the initial occupation of Rockwell Hall, "which began the 'Move the Gym' episode." After the program, Sooy "turned around" and "started running" toward Rockwell Hall, ahead of the crowd. "I remember one woman coming up to me," Sooy recalled, and she said 'Well, should we go back?' No, I'm not waitin' for the vanguard this time, I'm gonna go!" "Because I was kind of disgusted at this point with the institutionalized radicals, you know. Like my thing was entirely personal; I wanted to go talk to the members of the Board of Trustees because of the gymnasium situation." When others began to arrive, one of them, Cliff Burns, gave Sooy a bullhorn.

> Cliff says, "Okay, Nathan, you take the bullhorn; you tell everybody." And, so all of a sudden, I was on stage, and I said, "The Trustees that are right in here!" And people went, "Ohhhh!" And they started going into the building. Well, once people were inside, I was on the spot again because they'd given me the bullhorn all of the sudden I was supposed to be leading this thing. I had absolutely no idea what I was doing [laughing], and it's like, I found myself mouthing slogans like, "It's gonna be bodies against bulldozers—we're gonna go after 'em!" And, you know, that worked for a time, but it was a good thing that there was also somebody else there who was one of the speakers that day, Ron Kovic. Ron had been in demonstrations before and I hadn't. And Ron started whispering to me as to what to do. He says, "Well do this; get everybody to sit down." [laughing] So, I got everybody to sit down. And then he says, "Well, get everybody to do this," and then I did this. Then it was, "Okay, now Nathan, go call the press and tell them what happened." Now, Ron was being a sly organizer; he was doing two things. One, he was getting the press informed, and two he was getting this kid who didn't know what he was doing off of center stage [laughing].[25]

Following this, Sooy became involved more closely with radicals like Ken Hammond and Bill Arthell. Through them, Sooy was among the group that formed the May 4 Coalition.

On May 12, about 1,500 people gathered on the Commons and marched in support of the Coalition's demands, which the KSU Board of Trustees considered during its meeting, broadcast live in the student center. The trustees agreed to maintain the Center for Peaceful Change (they had previously voted to cut its budget) and not pursue action against those who occupied Rockwell Hall, but the trustees refused to offer an official acknowledgement that the shootings were an injustice and to never build on the site. At this point, about three hundred people walked out and gathered on the proposed site of the annex. Soon after, some pitched tents and Tent City was born.

The occupation continued into July, and after the university obtained a court order to remove the protesters, who chanted "we will not be moved," KSU police arrested 193 people on July 12. Some May 4 Coalition members including Alan Canfora, his sister Chic Canfora, and Dean Kahler traveled to Washington, D.C., to meet with university representatives, including then KSU interim president Michael Schwartz, Congressman John Seiberling, and staff from the offices of Ohio senators John Glenn and Howard Metzenbaum to discuss making the site of the shootings a national historic landmark.[26]

Michael Schwartz, who ultimately served as Kent State's president from 1982 to 1991, was vice president for graduate studies and research in 1977 and served as interim president that year at the height of the protests, in between Olds's leaving and the arrival of Brage Golding. He recalled the Washington, D.C., meeting in his 2008 interview. "The fear of somebody getting hurt was high on everybody's mind at the time, to the point that the Carter White House called me for conversations because they were very fearful of something more happening," Schwartz said.

> They already had a number of the protest leaders there when we arrived. We left at the end of the day, and there was no resolution of anything except we understood no one was supposed to get hurt. Well, we didn't need a trip to the White House to tell us that. But we had a trip to the White House and that's how far up in the political food chain that this concern had finally reached.[27]

Following the meeting, at a rally on the site of The Annex, over 150 protesters entered the roped-off construction site. Days later, Portage County sheriff Allen McKitrick filed arrest warrants against twenty-seven of the protesters, including members of the May 4 Coalition. More arrests followed another occupation of the construction site in late July and again in September, which by now had a chain-link fence around it. The Coalition filed legal briefs to block the construction. Meanwhile, attempts were made to negotiate shifting the footprint of the new building away from the hill and using the Kent State University School as a new site; both efforts failed. The legal case went to the U.S. Supreme Court, where in September 1977 Justice William Brennan rejected the Coalition's arguments and removed the temporary ban on construction. At this point, the Coalition had fractured between the more radical Revolutionary Student Brigade along with members from other schools who came to Kent to protest and who urged more violent action, and the majority, who formed their own group, the Blanket Hill Council. Construction began on September 19 and finished in July 1979—the same year as the legal settlement in *Krause v. Rhodes*.[28]

The battle over the physical site intermixed with the larger battles in American political culture and the continued tensions in Kent and on campus over the shootings. Some saw in the Gym Annex further evidence of a

KSU conspiracy to cover up—literally, in this case—the shootings and any university complicity in them. Coalition leader John Rowe argued that "the gym and the landscaping will completely destroy the historical perspective of the site."[29] Said KSU president Glenn Olds, "You can't memorialize the whole campus. This is a university, not a Gettysburg site."[30] Conservatives again lined up against the protesters in 1977, and this time their efforts indicated the growing influence of the political right. On campus, Students Maintaining and Advocating Cooperation and Constructiveness at Kent (SMACCK), a group inspired by the Young Americans for Freedom (YAF), led the drive with flyers and other literature titled "Move the Protesters not the Gym," "Remember Kent State—Build the Gym," and "I'm Tired of the Bullshit."[31] They again utilized the refrain about outside agitators (and there were some involved in this protest, unlike those active in May 4) in their support for the annex, "outsiders [who] . . . are not truly concerned nor empathetic with the wants, needs, and feelings of the student body."[32] Miriam Jackson, who wrote her dissertation on the 1977 protests, believed that the Tent City "echoed the communalism and antiwar feeling of the 1960s in its insistence on participatory democracy and nonviolent behavior." Newer issues of the 1970s, like land-use policy stemming from the environmental movement, merged with these, so that the May 4 Coalition fought "to protect the May 4 site from partial destruction both because the land was beautiful and because the Coalition members wanted the site recognized, at least henceforth, as an honored American battlefield. The comparisons to Gettysburg were not accidental."[33] For Jackson and others, the site—like Gettysburg—was sacred space; protesters saw as profane any altering of the area of the shootings.[34]

In the gym controversy, the memory of the shootings remained front and center. For Schwartz, there was the fear that more violence would come to the campus, but he remained undeterred in moving forward with construction.

> The best course that we could have taken we did take, and that was to get this thing under the umbrella of the courts. And we did that. I can't remember all the goings on there, but I thought as long as we were under the umbrella of the courts, and court orders had come about how conduct was going to go forward, then I thought we were okay. If something had to happen, I wanted a judge to tell me what that was going to be.
>
> I think finally once the construction went forward, that pretty much ended it, except for the fact that when President Golding arrived he was still in the tear gas business. That was, I think, in September when he started. End of August, September, I can't remember exactly. But he

still found himself standing on top of a building, maybe this one [the library], and there was a lot of tear gas flying. People had come in for a final shot at the protest stuff. Buses from all over the place, busloads of people, and they didn't stay very long. It was more or less under control, but the university paid an enormous price for it—which was, I suppose, that was supposedly the aim in from the beginning—and the price was that the enrollment just, the bottom dropped out. At one time I think we were down to 16,000 students, and it got kind of pricey fast. And Golding's job was to kind of figure out how to keep the place open and running on that basis of that loss. And he was masterful, he was absolutely masterful at that. He had to be kind of ruthless—and he was—but he was also capable of making it clear what had happened and what we were going to do about it.[35]

Ken Hammond had come back to work in the library on campus and was there when Tent City erupted.

[Interviewer]: You did set up the first tent?

Yeah. I set up the first tent. We had a march, a memorial march on May 4th that year. We went around, and I happened to have camping gear in the trunk of my car parked over in the visitor's lot here. And Bill Arthrell and I actually it was, we were, like, "Let's set up a tent." So we ran down, we got stuff out of my car, and we ran up there while the march was going on, and when the march came to the site, we were ready to put up this tent. Then it just grew from that. But when that came to an end, when it came time for everybody to get arrested, I felt that that was not the correct tactic at that point. So I didn't stay in Tent City, I didn't take the bust with everybody, because I didn't believe that that was the best way to achieve the objectives that we were working for at that point. Alan Canfora and Chic and those people who sort of were most heavily involved in that. We disagreed about that, but that's never been a problem.

[Interviewer]: You disagreed about?

About the effectiveness of having a mass arrest. I liked the gesture—the live-in as it were, the camp-in. But that was a symbolic gesture. As it went on, and people sort of got vested in the site and staying there, then the question became: at some point, the University's going to come

Tent City came about when activists Ken Hammond and Bill Arthrell set up a tent near the construction site of the Gym Annex. (Kent State University Libraries. Special Collections and Archives.)

in and want to clear this, and what's the best response to that? And the majority clearly felt that people should just take a stand and link arms, and stay and take the bust. I just disagreed with that. I thought that we could be more effective by pursuing other strategies, other approaches. I was very much in the minority at that point. But on the other hand, I was able to help organize bail funds and stuff like that.[36]

Barry Seybert pitched the second tent. He had been in ninth grade in Cleveland Heights, Ohio, when the shootings happened. He was acquainted with Allison Krause; Barry Levine, Allison's boyfriend in 1970, was the brother of Barry's Hebrew school teacher. Seybert attended Kent from 1974 to 1978 and was involved in helping create the May 4 Task Force and the Tent City protests. He recalled that

all the news crews [were] there, because they actually thought we were going to have another Kent State massacre on our hands. And so the day before the arrest, we sat down with the officers and discussed how the arrest procedure was going to take place and did a practice arrest. Everybody linking arms and the police breaking that apart and carrying us off as a practice arrest so that it would be peaceful. They didn't want another incident happening on campus.[37]

Professor John Guidubaldi was more dismissive of the 1977 protests, in line with the conservative view. Boundaries were more restrictive for him in terms of what may have counted as sacred. His use of the phrase "fabricate" suggests that the feelings and arguments about sacred space and preservation of memory of the shootings were illegitimate. He believed that perhaps, since leftists were involved, the protests were merely a subterfuge for those groups to cause disruption that was tangential to the memory and meaning of the shootings held by students and others.

> Tent City, I thought, was a fabrication. They didn't really plan on putting the gymnasium on the spot where the slain students fell. It was, in fact, not far from there, but you can't take up the whole area and say that's sacred ground. But they weren't putting it right on the spot; even if that were the case, even if you made that argument, they weren't putting it right on the spot. But it was another excuse to gather people 'round. And they came from all over.
>
> I went with my neighbor to Tent City because we were both curious about what was going on. We sat there one evening talking to people, and they were having little cookouts and it was kind of a communal atmosphere. Although I had argued with my uncle that it was not communist inspired, that evening when they were announcing the donations to Tent City, they were announcing a donation from the Buffalo Workers Party and a few other socialist and communistic groups that were organized groups. Now, that wasn't the only place they were getting money, they were getting from other places as well, but the students were, again, I think, trying to fabricate a situation. And every May 4th anniversary we were facing the same kind of thought that maybe this was going to be another time when we have a problem.[38]

Building a Memorial: Segal, Ast, and the Visitor Center

The struggle over the memory and meaning of the shootings continued when plans to construct a memorial on campus emerged in the 1970s. In 1978, a private foundation, the Mildred Andrews Fund of Cleveland, commissioned famed sculptor George Segal to do a memorial work for Kent State.[39] The university administration under the new president, Brage Golding, proceeded cautiously at first, entering into an agreement noting that "this matter is one of the greatest sensitivity" seeing that there were "strongly-polarized attitudes" over the shootings, and since also at the time

An aerial view of the Gym Annex (center), c. 1978. The final construction of the Annex constricted the space near the shootings from what it had been in May 1970. (Kent State University Libraries. Special Collections and Archives.)

the legal cases remained in the courts.[40] Segal visited the campus in March and went directly to work on a piece, photographs of which he submitted to Golding at the end of May. The university had wanted to review drawings first before any castings had begun. The title and form Segal chose, "Abraham's Sacrifice of Isaac," was similar to other works he had developed. Segal wrote in emotionally powerful language to Golding that his theme "was provoked by the response to the students and the older people in charge. The students struck me as genuinely idealistic in their demonstrations against the spreading of the war into Cambodia, yet so singleminded they disregarded law, democratic process, and, wittingly or unwillingly, fanned the fears of those in charge. The older people had fought willingly and altruistically in World War II, equated patriotism with obedience, were convinced of a Communist and Anarchist threat to our political structure, and a sexual threat to our religious morality. The fevered encounter between the students and the National Guardsmen reminded me so strongly of Abraham's willingness to sacrifice his only son, born late in his life, because God had ordered him to, ie [sic] he believed in an invisible, difficult abstraction." Segal went on:

> This controversy has gone on for five thousand years. The only fact we can agree on is that parents still have the power to either kill or nurture their young. The issues are difficult and contradictory. I don't pretend to have the answers. In this sculpture, I've tried to switch the attention from the youth to the complexities and moral dilemmas of the older man.[41]

In a June letter never sent to Segal, Golding noted that he, his advisors, and the KSU May 4 Observance Committee anticipated "that viewers will see your Isaac as a 'student-victim'" and your Abraham as a "National Guardsman-assassin." Facing declining enrollments, and in the wake of the Tent City controversy, Golding feared that Segal's sculpture would only add to KSU's problems; "we simply cannot afford to be further divided on this campus,"[42] he wrote. In a subsequent letter that looked for a meeting to talk about the sculpture, Golding expressed the deep concern to Segal with a "possible 'political' fall-out" should the university accept and display the sculpture.[43] After Segal agreed to include text from Genesis as an explanation of the story, Golding and his advisors seemed to shift back to accepting the sculpture—or at least the theme of Abraham and Isaac. Then, the incoming vice president for university affairs, Charles W. Ingler, wrote a powerful letter to Golding's assistant against acceptance: "I cannot escape the conclusion that such artistic treatment memorializes, not the victim nor the tragedy, but the violence itself." Ingler ended his letter, "Is there to be no end to this violence and its shadow?"[44] In the end, Golding decided against the sculpture and the final university public communication echoed Ingler's reason, stating that it would be "inappropriate" to commemorate the four deaths and nine wounded "with a statue which appears to represent an act of violence about to be committed."[45] Princeton University accepted the sculpture and it remains there on campus.

This did not end the row. Segal sent a letter to Kent State art students subsequently published in the *Daily Kent Stater* in which he accused the university of trying to push him to make a different sculpture. This was true. In correspondence, English professor Robert McCoy, Golding's executive assistant, offered a suggestion to the renowned sculptor of a young military man opposed by a girl. Segal disagreed that his theme was too violent. Segal quoted some of Golding's unsent June letter that McCoy had shown Segal and let him keep. McCoy sent a five-page reply in which he noted that by proceeding straight to a casting without showing the drawing first, Segal had violated the understanding he had sent Segal. McCoy claimed that the university did not reject the piece because it was too violent. Perhaps not surprisingly, the *Kent-Ravenna Record-Courier* agreed with Golding's decision, supporting university officials for acting "in what they considered to be the best interests of the university."[46]

After this failed attempt at a memorial, a second one emerged in 1982 after Golding had left KSU and Michael Schwartz was president. This effort, too, would erupt in controversy. Schwartz, as president, proved more willing to move KSU toward memorializing the shootings.

[Interviewer]: During that nine year term, what May 4–related events do you remember?

Early in my administration, I think that probably the first six to ten months, I felt we gotta come to terms with this thing. We'll never end this, because it's not gonna end, but we can get at least the beginning of an ending. An ending in the sense of the anger and bitterness. So we struck on the idea of having a memorial built. That is something that people had wanted. But it's also something that an awful lot of people did not want. So the trick was, somehow, to bring both sides together, let them hammer this thing out and see what sort of conclusion they could reach. It was miraculous that we got them to sit down at the same table.

The chair of that committee was a dean of fine professional arts. His name was Harry Alspritch, [and he] did a masterful job over a long term of getting folks to talk to one another and to come to some conclusion about this. It took most of the year. And the conclusion was, not that there should be a memorial to those killed and wounded, but there should be a memorial to the events of May 4th 1970. That's the way they put it, I think, in their report, which was fine with me. And at least that much they could agree on, without anything much of any dissent. I put together students and faculty and alumni and townspeople, and we got them all to sit down around the same table. And that's what they came up with.[47]

This occurred just one year after the opening of Maya Lin's Vietnam Veterans Memorial in 1982 on the Mall in Washington, D.C. The mission statement for the Vietnam monument to be built, funded initially by the Vietnam Veterans Memorial Fund, "set forth a theme of reconciliation"[48]: "The Memorial will make no political statement about the war or its conduct. It will transcend those issues. The hope is that the creation of the Memorial will begin a healing process."[49] But, as Edwin Martini notes, "it was impossible for anything related to the American war in Vietnam to be apolitical."[50] Those on the conservative side assailed it as not being patriotic enough. The Wall's open-ended, nonlinear structure is, as Marita Sturken has noted, "appropriate to a conflict that has no narrative closure."[51] Moreover, "the memorial was designed to leave the task of interpretation to the individual visitors."[52] It was meant as a space for personal reflection and private acts of memory, "leaving the larger questions 'about the war or its conduct' appropriately unresolved."[53]

The political battles over the Vietnam Veterans Memorial became part of a larger contest over the cultural memory of the war in Vietnam. In the 1980s, the dominant view held that Vietnam was "a rotten country" and that the United States, its people, and its soldiers (and not Vietnam or the Vietnamese) were the victims. The popularity of films including *Uncommon Valor* (1983), *Missing in Action* (1984), and especially *Rambo: First Blood Part II* (1985) perpetuated the dominant view, focusing especially upon the rescue of POWs ostensibly still held in Vietnam and the U.S. government's supposed complicity by covering up their existence. These ideas also supported the notion that the government, led by liberals including Kennedy and Johnson, not only failed to win in Vietnam but actively prevented the U.S. military from achieving victory. The films also played up the hypermasculinity so prevalent in the 1980s; these and other forms of popular culture allowed the white American male to regain his sense of power after Vietnam.[54]

The 1980s struggle over the meaning and memory of the war in Vietnam became one central part of a larger reconsideration of the meaning and memory of the 1960s. As conservatives, symbolized by President Ronald Reagan, gained more influence and power, the popular memory of the 1960s embraced the era (defined in this schema as mainly events after 1965) as a lost decade of chaos and mistakes caused by radicals and liberals. Conservatives—not without some counternarratives by liberals and former 1960s activists—depicted "the social movements of the 1960s as responsible for the destruction of traditional and natural hierarchies, an unwarranted increase in governmental intervention in the economy, and the devaluing of patriotism."[55]

As the battle over Lin's memorial, Vietnam, and the 1960s waged on in 1980s America, inevitably the shootings at Kent State and efforts to memorialize them would become part of this struggle. Our oral history narrators—whose own narratives can be open-ended, often nonlinear—recall the efforts at Kent State to construct a memorial to the shootings. As it was with those over the Vietnam Veterans Memorial, the political battles over memorialization at Kent State reflected the long duration of the shootings and the 1960s in American memory and political culture. As with those of the Vietnam Veterans Memorial Fund, efforts by those creating the Kent State memorial to remain apolitical proved elusive.

In 1983, the Kent State Board of Trustees authorized the establishment of a May 4 Memorial Committee. It included two faculty members (one of whom was Jerry Lewis), three students, two alums, the mayor of Kent, a Kent resident, and two KSU administrators. The group held its first meeting in March 1984 and issued a report to Schwartz in December. According to the report, the "charge of the Committee was to determine the meaning of the events of May 4, 1970" to the university and propose a memorial. This was a simple statement that belied the depth and contested nature of the meaning of the shootings. Nonetheless, the committee's report argued that by 1985, fifteen years after the shootings, it was now "appropriate for a sober reevaluation of the tragic event." May 4, the report stated, had become a "visible milestone" in the "nation's memory" of Vietnam. In keeping with the style of official committees and balancing the political views of the members, the report also crafted a narrative of the shootings as it argued for a memorial. The report argued that "the shock of May 4th revealed the limits of violent demonstration. Perceived and/or real threats to lives and property on the part of the Kent citizenry, evoked the power of the state in ways that were destructive for state and townspeople as well as students." Further, the report expressed hope "that National Guardsmen in future crises will be better prepared to deal with disorder that had been the case in 1970." It characterized the gym protests as a "demonstration both of the vulnerability of the University" to outsiders who used the campus "for their own causes" and "its ability to cope with a crisis through firm but peaceful action." It celebrated the Center for Peaceful Change "as a permanent reminder of May 4th as it seeks to understand and find some answers to violence at every level." The report argued that the existing memorials on campus "do not choose sides. All society was the victim on May 4th—students, Guardsmen, townspeople, and faculty. The four dead paid the ultimate price."[56]

This document is an intriguing one. Generally, it contains the early stages of constructing a tragic narrative of the events in which, as the report states, everyone was a victim. It bemoans violence and expressed hope for peaceful reconciliation of conflict. If any blame is assigned, it is directed at the students; their activities, the report indicates, precipitated a response that "evoked the power of the state." In stating that the Guard should have been better prepared, the report seems to shift responsibility away from individual Guardsmen and toward their leadership. It echoes the statement of regret issued at the end of the trials in putting blame on students for protesting and calling for better preparation for the Guard. The report shows a remarkable affinity to the statement Richard Nixon made following the shootings that implied protesters and the actions on the days before were to blame: "This should remind us all that once again that when dissent turns to violence, it invites tragedy."[57]

In endorsing a memorial on campus, the report noted "even after nearly fifteen years, there is no accepted explanation why" the "events" happened or "what might have prevented the violence and shootings." Hence, the committee recommended "a site which reflects the diverse constituencies and meanings would be most appropriate." To this end, the panel argued that the

> reflective site should present the visitor with the opportunity to inquire into the many reasons and purposes of the events that led to the

killing and wounding of students on May 4, 1970 and to encourage a learning process to broaden the perspective of these events. The site should encourage visitors to ask what differences were confronting this community and this nation at that time and to reflect on how those differences may have been resolved peacefully.[58]

Read another way, if all are victims, then none is responsible for the deaths of four students. The vagueness of listing the groups of people who count as victims deepens this sense of either evasion of the pain of assigning direct responsibility, the inability to do so, or purposeful ambivalence that embodies the forces of memory. First, "All of society" is so broad as to be meaningless. "Students" does not distinguish among protesters, bystanders, those wounded in the shootings, conservatives who supported the Guard, or those who remained apathetic. Are they all victims of the shootings? "Guardsmen" does not delineate among the shooters who aimed at students, those who shot randomly, those who shot in the ground or in the air, those who chose not to shoot, commanders on Blanket Hill, those in the area, and those elsewhere around campus and in town. How are they all victims? "Townspeople" lumps together business owners whose windows and other property were damaged in the days prior to May 4, those who had to stay in their homes during curfews, and the thousands of others who lived in town as victims of the shootings. Finally, "Faculty" includes marshals like Glenn Frank and Jerry Lewis, those who remembered the four killed as students in their classes, those sympathetic to the protesters, those dismissive of them, those who were apathetic, and all who had to teach in the immediate aftermath through correspondence courses and then in the first years following the shootings. Without being specific, the report ascribes and sanctifies victimhood upon all of these people in equal measure or at least places within the same discursive frame the four who were killed and all of the others. Such terminology is a concerted effort to flatten and level conflict and contested narratives as a pathway to reconciliation.

As Michael Schwartz's interview suggests, the move to create a memorial on campus was a university-sanctioned effort to find a "beginning of the ending," but it required evading directly an answer to why the Guardsmen shot and putting responsibility on the Guard, as the Kent Families and their supporters wanted, or on the students, as the Guard's defenders demanded. Hence, as Schwartz noted in a supportive fashion in his interview, "The conclusion was, not that there should be a memorial to those killed and

Michael Schwartz was acting president of Kent State in the summer of 1977, as well as vice president for Academic and Student Affairs before serving as president from 1982 to 1991. (Kent State University Libraries. Special Collections and Archives.)

wounded, but there should be a memorial to the events of May 4, 1970. That's the way they put it, I think, in their report, which was fine with me. And at least that much they could agree on." The report is an effort at finding some reconciliation, but it makes clear none yet existed in 1985.

In announcing the competition, the university followed recommendations in the report. University leaders were adamant in what they did not want: "In no way, however, is it the intention of the Sponsor that the memorial be either accusatory or laudatory." "The full purpose of the memorial," the booklet to prospective designers stated, "is to stimulate thoughtful reflection on the tragic events, and cause us to ponder the larger tenets of our society."[59] The design competition began in the fall of 1985 and continued into early 1986. In April, the committee announced that the team of Ian F. Taberner and Michael G. Fahey had won, with Bruno Ast coming in second. In a public statement announcing the winners, Schwartz reiterated the statements in the design brochure: "According to our purpose, it will be remembered in a manner that is neither heroic nor accusatory." He went on, "To reflect and inquire into our own values and ideals as Americans, knowing our past and concerned with our future has been our purpose."[60]

There was no consensus at KSU on the need for a memorial. As Kathryn Weiss notes, most faculty wanted to leave the issues alone and move on.[61] There was no consensus among students at KSU either. Lisa Lynott was on the May 4 Task Force in 1986 when the "Carol Paugh crisis," as she refers to it, erupted.

Carol Paugh was a freshman who wrote a letter to the *Daily Kent Stater* ["Students Knew Risk of Protesting on May 4," *Daily Kent Stater,* Feb. 19, 1986, 4] in which she got a few nasty digs in to the Task Force. I'll never forget this paragraph, she said, "It is my opinion those four people deserved what they got." And her last line—I don't remember the two paragraphs after that—but her last line was, "They knew the penalty. They were the ones to suffer." As if the penalty for walking to class 300 feet away from a bullet was to get shot and die for it. I remember seeing that letter and thinking, Oh, boy, this is gonna be a real bomb; I mean this is really gonna hit the fan.

And, what happened after that was just a flood of letters to the *Stater;* the *Stater* had almost never seen such a flood of letters. We were surprised the number of people who knew; that there were that many people on campus who knew so much about May 4th. We'd never seen them in the Task Force. And what happened after that actually did, was good for the Task Force in the long run, because at the next meeting we had about six new people. And those six new people stayed with the Task Force for the next year or two until they all graduated, and were very active, reliable members. And so I guess that little crisis turned out not too bad because it focused attention on the facts and the fact that there still are an awful lot of ignorant people out there who think May 4 is just the greatest thing in the world.[62]

Taberner and Fahey's victory was short-lived, however. Taberner was Canadian, which was against the rules of the contest; after Fahey refused the prize, Ast became the winner. Taberner filed a $2 million lawsuit against the university for breach of contract in February 1987 that was settled for $15,000 in May. And the May 4 Task Force issued a public statement supporting Taberner's design. Ast initially did not reply to the Task Force's request to speak at the upcoming May 4 commemoration. He did reply later that he declined the offer to speak.

A week after disqualifying Taberner, the resolution committee of the Ohio Unit of the American Legion approved a resolution titled "Kent State Memorial to Terrorists." The inclusion of the word "terrorists" reflects the rise of that term in public discourse and current events by the 1980s. In objecting to the proposed memorial, the resolution stated, "The construction of this memorial would be an insult to the patriotic veterans who served their country honorably and well."[63] The Fraternal Order of Police in Ohio passed a resolution similar to one considered by the Ohio American Legion. In response, KSU president Michael Schwartz issued a statement: "The Ohio Unit of the American Legion seriously misunderstands the purpose of this memorial. The purpose of the memorial is simple. It's a place for peace, reflection, and learning. A device to teach of the past to educate for the future. It is not to memorialize rioting or anything illegal. It's to talk about people and ideas."[64]

Ast's original design was estimated to cost Kent some $500,000 in construction costs, an amount revised upward to $1.3 million in 1988, which the university tried to raise in donations or through grants. No outside agencies came forward with donations; appeals to alumni and fund-raising events also came up short. After these failures, the KSU trustees passed a resolution stating that the cost could not exceed $100,000; Ast told the trustees he would build the memorial under the new guidelines. With enough money from private donors and Kent trustees, groundbreaking occurred on January 25, 1989, but only after the May 4 Task Force and Glenn Frank, then an emeritus professor—still dedicated to the Taberner design—tried to block construction through a court order. The parties settled this matter once the university agreed to offer refunds to those who intended their contribution only for the original design. Carl DeVaughn, the head of the May 4 Task Force on campus in 1989, believed that the decision to scale down was political. He argued that the trustees "never formed a committee. They never hired a fund-raiser. All that they can prove they did was send thirty-four thousand brochures to KSU alumni."[65] Florence Schroeder, mother of William Schroeder, added her own thoughts on the memorial: "Our children cannot be returned to us, and disfigured bodies cannot be restored totally, but it is now time for calm heads to prevail and to put an end to confrontation tactics."[66] Perhaps Dean Kahler, like Schroeder, hoped to bridge the divide. Kahler, then working as a county commissioner in Athens, Ohio, spoke at the groundbreaking: "There's still a stigma about Kent State and the whole incident. Today's events mark the culmination of that stigma. We now have healed the wound."[67]

Lisa Lynott and others on the May 4 Task Force had different feelings about the memorial:

I remember how upset a lot of us were that no representative from the Task Force or any of the victims' families or any of the wounded students or any people like that would be permitted to have any say or input in the design selection. That shouldn't have been surprising considering the University's twenty-year record of total blatant insensitivity about anything to do with May 4th, especially where the families are concerned. When the design was selected, we generally as a group, there were some dissensions in the Task Force as there usually are, but generally we approved of it, thought it was a good design, an appropriate design. And there was a feeling of a major, major weight being lifted; a feeling of real hope that finally, maybe, the University was starting to turn itself around in the way it dealt with May 4th issues, and that finally we were going to get something accomplished and get some action done. Well, of course, gee, a month later we found out how wrong we were.

We didn't like [Ast's] design very much, not nearly as much as Taberner's. At the Task Force, we all appreciated Ian Taberner a lot more because he had a lot more understanding of May 4th and the real significance of it. Bruno Ast didn't. He didn't even want to put the names of the students on the memorial, didn't think it was important, didn't think it was necessary. . . . He didn't answer our invitations to speak at any May 4th function, including the 1987 commemoration. Just totally ignored, ignored anybody that had anything to do with the Task Force. Things started to calm down a little bit when we realized at least they were going to build a full-scale, real memorial. It may not have been the design we wanted, we may not have liked the designer but at least they were going to do it.[68]

In discussing the costs, Schwartz elided the failure to raise the required amount for Ast's original concept in his recollection about the KSU trustees' limiting the spending: "There was a state senator, who was [a] Vietnam Veteran, I think a Marine [likely Eugene Watts, a historian at Ohio State and a Republican senator who earned a Bronze Star in Vietnam], who was a faculty member at Ohio State also—I think in political science—who, as part of the budget bill that was presented, said, 'No funds from this budget will be used to create a memorial at Kent State University,'"

which I thought was—not that we were going to [seek public funding] . . . because we weren't, we were going to raise it one way or another through private money. But it was as mean-spirited an act as I had really run across in all of this. . . . But we overcame that and we put some money together, one way or another, and we were able to build it. And we dedicated the memorial on May 4th of 1990, as you may have heard. But that great long piece of the saga probably has not been chronicled or told maybe anywhere else.[69]

At Schwartz's request, the Faculty Senate created the May 4 Twentieth Anniversary Commission to coordinate the events for 1990 and handle the dedication ceremony. That year the university established four scholarships in the names of the four slain students and Governor Richard Celeste apologized on behalf of the state of Ohio to the families of those who were killed and wounded.

Ast's memorial rests on a hillside adjacent to Taylor Hall on a two-and-one-half-acre site overlooking the Commons. It consists of a granite plaza seventy feet wide. As the May 4 Special Collections website notes, part of the memorial ends in a jagged border, "symbolic of disruptions and the conflict of ideas. Its fractured edge suggests the tearing of the fabric of society." As suggested by faculty member and artist Brinsley Tyrrell, surrounding the plaza are 58,175 daffodils, the number of the country's losses in Vietnam.

The Bruno Ast memorial as it appeared in 1990. (Kent State University Libraries. Special Collections and Archives.)

"Engraved in the plaza's stone threshold are the words 'Inquire, Learn, Reflect.' The inscription, agreed upon by the designer and Kent State University, affirms the intent that the memorial site provide visitors an opportunity to inquire into the many reasons and purposes of the events, to encourage a learning process, and to reflect on how differences may be resolved peacefully.

"A progression of four polished black granite disks embedded in the earth lead from the plaza to four freestanding pylons aligned on the hill. The disks reflect our own image as we stand on them; the pylons stand as mute sentinels to the force of violence and the memory of the four students killed.

"A fifth disk, placed to the south, acknowledges the many victims of the event. It implies a much wider impact, one that stretched far beyond the Kent campus."[70]

The design itself has not gone without controversy and commentary. Other than Ast's, no names are on the memorial itself, but on a plaque across from it are the names of the four killed and the nine wounded. The university agreed to the plaque after Sandy Scheuer's family met with Schwartz. Here is Timothy Moore reflecting on the design and its meaning:

[Interviewer]: Do you think the university has responded to these events better now than it did then?

Yes and no. As an artist, when I do artwork, I like to do artwork that is either self-explanatory or can become explained by the creator, so that I as the observer understand what was trying to be communicated. I think it, again, it was indicative of "Chaos U.," the way that for so long they tried to act like this thing would go away from the administration's vantage-point; and this was pre-Schwartz and then through Schwartz's administration. Then they come up with this contest which became a national embarrassment when the winner was a Canadian.

[Interviewer]: The Memorial Design Competition.

Right, the Memorial Design. The Memorial that is up there—help me understand what it represents. What it symbolizes in common-sense terms. For me, art should be able to communicate to most people when they see it. I see some interesting structures, but I don't know what the artist was thinking. I see this little brochure and, it's amazing, I don't even think I've ever read this brochure to see if it adequately explains it. But that's just my own personal view. It was an attempt. I think the university has been trying to do better, and I think over time they had to, when eventually you see that you can't sweep this under the rug. This is something that's national, international, and it's always going to be associated with Kent.[71]

The few scholarly works on the design have been critical. In his master's thesis, Kal Johal sees the design as reflecting the triumph of conservative viewpoints over the liberal-left ones. According to Johal, having the names on a plaque and not on the memorial itself is problematic, "since it is physically and thus emotionally detached from the main site." Johal sees the site as "a failure in that it falls short in reflecting the shootings as a seminal event in Ohio and American history. This has long been the goal of liberals but has met with little success."[72] His criticisms echo those of Kathryn Weiss. In examining the memorial, Weiss sees "institutional ambivalence," containing "material traces of a struggle between the desire to remember and the impulse to move on."[73] Even her experiment in bringing visitors to the site, with different levels of knowledge about May 4, resulted in their being confused and uncertain about the memorial and its meaning. So if there seems to be a sense of acceptance on campus regarding the shootings, these scholars ask, "Acceptance of what?" In examining the Bruno Ast memorial, ambivalence is their conclusion.

From Bruno Ast to the May 4 Visitors Center

The Ast memorial was perhaps the first step in forging greater acceptance and ownership of the shootings on the part of KSU, although the precise meaning ascribed to them remained open for debate. The May 4 commemoration continued, as did the May 4 Task Force in charge of the event, but the Ast memorial left open an ambivalent legacy to the shootings. Under the presidency of Carol Cartwright (1991–2006), the university pushed forward toward further institutionalizing the history and memory of the events. In this 2008 interview, she recalled how the KSU administration began to confront directly the issue of the shootings by inviting the university community into the conversation.

> We did in the mid-90s a deep cultural analysis of the university. One of the surprising results was the deep angst that was felt throughout the community about May 4th. People really kind of poured out their souls, and it was a very long, very complicated questionnaire; and the consultants that worked with us said they'd never seen anything quite like it, in terms of how much narrative the respondents provided. They turned pages over, wrote on the back, wrote in the margins; and basically they were saying that the university has been ambivalent. [May 4th is] not really owned by the university, and yet the university dares not reject it. The bottom line was: Would somebody please make a decision one way or the other? Either embrace it or forget it, but don't leave us hanging in the middle, because we feel like we're responsible for carrying this burden because the university hasn't taken a stand.
>
> And that, for me, was the defining moment in terms of thinking about what the university needed to do differently. And I wasn't here

during the immediate years after the shootings; I have no idea how I might have reacted had I been in that role. But I know the situation that I inherited as I became President, and I know what I learned in the presidency after several years, and I felt that I had some responsibility to deal with it differently.

Cartwright's assertiveness in addressing May 4—unpopular from some vantage points—included becoming the first KSU president to participate in the annual Candlelight Vigil. Additionally, in 1999, permanent markers were installed in the Prentice Hall parking lot to designate where the four students were killed. In 2000, KSU initiated a Democracy Symposium whose inaugural topic was May 4. "I began to think that everything that was done around May 4th was, in a way, negative," Cartwright explained.

It was looking back, never looking forward. It was always about protest, anger, shooting, dying, et cetera. And there was never really anything about the cost of being a democracy. . . . And I became convinced that we could do something that was much more in keeping with our academic mission, because we really had done very little. We had scholarships, and we had the Center for Conflict Resolution, which has had several names over time. But we hadn't really done anything bold in terms of trying to anchor all of this in the academic mission of the institution.[74]

Following this, under President Lester Lefton (2006–2014) came the historical marker, the walking tour, and the May 4 Visitors Center. The Center opened in October 2012 and was officially dedicated during the May 4 commemoration in 2013. The official dedication offered a panel of historians, including Thomas Grace, examining the shootings and their significance. Other events included talks by Tom Hayden (who later wrote about his experience at the dedication and events) and William Ayers, formerly of the Weather Underground (accompanied by his wife and co-member Bernardine Dohrn).[75] Oliver Stone also gave a talk as part of the official dedication in which he revived the idea that it was likely Terry Norman, as an agent provocateur of the FBI, who fired his gun to get the Guard to fire in return. This was Stone's version of the sniper theory, which the FBI and activists like Alan Canfora dismissed.[76] Canfora has been the leading voice seeking to use the Strubbe tape as evidence of an order to fire, in the hopes of ending much of the speculation about the motives and reasoning behind

Carol Cartwright served as president of Kent State from 1991 to 2006, the first female president of a state university in Ohio. (Kent State University Libraries. Special Collections and Archives.)

the shootings that have been at the heart of the Kent State controversy since 1970. Canfora claims that a member of the National Guard can be heard on the tape shouting "Right here! Get set! Point! Fire!" In his book, *Kent State: Death and Dissent in the Long Sixties,* Tom Grace agrees that the Stubbe tape, combined with various statements of witnesses, confirms an order to fire.[77]

The Visitors Center's permanent exhibit contains the context and interpretation that many had called for in getting KSU to accept, if not embrace, the shootings as part of its history and as part of the national memory of the 1960s. It consists of three galleries, and visitors move through each in order. The first presents the larger context of the shootings by focusing on three themes prevalent during the 1960s: social justice, generation gap, and the Vietnam War. The idea is to show how the events on May 4 illustrated a nation divided and how the demonstration at Kent against the Vietnam War was part of a larger set of developments that connected the protests and acts of civil disobedience of the civil rights movement to youth culture and the antiwar movement. The second gallery focuses on the shootings themselves, while the third and final gallery examines the reaction to and the significance and legacy of the event. The Center makes use of oral history and video interviews in the last section and in the film shown in Gallery Two. The film closely suggests, but does not audibly present, the evidence for an order to fire. The word *Point* is displayed on the film's captioning as the audience hears that part of the Terry Strubbe tape, followed by the thirteen seconds of gunfire. As cofounder of the Center, Carole Barbato noted concerning the Center's interpretation, "This is a story that is not concluded and we realize that. . . . This is the best documented evidence that we know at this time."[78]

This has not satisfied Laurel Krause, sister of Allison, who continues to insist that there were four shots fired before the Guardsmen's shots, something Stone says the Strubbe tape proves. Tom Grace has stated that neither he nor Canfora, both wounded and in the area, heard these shots, nor are there "any other witnesses of whom I am aware, [who] heard low-velocity shots before the National Guard salvo."[79] Even if the tape can be definitively analyzed again by outside experts (the Obama Justice Department and FBI both deny there was an order on the tape after they analyzed it), it is unlikely to end the debate over the history and memory of the shootings. Krause, for example, initiated the Kent State Truth Tribunal, an effort to "heal those involved, establish cause and effect, and shed light on command responsibility for the Kent State shootings on May 4, 1970."[80] But Krause has also stated that "any exhibit is good if it's talking about Kent State," but "when it's only more of the same cover-up, my only word on that is shame." She added that in the Visitors Center there is "no commentary about the truth of what really happened."[81]

In contrast to the Ast memorial and more in line with the annual commemoration, the Visitors Center focuses more intently on names, on context, on causes. In this way, it represents on one level an assertion against forgetting, moving on, and it interprets the events as a tragic exercise in the abuse of power against the rights of people to demonstrate and criticize their government. The Center moves, like oral history often does, between the personal and the collective memory. Moreover, being crafted by those with a lived experience of the events, the Visitors Center is—like the commemoration and vigil—a mixture of historical memory and collective memory in the process of becoming official memory. As Lynn Abrams writes, following Maurice Halbwachs, historical memory is a memory of the past "that is lost, whereas collective memory is anchored in the social group that actively preserves and reinterprets the past via the consciousness of those who are still alive."[82] Official memory is a public interpretation, one sanctioned and fixed to a site. At times, official memory can, in the words of John Gillis, "appear consensual" when in fact it is the "product of processes of intense contest, struggle, and in some instances, annihilation."[83]

In the case of the Visitors Center, the memorial, and the walking tour, they represent the effort to preserve the site of the shootings. Yet the internal struggle at KSU over whether or not to remember the shootings and the reluctance of state officials to recognize the events is absent. Laura Davis, who witnessed the shootings, and Carole Barbato, a student at Kent in 1970, together were the driving forces behind the creation of the Center.[84] In this sense, they have brought their personal memory to bear with the scholarly and collective understanding of the events on and near May 4 and the 1960s era more generally. In using personal artifacts such as photographs and oral history, the Center has also woven together the personal and the collective, the individual and the scholarly memories. Indeed, there is throughout a focus on the students, especially those killed, and making their deaths meaningful. As the exhibit script notes, "In this exhibit, see how the youth of America made a difference."[85] Since Kent State's mission is to educate the youth, the Center has placed itself inside this mission. As Laura Davis stated when the Center opened, "Historians cite the Kent State shootings as a watershed moment in U.S. history and an important turning point in the consciousness of Americans about the Vietnam War. The May 4 Visitors Center offers a powerful and immersive experience that provides context and perspective on the tragedy, and examines the lasting impact that still resonates today." Davis added that "from the perspective of more than 40 years, the visitors center experience remembers the students who lost their lives on May 4—Allison Krause, Jeffrey Miller, Sandra Scheuer and William Schroeder—while offering meaning for today in their loss."[86]

Kent State: Memory and Meaning

What have the oral history narrators said about these issues and the overall significance of the shootings and the 1960s more generally? At one level, they demonstrate affinity with the more abstract lessons that the Center wished to convey: democracy, power, and rights. At times, they affirm the interpretation of the 1960s as an era of division and discord but also hope and possibility. For some, especially more conservative narrators, the events and the era were signs of society in chaos; they've adopted and reinforced the cultural memory so prevalent in the 1980s of the era—really the period after 1965—of being a time of lawlessness and disrespect for authority and tradition. In short, they allow us to hear the continued differences and divisions over the shootings themselves and their meaning. As Katharine Hodgkin and Susannah Radstone note, "Memory, in both private and public manifestations, makes claims about the past, which will not be acceptable to everybody. And if these differences in some instances seem reconcilable, in others there is a sense of intractability."[87]

No doubt, over the intervening years these narrators have absorbed the many books, articles, films, and other public forms of memory about the events. Their narratives represent the amalgam of personal and collective memory. They show the continued struggle between interpretations of events, between past and present, and between individual and collective memory. Alongside the more abstract and political, these oral histories also reveal the deeply personal and emotional memory of the four days in May. Some eschew larger concepts and concerns and focus on the personal relationships they had or the emotional response and meanings they have drawn—and for many, continue to draw—from the experience. Whether personal, political, or an amalgam of both, as Alessando Portelli reminds us, these narrators demonstrate that "memory is not a passive depository of facts, but an active process of creation of meanings."[88] We close with the words of several of our narrators and their sense of purpose, significance, and meaning pertaining to the shootings.

For some, the lessons are political. As before, John Guidubaldi adopted a more conservative interpretation of the shootings when asked about their consequences.

Well, one of the consequences that was rather apparent was that there weren't any further demonstrations. That is to say, there weren't demonstrations of the sort that we had or that were going on that I saw so much of on the East Coast. It was like all of sudden people realized this was a deadly game. This was not a panty-raid kind of mentality. This was not something that could be done on a whim without regard to consequences; that the consequences were indeed dramatic and severe. I think it was a sobering moment nationally to see that we could have an occasion where the youth of our country were actually killed by the military units that were there to preserve the peace.

Of course, there was a lot of sympathy for slain students . . . but they weren't children, first of all. They were beyond the age of reason, they were grown people. Now, we had innocent victims, but I'm talking about the people who were leading the rebellion, who were fomenting unrest among the student body. These were people fully in control of their faculties and they were people who had a mission. And I just showed you right before this interview some quotes from Mark Rudd from Columbia and others who talked very pointedly about the importance of confrontation politics: just keep pushing, pushing until you get a response; and then if you get a response that involves somebody getting hurt, then you have a cause, you have a sympathy that you can exploit. And I'm sorry to say I think that was one of the outcomes. There was that for these past demonstrations and for the Harvard riot, the Harvard demonstration, and also for the Kent State one.[89]

Mike Alewitz took the opposite, radical view as he considered the shootings in a larger context.

The real memorial is the anti-war movement. That's the living memorial. I think it's very important that people keep alive the memory of Kent. I applaud the efforts of the people in Kent to do this. I think that efforts like Laurel Krause, Emily Kunstler and others who did the [Kent State Truth Tribunal], who put some of these things down and recorded some of the stuff are very important. I think we have to educate widely about what happened at Kent. The main thing is we have to write the history of the mass anti-war movement into the real history of what happened at Kent. Because when you pose this thing as an individual tragedy or an event that just involved a handful of radicals or that it was unique to the experience, just to Kent State and that this was not something that happened other places . . . we have to draw the real lessons from this stuff in my opinion. Perhaps that's why I don't go to the memorials—I always do slide shows on May 4 and I've given thousands of slide shows.[90]

Joe Cullum framed the significance in terms of power and political issues from the liberal-left perspective.

The shootings at Kent demonstrated to me, and I think a lot of other people, the extent to which any government might go when it feels threatened. And I think that that's an important lesson. Because having taught the last 19 years, and a good bit of that teaching government, I have used the shootings at Kent State as a case study in First Amendment, freedom of assembly and freedom of speech and government repression. It's been a good teachable moment for me. So, what I've noticed over the years, as this fades more and more from collective memory . . . students that I have had were born well after any of this occurred and maybe their parents remembered it. But I guess what surprised me a little bit was that they were not as shocked that this would happen as my generation was when it happened. I think in a sense what Kent State meant is that never again would young people be so naive as to think that they would not have to, you know, pay some significant consequence for their actions. There's clear evidence that hanging on to power is something that that people in power do. Almost at any cost. . . . I think the divisions in the country are gonna continue to be exploited as they were then. I don't think a lot of people have learned that lesson that you can be turned against your own interests by somebody banging a table and complaining about gays and guns and God and all the things that divide people.[91]

For former radical Ken Hammond, the only

real way to honor that is to carry those struggles on, to continue to fight for, you know, a better world and for justice and, you know, all those good things. We want to remember the pain and the suffering and the sorrow, but the only way to overcome that and assuage that is to continue to work and struggle for the justice and the causes that we believed in then.[92]

For undergraduate Catherine Delattre, the lack of closure exacerbated the atmosphere in not only the days but years that followed.

I think there was a part of me that waited for years, was always looking for there to be somebody to take the blame for this, and that was a hard thing to accept all those years as a student and having been there. But nobody was ever, no one was really punished for what happened, that those poor families—it took years and years and years for the families of the students who were killed to get anything. And I can only, I can't even imagine what it must have been like for those parents all those years, and I think finally there was money paid to the families, right? At the time, you just, you didn't know what exactly had happened, and you wanted to know.[93]

Diane Yale-Peabody put the events on a more personal yet still political note.

So year after year we came back, and we've come back to the candle-light march and the vigils and memorial services until we moved away from this area and we had children. But I've always told my children what happened. I want them to know, because if we forget, it'll happen again. I have a boy and a girl, the boy's 13 and the girl's 11, and I've raised them to be conscientious objectors. I never want them to go to war. War is wrong. And I'm just as much a victim of the Vietnam War as all the veterans that died in Vietnam. I came back this year and I brought my children because I want them to remember. I want them to be a part of this. I want them to fight and have passion for the things that are right. I don't want them to be apathetic. I feel a real affinity with the men and women who fought for freedom in the first place in this country in 1776. And if we don't help them remember; if people say it's time to forget—and the students on campus today who say they want to put it behind them—then it's gonna happen to them, and it's gonna happen to their children and it's gonna happen to my children. And those four people would have died for nothing. And I can't accept that.[94]

Kent resident Rosann Rissland sees improvement in the relations between students and the residents of Kent.

It has only been in the last few years, really, as students have started volunteering or that go to the different churches in the community, that I've seen less of a demarcation. Because these students become people to the town people, you know? You can't say so-and-so who you sang in the choir with and is a student is a bad person. So it makes you realize more who the individual students are, and not just take the actions of a few and make the rest carry the burden of those actions.[95]

Former KSU president Schwartz framed the events in terms of an epic saga:

You know, if you back out of it, it was all part of a piece. It was the creation of this enormous great saga, almost like an Icelandic saga. A great heroic story that was developing, and it has developed to the point now where it is such a massive part of that's now the legend of Kent State. Never mind the reality of it, it's part of the legendary Kent

State. I never really thought about it too much while it was happening, but it sure did occur to me, while it was happening, that something like that could happen. And it did, and I'm sure that it still arouses all kinds of feelings on both sides of the event. Very much in the tradition of, you know, there are southerners who call it [the Civil War] the War of Northern Aggression, and there are northerners who, well—there's that kind of thing continues to develop now, as far as I can tell.[96]

Janice Wascko reflected that

there's a favorite line from Dante that there's a special circle of hell for those who won't cry out against murder. And I guess I need to make this tape because I need to cry out against murder, and the sickness that can take over a society. I'd become Christian in the intervening years, and today was real interesting to me, it really pointed out some things to me, made things clearer. I never found the middle ground for myself, and I hadn't found healing yet or resolution. But if there's no forgiveness there's no healing, and the murder goes on forever.[97]

Chuck Ayers conveyed the emotional elements for some in remembering.

I never am able to stop talking about it. I was on campus for the thirtieth anniversary. And that was one of the most emotional couple of days that I've ever gone through. I was with Jim Russell quite a bit of that time. Jim introduced me to most of the other survivors, so I think I've met all of them. Those days on campus, being with Jim, being with the other survivors who were actually shot, being with the other people that I was with on those days—there were a couple of people that I'm sure I hadn't seen since the morning of May 4th. And it was wild to see so many grown men—we were all older by that time, lots of gray beards around—just openly weeping over what we had gone through. And you could tell talking to some of these people that they'd held it in and never let it out ever before. It was very moving, very moving. And that's a big part of why Tom [Batiuk] and I did the comic strip, the *Crankshaft* series, about May 4th for the 30th anniversary. And I've gone through it again now with the passing of Jim Russell, because I wasn't on campus this May 4th. . . .

As a former Kent student, I would go places and have a Kent State t-shirt on, and people will say, "Well, were you there?" This had gotten to the point where you can answer that question basically before they even finish that sentence, because you can see the look in their faces, you know what the question is going to be. [I'd say], "Yeah, I was there."[98]

As Ayers tells us, the memory of the shootings at Kent State on May 4, 1970, lingers, despite counterefforts to forget or ignore what happened. It reminds us that, as David Lowenthal has noted, places that evoke pride are often safeguarded, while those "that reflect shame may be ignored or expunged from the landscape."[99] Violence and tragedy, according to Kenneth Foote, "have the power to transform landscape,"[100] but they can also transform individuals, institutions, and societies.

As we conclude, Robert Smithson's *Partially Buried Woodshed*, mentioned at the start of this book, serves here as a useful point of return. A piece of land art created by Smithson on the KSU campus four months before the shootings, the structure—possessing no political content or symbolism, and located far away from the site of the shootings—had the words "MAY 4 KENT 70" spray painted by an unknown individual not long after the shootings and was soon absorbed into the event's folklore. Scorned by the Kent State administration, who thought it a blemish on campus, the *Woodshed* was eventually set ablaze by an unidentified arsonist in 1975. Yet still the edifice remains, such as it is, in the same spot where it was built. Barely visible behind several trees, it is there—its entropy the opposite of the individual and collective memories of the shootings, which are ongoing and evolving, always in a state of revision as facts, feelings, and impressions are recalled, forgotten, or reassembled.

Richard Bentley, who taught in the KSU School of Journalism, knew this all too well. On May 4, he had let his photography class out early to witness and document the rally. Interviewed twenty years later at the annual commemoration in 1995, Bentley's testimony indicates that memories, while they yearn to be shared, can often be hard to express.

But as I said, I was one of the lucky faculty, I didn't have to come back for a year and a half. I taught at Ohio State the next year, and then came back the following year. This is the first time that I've looked at this book.

[Interviewer]: Your diary, right?

I noticed it was for 1970, and that's when I turned to May just to see if there was anything written down there. Then I see that, yes, I was in Ohio State, and then all hell broke loose. I think that I wrote some brief comment on May 4th.

[Interviewer]: Would you like to share those?

Well, let's see here. Well, on May 1st, Ohio State, J-School 10:45 to 12:00. And then Monday, and then just all hell [voice breaks], and to pick up the kids—[long pause]—and then everything else is blank. . . . [end of tape][101]

Notes

Introduction: The Memory

1. H. R. Haldeman, *The Ends of Power* (New York: Dell, 1978).

2. Thomas M. Grace, "Kent State and Historical Memory," in Carole A. Barbato and Laura L. Davis, eds., *Democratic Narrative, History, & Memory* (Kent, Ohio: Kent State Univ. Press, 2012), 8–29; quote, 13.

3. U.S. President's Commission on Campus Unrest (Scranton Commission), *The Report of the President's Commission on Campus Unrest* (Washington, D.C.: Government Printing Office, 1970), 289.

4. For a thorough chronology of the events, see the Kent State Library Special Collections website on the May 4 events, http://www.library.kent.edu/page/13950 (accessed July 15, 2013).

5. For a chronology of the memorial, see the Kent State Library Special Collections website on the May 4 events, http://www.library.kent.edu/page/14887 (accessed July 22, 2013).

6. Laurel Krause's blog on the events can be found on Michael Moore's website, http://www.michaelmoore.com/blogger/laurelk (accessed July 15, 2013).

7. One of the stories on the tape is "New Analysis of 40-year-old recording of Kent State shootings reveals that Ohio Guard was given an order to prepare to fire," Cleveland.com, May 9, 2010, http://blog.cleveland.com/metro/2010/05/new_analysis_of_40-year-old_re.html (accessed July 15, 2013).

8. For one of the many newspaper stories, see "Justice Department Won't Reopen Probe of 1970 Kent State Shootings," *Cleveland Plain Dealer,* Apr. 24, 2012, http://www.cleveland.com/science/index.ssf/2012/04/justice_department_wont_re-ope.html (accessed July 15, 2013).

9. Kenneth E. Foote, *Shadowed Ground: America's Landscapes of Violence and Tragedy,* rev. ed. (Austin: Univ. of Texas Press, 2003), 8.

10. Katharine Hodgkin and Susannah Radstone, eds., *Contested Pasts: The Politics of Memory* (London: Routledge, 2003), 1.

11. Grace, "Kent State and Historical Memory," 8–29, quotes on 8.

12. David Steigerwald, *The Sixties and the End of Modern America* (New York: St. Martin's Press, 1995), 2.

13. Daniel Marcus, *Happy Days and Wonder Years: The Fifties and the Sixties in Contemporary Cultural Politics* (New Brunswick, N.J.: Rutgers Univ. Press, 2004), 2.

14. Ibid., 9.

15. Lynn Abrams, *Oral History Theory* (New York: Routledge, 2010), 38–39. See also Charlotte Linde, *Life Stories: The Creation of Coherence* (London: Oxford, 1993).

16. Abrams, *Oral History Theory*, 64.

17. Ibid., 57.

18. Ibid., 35.

19. Ibid., 124.

20. Alessandro Portelli, *The Death of Luigi Trastulli and Other Stories: Form and Meaning in Oral History* (Albany, N.Y.: SUNY Press, 1991), 50.

21. Portelli, *Death of Luigi Trastulli*, 51.

22. Abrams, *Oral History Theory*, 80.

23. Ibid., 22.

24. Ronald J. Grele, *Envelopes of Sound: The Art of Oral History*, 2nd rev. ed. (New York: Praeger, 1991), 245.

25. Abrams, *Oral History Theory*, 136–39.

26. Ibid., 159.

27. Maurice Halbwachs, *On Collective Memory*, ed. and trans. Lewis A. Coser (Chicago: Univ. of Chicago Press, 1992).

28. See Jeffrey K. Olick, "From Collective Memory to the Sociology of Mnemonic Practices and Products," in Astrid Eril and Ansgar Nünning, eds., *Cultural Memory Studies: An International and Interdisciplinary Handbook* (Berlin: Walter de Gruyter, 2008), 151–61

29. Astrid Eril and Ansgar Nünning, eds., *Cultural Memory Studies: An International and Interdisciplinary Handbook* (Berlin: Walter de Gruyter, 2008), 5.

30. Geoffrey Cubitt, *History and Memory* (Manchester, UK: Manchester Univ. Press, 2007), 9.

31. Abrams, *Oral History Theory*, 99. For more on collective and individual memory, see also Eril and Nünning, eds., *Cultural Memory Studies*.

32. Eril and Nünning, eds., *Cultural Memory Studies*, 2

33. Michael Schudson, *Watergate in American Memory: How We Remember, Forget, and Reconstruct the Past* (New York: Basic Books, 1992), 4.

34. Ibid., 51.

35. Ibid., 56.

36. See Hodgkin and Radstone, eds., *Contested Pasts*, 11–12.

37. Nicholas DiFonzo, *The Watercooler Effect: A Psychologist Explores the Extraordinary Power of Rumors* (New York: Penguin, 2008), 38.

38. Gordon W. Allport and Leo Postman, *The Psychology of Rumor* (New York: Henry Holt, 1947), 33.

39. Ibid., x.

40. Ibid., 86.

41. Ibid., 193.

42. Tamotsu Shibutani, *Improvised News: A Sociological Study of Rumor* (Indianapolis, Ind.: Bobbs-Merrill, 1966), 9.

43. DiFonzo, *Watercooler Effect*, 3.

44. Ibid., 9.

45. Ibid., 10.

46. Gary Alan Fine and Bill Ellis, *The Global Grapevine: Why Rumors of Terrorism, Immigration, and Trade Matter* (New York: Oxford Univ. Press, 2010), 5.

47. Ibid., 9–10.

1. "The largest unknown university in the world"

1. Issues of the *Daily Kent Stater* (*DKS*) from 1959 to 1969 are available online through the Kent State Library. Quote from May 20, 1960.

2. Phillip R. Shriver, *The Years of Youth: Kent State University, 1910–1960* (Kent, Ohio: Kent State Univ. Press, 1960), 129.

3. *DKS*, Apr. 12, 1960.

4. Ibid., May 20, 1960.

5. Ibid.

6. Kent's enrollment in 1970 is found at the online e-Inside magazine of Kent State, http://einside.kent.edu/?type=art&id=92356.

7. Scott Bills, ed., *Kent State/May 4: Echoes through a Decade* (Kent, Ohio: Kent State Univ. Press, 1982), 3.

8. Ibid.

9. John Peach, interview by Craig Simpson, August 6, 2009, http://www.library.kent.edu/page/13894. (Hereafter, all web citations are removed; all interviews are part of the May 4 Collection.)

10. David Hansford, interview by Craig Simpson, August 3, 2007.

11. John Guidubaldi, interview by Craig Simpson, April 11, 2008.

12. James Mueller, interview by Craig Simpson, October 24, 2007.

13. Diane Yale-Peabody, recorded remembrance, 1990. We use the term *recorded remembrance* for those files where the narrator recorded a memory without the person from KSU asking questions.

14. Ellis Berns, interview by Craig Simpson, May 4, 2010.

15. U.S. President's Commission, *Report,* 234.

16. Douglas Kneeland, "Kent State in Flux but Still Attuned to Mid-America," *New York Times,* May 7, 1970.

17. For how conservatives since the 1970s have positioned the 1960s in public memory and political rhetoric, see Daniel Marcus, *Happy Days and Wonder Years: The Fifties and the Sixties in Contemporary Cultural Politics* (New Brunswick, N.J.: Rutgers Univ. Press, 2004).

18. Bernard von Bothmer, *Framing the Sixties: The Use and Abuse of a Decade from Ronald Reagan to George W. Bush* (Amherst: Univ. of Massachusetts Press, 2010).

19. Rick Byrum, interview by Gregory Wilson, Mar. 30, 2013.

20. Joe Cullum, interview by Gregory Wilson, May 11, 2013.

21. Helen Carringer, "KSU to Assist Students Through New Center," September 26, 1968, *Akron Beacon Journal*; Milton E. Wilson Jr., "Involvement/Two Years Later": A Report on Programming in the Area of Black Student Concerns at Kent State University 1968–1970," Box 1, Milton E. Wilson Jr., Papers, KSU May 4 Collection. For more on the history of activism at Kent prior to the shootings, see the upcoming book

by Tom Grace, *Kent State: Death and Dissent in the Long Sixties* (Amherst: Univ. of Massachusetts Press, forthcoming). Information here is from the first chapter of the manuscript made available to the authors.

22. Bills, ed., *Kent State/May 4*, 31.

23. *DKS*, March 11, 1960, http://dks.library.kent.edu/cgi-bin/kentstate?a=d&d =dks19600311-01.2.5&e=-------en-20--1--txt-IN------ (accessed Dec. 2013).

24. Ibid., Apr. 14, 1960, http://dks.library.kent.edu/cgi-bin/kentstate?a=d&d =dks19600414-01.2.5&e=-------en-20--1--txt-IN------ (accessed Dec. 2013).

25. Ibid., May 13, 1960, http://dks.library.kent.edu/cgi-bin/kentstate?a=d&d =dks19600513-01.2.2&e=-------en-20--1--txt-IN------ (accessed Dec. 2013).

26. See the following issues of the DKS, all accessed at the DKS website: http:// dks.library.kent.edu/cgi-bin/kentstate?a=cl&cl=CL1&sp=dks&e=-------en-20--1-- txt-txIN-------: Feb. 12, 1960, Mar. 11, 1960, Apr. 19, 1960, Apr. 26, 1960, May 13, 1960, May 20, 1960.

27. Ibid., February 20, 1964, http://dks.library.kent.edu/cgi-bin/ kentstate?a=d&d=dks19640220-01&e=-------en-20--1--txt-txIN-------.

28. Kenneth J. Heineman, *Campus Wars: The Peace Movement at American State Universities in the Vietnam Era* (New York: New York Univ. Press, 1993), 7, 70, 37.

29. Murvin Perry, interview by Robin Katz, Apr. 18, 2008.

30. Joann Peterangelo Gavacs, interviewed by Henry Halem, May 4, 2000.

31. Rosann Rissland, interview by Craig Simpson, May 19, 2009.

32. John Peach, interview by Craig Simpson, Aug. 6, 2009.

33. Thomas R. Hensley, *The Kent State Incident: Impact of Judicial Process on Public Attitudes* (Westport, Conn.: Greenwood Press, 1981), 31.

34. Heineman, *Campus Wars*, 37.

35. Kent State University Summer News, July 3, 1969, http://dks.library.kent.edu/ cgi-bin/kentstate?a=d&d=ksn19690703-01.2.2&e=-------en-20--1--txt-IN------.

36. Jerry Lewis, interview by Craig Simpson, Feb. 24, 2010.

37. Mike Alewitz, interview by Gregory Wilson, Aug. 6, 2012.

38. Peter Jedick, interview by Craig Simpson, Feb. 9, 2010.

39. Ken Hammond, interview by Craig Simpson, Mar. 24, 2010.

40. Curtis Pittman, interview by Sandra Perlman Halem, May 4, 2000.

41. "History Lesson: Kent State, a Participant's Memoir," Folder 13, Box 21, Bill Gordon, Ken Hammond, Thomas Lough Papers, KSU May 4 Collection.

42. Ibid.

43. Chuck Ayers, interview by Craig Simpson, Aug. 16, 2007.

44. *DKS*, Apr. 9, 1969, http://dks.library.kent.edu/cgi-bin/kentstate?a=d&d =dks19690409-01&e=-------en-20--1--txt-IN------.

45. Ibid., Apr. 17, 1969, http://dks.library.kent.edu/cgi-bin/kentstate?a=d&d =dks19690417-01&e=-------en-20--1--txt-IN------.

46. See James J. Best, "The Tragic Weekend of May 1 to 4, 1970," in *Kent State & May 4: A Social Science Perspective,* ed. Thomas R. Hensley and Jerry M. Lewis, 3rd. ed. (Kent, Ohio: Kent State Univ. Press, 2010), 7.

47. Carl M. Moore and D. Ray Heisey, "Not a Great Deal of Error . . . ?," Folder 31, Box 20A, Carl M. Moore Papers, KSU May 4 Collection.

48. Carl Moore, interview by Les Stegh, Sept. 10, 1973.

49. Chuck Ayers, interview by Craig Simpson, Aug. 16, 2007.

50. Catherine Delattre, interview by Craig Simpson, Nov. 13, 2008.

51. Timothy DeFrange, interview by Helene Cooley, Apr. 30, 1990.

52. DKS, Oct. 16, 1969, http://dks.library.kent.edu/cgi-bin/kentstate?a=d&d =dks19691016-01&e=-------en-20--1--txt-IN------ (accessed Dec. 2013).

53. David Farber and Jeff Roche, eds., *The Conservative Sixties* (New York: Peter Lang, 2010), 2.

54. Archie C. Epps III, "The Harvard Student Rebellion of 1969: Through Change and Through Storm," *Proceedings of the Massachusetts Historical Society,* 3rd ser., 107 (1995): 1–15; Gaston de Los Reyes, "University Hall, 1969, Is Revisited," *Harvard Crimson,* Sept. 4, 1999, http://www.thecrimson.com/article/1999/9/4/university-hall-1969-is-revisited-ptwenty-five/?page=1 (accessed Dec. 16, 2014); Jennifer Stetzer, "From Sympathizers to Organizers," in *Yards and Gates: Gender in Harvard and Radcliffe History,* ed. Laurel Ulrich (New York: Palgrave, 2004), 271–84.

55. John Guidubaldi, interview by Craig Simpson, Apr. 11, 2008.

56. William Barry Furlong, "The Guardsmen's View of the Tragedy at Kent State," *New York Times Magazine,* June 21, 1970, 12.

57. Ibid., 13.

58. From chapter 12, provided to the authors, in Grace, *Kent State: Death and Dissent in the Long Sixties.*

59. Drawn from Appendix A, "National Guard Call Outs," in Joseph Kelner and James Munves, *The Kent State Coverup* (New York: Harper and Row, 1980).

60. J. Ronald Snyder, interview by Craig Simpson, Nov. 1, 2007.

61. Ibid.

62. Arthur Krummel, interview by Craig Simpson, Jan. 11, 2008.

2. "An edge in the air"

1. David L. Anderson, ed., *The Columbia Guide to the Vietnam War* (New York: Columbia Univ. Press, 2002), 56.

2. Ibid., 113.

3. Chuck Ayers, interview by Craig Simpson, Aug. 16, 2007.

4. Richard Nixon, "Vietnamization—The Great Silent Majority," Nov. 3, 1969, http://www.presidentialrhetoric.com/historicspeeches/nixon/vietnamization.html (accessed Mar. 25, 2015).

5. See Jeffrey Kimball, *Nixon's Vietnam War* (Lawrence: Univ. Press of Kansas, 1998).

6. Richard Nixon, "Special Message to Congress on Draft Reform," Apr. 23, 1970, http://www.presidency.ucsb.edu/ws/?pid=2483 (accessed Mar. 25, 2015).

7. Richard Nixon, "Address to the Nation on the Situation in Southeast Asia," Apr. 30, 1970, in The American Presidency Project, http://www.presidency.ucsb.edu/ws/index.php?pid=2490 (accessed Nov. 21, 2013).

8. Ibid. (accessed Mar. 25, 2015).

9. Catherine Delattre, interview by Craig Simpson, Nov. 13, 2008.

10. Rob Fox, interview by Henry Halem, May 4, 2000.

11. Chuck Ayers, interview by Craig Simpson, Aug. 16, 2007.

12. Heineman, *Campus Wars,* 245.

13. Ken Hammond, interview by Gregory Wilson, July 16, 2012.

14. Carole A. Barbato and Laura L. Davis, eds., *Democratic Narrative, History and Memory* (Kent, Ohio: Kent State Univ. Press, 2012), 196.

15. Rob Fox, interview by Henry Halem, May 4, 2000.

16. Chuck Ayers, interview by Craig Simpson, Aug. 16, 2007.

17. Ken Hammond, interview by Craig Simpson, Mar. 24, 2010.

18. U.S. President's Commission, *Report,* 240.

19. Carol Mirman, interview by Sandra Perlman Halem, Apr. 1, 2000.

20. U.S. President's Commission, *Report,* 242.

21. John Carson, interview by Craig Simpson, June 17, 2006.

22. Ronald Sterlekar, interview by Craig Simpson, Oct. 12, 2007.

23. Chuck Ayers, interview by Craig Simpson, Aug. 16, 2007.

24. Anonymous, interview by Sandra Perlman Halem, n.d.

25. Winonna Vannoy, interview by Tina Boeder, May 3, 1990.

26. John Peach, interview by Craig Simpson, Aug. 6, 2009.

27. "Nancy Hansford, Former Kent Mayor, Dies at 83," http://www.recordpub. com/news%20local/2013/10/27/nancy-hansford-former-kent-mayor-dies-at-83 (accessed Mar. 25, 2015).

28. David Hansford, interview by Craig Simpson, Aug. 3, 2007.

29. Carole A. Barbato, Laura L. Davis, and Mark F. Seeman, "Appendix: This We Know," in Carole A. Barbato and Laura L. Davis, eds., *Democratic Narrative, History and Memory* (Kent, Ohio: Kent State Univ. Press, 2012), 199.

30. This comes from the 1970 summary of the events at Kent by the Justice Department, as published in I. F. Stone, *The Killings at Kent State: How Murder Went Unpunished* (New York: Vintage, 1971), 66.

31. Anonymous, interview by Sandra Perlman Halem, n.d.

32. Ruth Gibson, interview in Bills, *Kent State/May 4,* 87.

33. Anonymous, interview by Sandra Perlman Halem, May 3, 2000.

34. Catherine Delattre, interview by Craig Simpson, Nov. 13, 2008.

35. John Carson, interview by Craig Simpson, June 17, 2006.

36. See Peter Davies, *The Truth About Kent State: A Challenge to the American Conscience* (New York: Farrar, Straus, Giroux, 1973), 17–19; Peter Davies, "The Burning Question: A Government Coverup?," in Bills, *Echoes,* 150–59; and Joseph Kelner and James Munves, *The Kent State Coverup* (1980; repr., Lincoln, Neb.: Authors Guild, 2001), 204–5.

37. Barbato, Davis, and Seeman, "Appendix: This We Know," 200–201.

38. Anonymous, interview by Sandra Perlman Halem, May 3, 2000.

39. William A. Gordon, *Four Dead in Ohio,* links to the video for a kickstarter campaign for a documentary on Devo in his blog, http://kentstatedevelopments. blogspot.com/2014/04/devo-founder-admits-helping-burn-rotc.html. The video is at https://www.kickstarter.com/projects/1409838010/authorized-devo-documentary-film/posts/278030, in which Bob Mothersbaugh (not Mark as Gordon's blog notes) states his involvement in the fire.

40. Ellis Berns, interview by Craig Simpson, May 4, 2010.

41. J. Ronald Snyder, interview by Craig Simpson, Nov. 1, 2007.

42. J. Ronald Snyder, interview by Gregory Wilson, May 3, 2013. On the afternoon of this interview, Guardsman Lawrence Shafer, who shot Joe Lewis, died.

43. Arthur Krummel, interview by Craig Simpson, Jan. 11, 2008.

44. Ohio National Guardsman, interview by Sandra Perlman Halem, May 2, 2000.

45. Eldon Fender, interview by Craig Simpson, Nov. 28, 2007.

46. U.S. President's Commission, *Report,* 253.

47. An audio file of the speech and press conference can be heard at http://www.kentstate1970.org/timeline/may3rd1970, a repository of information hosted by WKSU. We transcribed the quotes from the audio file; a text version can be found at Gregory Payne's site: http://www.may4archive.org/appendices.shtml (accessed Mar. 25, 2015).

48. See http://www.kentstate1970.org/timeline/may3rd1970. We transcribed the quotes from the audio file; in some cases, our transcription differs slightly from quotes found in the U.S. President's Commission's (Scranton Commission's) *Report.*

49. U.S. President's Commission, *Report,* 255.

50. See http://www.kentstate1970.org/timeline/may3rd1970. We transcribed the quotes from the audio file; in some cases, our transcription differs slightly from quotes found in the U.S. President's Commission's *Report.*

51. U.S. President's Commission, *Report,* 255.

52. See http://www.kentstate1970.org/timeline/may3rd1970. We transcribed the quotes from the audio file; in some cases, our transcription differs slightly from quotes found in the U.S. President's Commission's *Report.*

53. U.S. President's Commission, *Report,* 255.

54. Rosann Rissland, interview by Craig Simpson, May 19, 2009.

55. Linda Cooper-Leff, interview by Craig Simpson, May 21, 2008.

56. Arthur Krummel, interview by Craig Simpson, Jan. 11, 2008.

57. James Vacarella, interview by Sandra Perlman Halem, Apr. 3, 2000.

58. Quote found on Gregory Payne's website, http://www.may4archive.org/allison_krause.shtml (accessed Mar. 25, 2015).

59. Carol Mirman, interview by Sandra Perlman Halem, Apr. 1, 2000.

60. Ken Hammond, interview by Gregory Wilson, July 16, 2012.

61. Mike Alewitz, interview by Gregory Wilson, Aug. 6, 2012.

62. Ohio National Guardsman, interview by Sandra Perlman Halem, May 2, 2000.

63. Descriptions of the events are drawn from Barbato, Davis, and Seeman, *This We Know,* the U.S. President's Commission's *Report,* and James J. Best, "The Tragic Weekend of May 1 to 4, 1970, in Thomas R. Hensley and Jerry M. Lewis, eds., *Kent State & May 4: A Social Science Perspective,* 3rd. ed. (Kent, Ohio: Kent State Univ. Press, 2010), 4–31.

64. Arthur Krummel, interview by Craig Simpson, Jan. 11, 2008.

65. Dean Kahler, interview by Gregory Wilson, May 2012.

66. Eldon Fender, interview by Craig Simpson, Nov. 28, 2007.

67. Rebecca Howe, recorded remembrance, May 2, 1990.

68. Rick Byrum, interview by Gregory Wilson, Mar. 30, 2013.

69. Arthur Krummel, interview by Craig Simpson, Jan. 11, 2008.

70. Janice Marie (Gierman) Wascko, interview by Nancy Brendlinger, May 4, 1990.

3. "A bullet is a drastic answer"

1. U.S. President's Commission on Campus Unrest, *Report*, 259.

2. Ohio National Guardsman, interview by Sandra Perlman Halem, May 2, 2000.

3. U.S. President's Commission on Campus Unrest, *Report*, 260.

4. Ibid., 261.

5. Best, "Tragic Weekend," 55.

6. See Davies, *Truth About Kent State*, 31; and Phillip K. Tompkins and Elaine Vanden Bout Anderson, *Communication Crisis at Kent State: A Case Study* (New York: Gordon & Breach, 1971).

7. U.S. President's Commission on Campus Unrest, *Report*, 261; Best, "Tragic Weekend," 56–57.

8. McMillen also served as assistant to President White, acting as Special Counsel for Student Rights from 1968 to 1969. See Joe Eszterhas and Michael D. Roberts, *Thirteen Seconds: Confrontation at Kent State* (Cleveland: Gray & Company, 1970), Kindle location 322–23.

9. The full audio of his speech is available on the WKSU website, "Kent State 1970," http://www.kentstate1970.org/timeline/may4th1970/mcmillen# (accessed Mar. 25, 2015).

10. Dean Kahler, interview by Gregory Wilson, May 14, 2012.

11. "Sequence of Events at Kent State," Ohio National Guard Documents [includes reports and statements] Folder, Box 64D, Charles Thomas Papers, May 4 Collection, KSU.

12. See Barbato, Davis, and Seeman, *This We Know*, 13, Best, "Tragic Weekend," 57; and U.S. President's Commission on Campus Unrest, *Report*, 263.

13. Chuck Ayers, interview by Craig Simpson, Aug. 16, 2007.

14. Richard Bentley, interview by Gina Bodra, May 4, 1990.

15. Dean Kahler, interview by Gregory Wilson, May 14, 2012.

16. U.S. President's Commission on Campus Unrest, *Report*, 263.

17. Ron Snyder, interview by Gregory Wilson, May 3, 2012.

18. William Derry Heasley, interview by John Burnell, May 4, 1990.

19. Dean Kahler, interview by Gregory Wilson, May 14, 2012.

20. Rick Byrum, interview by Gregory Wilson, Mar. 30, 2013.

21. Ken Hammond, interview by Craig Simpson, Mar. 24, 2010.

22. "Report of Investigation, Riot Kent State University, May 12, 1970," State Series 6524, Ohio Historical Society, Columbus.

23. U.S. President's Commission on Campus Unrest, *Report*, 265.

24. Ron Snyder, interview with Gregory Wilson, May 3, 2012.

25. Ibid.

26. Ibid.

27. Chuck Ayers, interview by Craig Simpson, Aug. 16, 2007.

28. Lowell Zurbuch, interview by Craig Simpson, Oct. 17, 2007.

29. Joe Cullum, interview by Gregory Wilson, May 11, 2012.

30. Michael Erwin, interview by Sandra Perlman Halem, Apr. 4, 2000.

31. Carol Mirman, interview by Sandra Perlman Halem, Apr. 1, 2000. Like others, she remembers tanks, which were likely armored personnel carriers.

32. Mike Alewitz, interview by Gregory Wilson, Aug. 6, 2012.

33. See chapter 12 in Thomas Grace, *Death and Dissent in the Long Sixties* (Amherst: Univ. of Massachusetts Press, 2015).

34. Chuck Ayers, interview by Craig Simpson, Aug. 16, 2007.

35. U.S. President's Commission on Campus Unrest, *Report,* 267.

36. Best, "Tragic Weekend," 61.

37. Davies, *Truth About Kent State,* 36; Grace, *Death and Dissent,* chapter 12.

38. Although many Guardsmen and those defending the Guard used this idea at the time and as noted later still refer to it.

39. Chuck Ayers, interview by Craig Simpson, Aug. 16, 2007.

40. Ibid.

41. Catherine Delattre, interview by Craig Simpson, Nov. 13, 2008.

42. Carol Mirman, interview by Sandra Perlman Halem, Apr. 1, 2000.

43. The film is housed at the Ohio Historical Society but remains as of this writing fragile and perhaps unplayable. See the U.S. President's Commission on Campus Unrest, *Report,* as well as Barbato, Davis, and Seeman, *This We Know,* and Davies, *Truth About Kent State.*

44. Joe Cullum, interview by Gregory Wilson, May 11, 2012.

45. See Barbato, Davis, and Seeman, *This We Know,* 22.

46. The distance he is reported to have been from the Guard is also sixty feet.

47. Carol Mirman, interview by Sandra Perlman Halem, Apr. 1, 2000.

48. Catherine Delattre, interview by Craig Simpson, Nov. 13, 2008.

49. Jerry Lewis, interview by Craig Simpson, Feb. 24, 2010.

50. Ellis Berns, interview by Craig Simpson, May 4, 2010.

51. Ron Snyder, interview by Craig Simpson, Nov. 1, 2007.

52. "Ohio State Highway Patrol Report of Investigation, interview with Captain J. R. Snyder, September 9, 1970," Box 208, *Akron Beacon Journal* collection, May 4 Collection, KSU. See Barbato, Davis, and Seeman, *This We Know,* 25; and Kelner and Munves, *The Kent State Coverup,* 123.

53. Ohio National Guardsman, interview by Sandra Perlman Halem, May 2, 2000.

54. See the FBI summary report in I. F. Stone, *The Killings at Kent State: How Murder Went Unpunished* (New York: Vintage Books, 1971), 87.

55. Rob Fox, interview by Henry Halem, May 4, 2000.

56. Barbarto, Davis, and Seeman, *This We Know,* 25.

57. The high school closed in 1972, and the remainder of the school closed in 1982.

58. Ellen Mann, interview by Stephanie Tulley, May 3, 2010.

59. Ken Hammond, interview by Gregory Wilson, July 16, 2012.

60. Julio Fanjul, interview by Sandra Perlman Halem, May 3, 2000.

61. Chuck Ayers, interview by Craig Simpson, Aug. 16, 2007.

62. Janice Wasko, interview by Nancy Brendlinger, May 4, 1990.

63. E. Timothy Moore, interview by Craig Simpson, May 14, 2009.

64. Three recent pieces on oral history and new media are Steven High, "Telling Stories: A Reflection on Oral History and New Media," *Oral History* 38 (Spring 2010): 101–12; James Evans and Phil Jones, "The Walking Interview: Methodology, Mobility, and Place," *Applied Geography* 31 (Apr. 2011), 849–58; and Simon Bradley, "History to Go: Oral History, Audiowalks, and Mobile Media," *Oral History* 40 (Spring 2012): 99–110.

65. Eldon Fender, interview by Craig Simpson, Nov. 28, 2007.

66. Anonymous female, interview by Sandra Perlman Halem, (May?) 2000.

67. John Panagos, recorded remembrance, May 4, 1990.

68. Rosann Rissland, interview by Craig Simpson, May 19, 2009.

69. John Mangels, "Kent State Shootings: Does Former Informant Hold the Key to the May 4 Mystery?," *Cleveland Plain Dealer,* December 19, 2010; Davies, *Truth About Kent State,* 183–85.

70. See Barbato, Davis, and Seeman, *This We Know,* 25–29, and Michener, *Kent State,* 358–63.

71. Jerry Lewis, interview by Craig Simpson, Feb. 24, 2010.

72. The recording of Frank's plea can be heard on the WKSU site, http://www.kentstate1970.org/timeline/may4th1970.

73. Willam Brauning, interview by Sandra Perlman Halem, Apr. 24, 2000.

74. Naomi Goelman Etzkin, recorded remembrance, May 4, 1990.

75. Janice Wascko, interview by Nancy Brendlinger, May 4, 1990.

76. Naomi Goelman Etzkin, recorded remembrance, May 4, 1990.

4. "The divide in this country"

1. Schudson, *Watergate in American Memory,* 51.

2. Barbara Becker Agte, *Kent Letters: Students' Responses to May 1970 Massacre* (Deming, N.Mex.: Bluewater Press, 2012), 18–19, 21, 23.

3. See Christian Appy, *Patriots: The Vietnam War Remembered From All Sides* (New York: Penguin Books, 2004), 388.

4. Joan Morrison and Robert K. Morrison, *From Camelot to Kent State: The Sixties Experience in the Words of Those Who Lived It* (New York: Random House, 1987), 333.

5. See Appy, *Patriots,* 388.

6. J. Morrison and R. K. Morrison, *From Camelot to Kent State,* 333.

7. Joe Cullum, interview by Gregory Wilson, May 11, 2012.

8. Ibid.

9. John Cleary, interview by Craig Simpson, May 3, 2010.

10. Timothy DeFrange, interview by Helene Cooley, Apr. 30, 1990.

11. Dean Kahler, interview by Gregory Wilson, May 14, 2012.

12. Ibid.

13. Quote in Barbato, Davis, and Seeman, *This We Know,* 29.

14. Bruce Dzeda, interview by Connie Sickels, May 2, 1995.

15. Catherine Delattre, interview by Craig Simpson, Nov. 13, 2008.

16. John Carson, interview by Craig Simpson, June 17, 2006.

17. Chuck Ayers, interview by Craig Simpson, Aug. 16, 2007.

18. James Mueller, interview by Craig Simpson, Oct. 24, 2007.

19. Urban Research Corporation, *On Strike . . . Shut It Down: A Report on the First National Student Strike in U.S. History* (Chicago: Urban Research Corporation, 1970), 1.

20. "Antiwar Leaders Advocate Seizing Closed Campuses," *Cleveland Plain Dealer,* newsclipping, Saturday, May 8, 1970, in Folder 4, Box 179, Bob Carpenter Papers, KSU Special Collections and Archives, Kent, Ohio. Carpenter was the news director

of Kent's local radio station, WKNT.

21. Mike Alewitz, interview by Gregory Wilson, Aug. 6, 2012.

22. Christopher Powell, "Kent State Comes to Canada: Internationalizing the Antiwar Movement," in Carole A. Barbato and Laurel L. Davis, eds., *Democratic Narrative, History, and Memory,* 30–48.

23. Bruce Dzeda, interview by Connie Sickels, May 2, 1995.

24. "Tragedy at Kent State," *Chattanooga Times,* May 5, 1970, Folder 7, Box 1779, Bob Carpenter Papers.

25. "Outrage at Kent State," *Lorain Journal,* May 5, 1970, in Bob Carpenter Papers, Box 179, Folder 7.

26. *Kent Record-Courier,* Monday, May 4, 1970, in "News Clips: Ohio, Kent May 4, 1970" Folder, May 4 Collection: News Clippings, July 1969-May 4, 1970, Box. KSU Special Collections and Archives, Kent, Ohio.

27. "Del Corso says sniper fired before Guard" and "Colonel: guard has right to self-defense," *Kent Record-Courier,* May 5, 1970, in "News Clips: Ohio, Kent May 4, 1970" Folder, May 4 Collection: News Clippings, "July 1969-May 4, 1970" Box.

28. Joe Eszterhas and Michael D. Roberts, *13 Seconds: Confrontation at Kent State* (Gray & Company, 1970), location 100, Kindle.

29. Eszterhas and Roberts, *13 Seconds.*

30. Newsclipping, *Record-Courier,* May 8, 1970, in Bob Carpenter Papers, Box 179, Folder 4.

31. Michener, *Kent State,* 390–91.

32. For more, see esp. Ottavio M. Casale and Louis Paskoff, eds., *The Kent Affair: Documents and Interpretations* (Boston: Houghton Mifflin, 1971).

33. Letter to editor, *Kent Record-Courier,* Saturday, May 8, 1970, in Bob Carpenter Papers, Box 179, Folder 4.

34. News clipping, Jerry Lewis Papers, Box 20B, KSU Special Collections and Archives, Kent, Ohio.

35. Flamm, *Law and Order,* 3–4.

36. Ronald Snyder, interview by Gregory Wilson, May 3, 2013.

37. News clipping, Jerry Lewis Papers, Box 20B, KSU Special Collections and Archives, Kent, Ohio.

38. See the tables in Stuart Taylor, Richard Shuntich, Patrick McGovern, and Robert Genther, *Violence at Kent State, May 1 to 4, 1970: The Students' Perspective* (New York: College Notes and Text, 1971), 112–17.

39. Agte, *Kent Letters,* 66.

40. "Resolution Passed by Faculty of Kent State University May 5, 1970," in Folder 8, Box 70, May 4 Collection, Kent State University Department of Political Science May 4 records, KSU Special Collections and Archives, Kent, Ohio.

41. "Speech by President White (questions and answers)," May 22, 1970, Folder 1, Box 127, May 4 Collection, Administrative Offices Papers, KSU, Kent, Ohio.

42. Grace, "Kent State and Historical Memory," 13–14.

43. Ibid., 13. See Tom Grace, *Death and Dissent,* for more detail.

44. Kathy Stafford, interview by Craig Simpson, June 10, 2008.

45. CKSUV report, May 4 Archives, KSU, Kent, Ohio.

46. Albert Van Kirk, interview by Craig Simpson, Oct. 9, 2009.

47. FBI report, May 10, 1970, provided by Alan Canfora and Tom Grace; "Test Shoots Hole in Part of KSU Sniper Rumors," *Akron Beacon Journal,* May 10, 1970.

48. Albert Van Kirk, interview by Craig Simpson, Oct. 9, 2009.

49. John Mangels, "Kent State Shootings: Does Former Informant Hold the Key to the May 4 Mystery?," *Cleveland Plain Dealer,* Dec. 19, 2010, http://www.cleveland.com/science/index.ssf/2010/12/kent_state_shootings_does_form.html.

50. For a brief summary of the questions surrounding Norman, see "Kent State tape indicates altercation and pistol fire preceded National Guard shootings (audio)," *Cleveland Plain Dealer,* http://www.cleveland.com/science/index.ssf/2010/10/analysis_of_kent_state_audio_t.html (accessed June 15, 2014).

51. Joseph M. Sima, interview by Craig Simpson, October 16, 2007; John Mangels, "Kent State Shootings: Does Former Informant Hold the Key to the May 4 Mystery?," *Cleveland Plain Dealer,* December 19, 2010, http://www.cleveland.com/science/index.ssf/2010/12/kent_state_shootings_does_form.html.

52. Pamela Donovan, "How Idle Is Idle Talk? One Hundred Years of Rumor Research," *Diogenes* 54 (Feb. 2007): 62.

53. Fine and Ellis, *Global Grapevine,* 9.

54. Quoted from I. F. Stone, *The Killings at Kent State: How Murder Went Unpunished* (New York: Random House, 1970), 105–6. The proceeds from Stone's book went to the Kent Legal Defense Fund.

55. Catherine Delattre, interview by Craig Simpson, Nov. 13, 2008.

56. Chuck Ayers, interview by Craig Simpson, Aug. 16, 2007.

57. See the summary of the FBI report in "Excerpts from Summary of the F.B.I. Report on Kent State U. Disorders, Last May," *New York Times,* Oct. 31, 1970. The Justice Department's summary of the FBI report is published in Stone, *Killings at Kent State,* 1971.

58. "Statement of SP5 William James Case," Series 1981, Adjutant General's Kent State University Investigation Files, Ohio Historical Society, Columbus.

59. "Statement of Sp4 James D. McGee," Series 1981, Adjutant General's Kent State University Investigation Files, Ohio Historical Society. The misspellings in this statement and others are in the originals.

60. "Statement of SSG Barry W. Morris," Series 1981, Adjutant General's Kent State University Investigation Files, Ohio Historical Society.

61. "Statement of SP4 James Edward Pierce," Series 1981, Adjutant General's Kent State University Investigation Files, Ohio Historical Society. The misspellings have been left intact.

62. "Statement of Howard R. Fallon," Series 6524, Department of Public Safety, Investigation and Report, Kent State Riot and Shootings, 56–60.

63. "Statement of James W. Farriss," Series 6524, Department of Public Safety, Investigation and Report Kent State Riot and Shootings, 61–64.

64. "Statement of Charles Fassinger," Series 6524, Department of Public Safety, Investigation and Report Kent State Riot and Shootings, 66–70.

65. In his 2013 interview, Ron Snyder showed the Beretta, saying "I have the only weapon that was on the hill that day."

66. It is not clear that Miller was throwing rocks at this moment. If Jones was hit, it was likely to have been by Jim Minard, who stated in a May 18 *Time* report on the

shootings that he "was harassing this officer. I threw a stone at him." See "At War with War," *Time,* May 18, 1970, http://cgi.cnn.com/ALLPOLITICS/1996/analysis/back.time/9605/20/.

67. "Statement of Harry D. Jones," Series 6524, Department of Public Safety, Investigation and Report Kent State Riot and Shootings, 105–6.

68. "Statement of Lawrence A. Shafer," Series 6524, Department of Public Safety, Investigation and Report Kent State Riot and Shootings, 200–201.

69. Ed Grant and Mike Hill, *I Was There: What Really Went on at Kent State* (Lima, Ohio: C.S.S. Publishing, 1974), quoted in Best, "Tragic Weekend," 59.

70. Quote in Best, "Tragic Weekend," 59.

71. An excerpt from and story on the Strubbe tape can be found at http://blog.cleveland.com/metro/2010/05/new_analysis_of_40-year-old_re.html (accessed June 7, 2014).

72. Ronald Snyder, interview by Gregory Wilson, May 3, 2013.

73. Best, "Tragic Weekend," 75

74. Report, "May 1, 1970-May 5, 1970," Series 6524, Department of Public Safety, Investigation and Report Kent State Riot and Shootings.

75. U.S. President's Commission on Campus Unrest, *Report,* 287.

76. Ibid., 289–90.

77. "Special State Grand Jury Report," Oct. 16, 1970, published in Stone, *Killings at Kent State,* 145–58.

78. Michael Erwin, interview by Sandra Perlman Halem, Apr. 4, 2000.

79. Joe Cullum, interview by Gregory Wilson, May 11, 2012.

80. Ken Hammond, interview by Craig Simpson, Mar. 24, 2010.

81. Carl M. Moore, interview by Les Stegh, Sept. 10, 1973.

82. "May 4, 1970, Kent State Shootings Site," National Register of Historic Places Application, http://ww2.ohiohistory.org/resource/histpres/docs/nr/kent1.pdf (accessed June 6, 1944).

83. See Hensley, *Kent State Incident,* 77, and May 4 Special Collections Legal Chronology, http://speccoll.library.kent.edu/4may70/legalchronology.html#1974.

84. Hensley, *Kent State Incident,* 78.

85. Linda Fifer, recorded remembrance, May 4, 1990.

86. Joseph Kelner and James Munves, *The Kent State Coverup* (Lincoln, Neb.: Authors Guild, 1980), 268–69; Hensley, *Kent State Incident,* 81.

87. Ronald Snyder, interview by Gregory Wilson, May 3, 2013.

88. Dean Kahler, interview by Gregory Wilson, May 14, 2012.

89. Rosanne Kennedy, "Stolen Generations Testimony: Trauma, Historiography, and the Question of 'Truth,'" in Robert Perks and Alistair Thomson, eds., *The Oral History Reader,* 2nd ed. (New York: Routledge, 2006), 506–20, quote on 514.

90. James Young, *Writing and Rewriting the Holocaust: Narrative and the Consequences of Interpretation* (Bloomington: Indiana Univ. Press, 1988), 165.

91. Dominick LaCapra, *History and Memory after Auschwitz* (Ithaca, N.Y.: Cornell Univ. Press, 1998), 8.

92. Ibid.

93. Hodgkin and Radstone, eds., *Memory, History, Nation,* 5.

5. "The beginning of an ending"

1. Foote, *Shadowed Ground,* 7–8.

2. Ibid., 18.

3. Ibid., 8.

4. John Fitzgerald O'Hara, "Kent State/May 4 and Postwar Memory," *American Quarterly* 58, no. 2 (June 2006): 301–28; quotes on 306.

5. Bills, *Kent State/May 4,* 33.

6. Linda Fifer, recorded remembrance, May 4, 1990.

7. Peter Jedick, interview by Craig Simpson, Feb. 9, 2010.

8. William Wilen, recorded remembrance, May 4, 1990.

9. Grace, "Kent State and Historical Memory," 15.

10. Flyer, Folder 3, Box 117, Annual Commemoration Records, May 4 Collection, KSU.

11. Grace, "Kent State and Historical Memory," 16.

12. "Position Paper, May 1–4 Memorial Observance," Folder 2, Box 117, Annual Commemoration Records, May 4 Collection, KSU; Bills, *Kent State/May 4,* 32.

13. Grace, "Kent State and Historical Memory," 17.

14. Miriam R. Jackson, "The Kent State Legacy and the 'Business at Hand,'" in Bills, *Kent State/May 4,* 177–86; quote on 178.

15. Ibid., 177–86; quote on 179.

16. *Daily Kent Stater,* May 2, 1973.

17. Ken Hammond, interview by Gregory Wilson, July 16, 2012.

18. Bills, *Kent State/May 4,* 34, citing the *Daily Kent Stater,* May 7, 1974.

19. Jerry Lewis, interviewed by Craig Simpson, Feb. 24, 2010.

20. Jeffrey C. Alexander and Philip Smith, eds., *The Cambridge Companion to Durkheim* (Cambridge: Cambridge Univ. Press, 2005), 215–16. Emphasis in original.

21. Alexander Riley, *The Social Thought of Émile Durkheim* (Los Angeles: SAGE Publications, 2015), 197.

22. Linda Fifer, recorded remembrance, May 4, 1990.

23. Cubitt, *History and Memory,* 210.

24. Shirley Ohles, recorded remembrance, May 2, 1990.

25. Nathan Sooy, interview by Nancy B. Brendlinger, May 4, 1990.

26. The Department of the Interior rejected this effort in 1978.

27. Michael Schwartz, interview by Craig Simpson, Nov. 20, 2008.

28. See the "Tent City Chronology" on the KSU Library May 4 page, http://spec-coll.library.kent.edu/4may70/citychron.html.

29. "Kent State Tent City Protesters Given Ultimatum to Leave Camp," *Toledo Blade,* July 10, 1977, 15, http://news.google.com/newspapers?nid=1350&dat=19770710&id=8cYxAAAAIBAJ&sjid=ogoEAAAAIBAJ&pg=6734,5883965 (accessed June 15, 2014).

30. "Kent State Tent City Protesters Given Ultimatum to Leave Camp," *Toledo Blade,* July 10, 1977, 15, http://news.google.com/newspapers?nid=1350&dat=19770710&id=8cYxAAAAIBAJ&sjid=ogoEAAAAIBAJ&pg=6734,5883965 (accessed June 15, 2014).

31. Kal Johal, "The Battle over the Kent State Shootings and the Monopoly of Memorialization" (MA thesis, Univ. of Akron, 2009), 94.

32. Ibid., 44.

33. Bills, *Kent State/May 4*, 184.

34. On battlefields like Gettysburg being sacred space, see Edward T. Linenthal, *Sacred Ground: Americans and Their Battlefields* (Urbana: Univ. of Illinois Press, 1991).

35. Michael Schwartz, interview by Craig Simpson, Nov. 20, 2008.

36. Ken Hammond, interview by Craig Simpson, Mar. 24, 2010.

37. Barry Seybert, interview by Betsy Zajko, May 3, 2000.

38. John Guidubaldi, interview by Craig Simpson, Apr. 11, 2008.

39. Peter Putnam to Brage Golding, Jan. 5, 1978, Folder 9, Box 90, KSU May 4 Collection.

40. Brage Golding to Peter Putnam, Feb. 15, 1978, Folder 9, Box 90, KSU May 4 Collection.

41. George Segal to Brage Golding, May 31, 1978, Folder 9, Box 90, KSU May 4 Collection.

42. Brage Golding to George Segal, June 28, 1978, Folder 9, Box 90, KSU May 4 Collection.

43. Brage Golding to George Segal, June 30, 1978, Folder 9, Box 90, KSU May 4 Collection.

44. George W. Ingler to Robert McCoy, Aug. 1, 1978, Folder 9, Box 90, KSU May 4 Collection.

45. News Release re: Memorial Sculpture, Aug. 28, 1978, Folder 9, Box 90, KSU May 4 Collection.

46. "KSU rejection of sculpture correct," *Kent-Ravenna Record-Courier*, Aug. 29, 1978, Folder 9, Box 90, KSU May 4 Collection.

47. Michael Schwartz, interview by Craig Simpson, Nov. 20, 2008.

48. Edwin A. Martini, *Invisible Enemies: The American War on Vietnam, 1975–2000* (Amherst: Univ. of Massachusetts Press, 2007), 207.

49. Ibid.

50. Ibid.

51. Marita Sturken, *Tangled Memories* (Berkeley: Univ. of California Press, 1997), 61.

52. Martini, *Invisible Enemies*, 208.

53. Ibid., 209.

54. Ibid., 126.

55. Daniel Marcus, *Happy Days and Wonder Years: The Fifties and the Sixties in Contemporary Cultural Politics* (New Brunswick, N.J.: Rutgers Univ. Press, 2004), 6.

56. "Report to the Kent State University's May 4th Memorial Committee," Folder 20, Box 20, Jerry M. Lewis Papers, KSU May 4 Collection.

57. Quoted in Jeffrey Kimball, *Nixon's War* (Lawrence: Univ. Press of Kansas, 1998), 216.

58. "Report to the Kent State University's May 4th Memorial Committee," Folder 20, Box 20, Jerry M. Lewis Papers, KSU May 4 Collection. Underlining in original.

59. "Kent State May 4 Memorial: National Open Design Competition," Folder 22, Box 20, Jerry M. Lewis Papers, KSU May 4 Collection.

60. KSU news release, n.d., Folder 22, Box 20, Jerry M. Lewis Papers, KSU May 4 Collection.

61. Kathryn Weiss, "Preconceiving Material Rhetoric: Literacy beyond Language at Kent State's May 4 Memorial" (PhD diss., Kent State Univ., 2006).

62. Lisa Lynott, recorded remembrance, May 4, 1990.

63. News clipping, "Legion panel votes to halt memorial at KSU," July 12, 1986, *Akron Beacon Journal,* Folder 28, Box 20, Jerry M. Lewis Papers, KSU May 4 Collection.

64. Ibid.

65. News clipping, "At Kent State, They Still Hear the Drumming," *Newsday,* Mar. 15, 1989, Folder 22, Box 20, Jerry M. Lewis Papers, KSU May 4 Collection.

66. Ibid.

67. Ibid.

68. Lisa Lynott, recorded remembrance, May 4, 1990.

69. Michael Schwartz, interview by Craig Simpson, Nov. 20, 2008.

70. See the May 4 Special Collections website, http://speccoll.library.kent.edu/4may70/exhibit/memorials/m4mem.html.

71. E. Timothy Moore, interview by Craig Simpson, May 14, 2009.

72. Johal, "Battle Over the Kent State Shootings," 56.

73. Weiss, "Preconceiving Material Rhetoric," 67, ix.

74. Carol Cartwright, interview by Craig Simpson, June 30, 2008.

75. "Kent State Announces Events for 43rd Annual Commemoration of May 4," http://www2.kent.edu/news/newsdetail.cfm?newsitem=567FFCA0-C1E7-A939-2261548DDF4F65E3 (accessed June 12, 2014).

76. Tom Hayden, "Closure at Kent State?," *The Nation,* May 15, 2013, http://www.thenation.com/article/174348/closure-kent-state# (accessed June 12, 2014).

77. Chapter 12 in his book is titled "Right here, get set, point, fire!"

78. "Kent State University to Open May 4 Visitors Center," *Cleveland Plain Dealer,* Oct. 19, 2012, http://www.cleveland.com/metro/index.ssf/2012/10/kent_state_university_opens_ma.html (accessed June 15, 2014).

79. Hayden, "Closure at Kent State?"

80. See the Truth Tribunal website, http://truthtribunal.org/about (accessed June 14, 2014).

81. Matt Fredmonsky, "Family of May 4 Victim Says New Visitors Center Presents Unbalanced View of Kent State Shootings," *Kent Patch,* Oct. 22, 2012 (accessed Mar. 29, 2015).

82. Abrams, *Oral History Theory,* 100–101.

83. John R. Gillis, ed. *Commemoration: The Politics of National Identity* (Princeton, N.J.: Princeton Univ. Press, 1994), 5.

84. Carol Barbato passed away suddenly on April 30, 2014.

85. May 4 Visitors Center, Kent State University, Exhibit Script, 5/18/2012.

86. "May 4 Visitors Center Now Open," KSU News, http://www.kent.edu/news/kent-state%E2%80%99s-may-4-visitors-center-now-open (accessed June 14, 2014).

87. Hodgkin and Radstone, eds., *Contested Pasts,* 5.

88. Alessandro Portelli, "What Makes Oral History Different," in Perks and Thomson, eds., *Oral History Reader,* 37.

89. John Guidubaldi, interview by Craig Simpson, Apr. 11, 2008.

90. Mike Alewitz, interview by Gregory Wilson, Aug. 6, 2012.

91. Joe Cullum, interview by Gregory Wilson, May 11, 2012.

92. Ken Hammond, interview by Gregory Wilson, July 16, 2012.

93. Catherine Delattre, interview by Craig Simpson, Nov. 13, 2008.

94. Diane Yale-Peabody, recorded remembrance, May 4, 1990.

95. Rosann Rissland, interview by Craig Simpson, May 19, 2009.

96. Michael Schwartz, interview by Craig Simpson, Nov. 20, 2008.

97. Janice Wascko, interview by Nancy Brendlinger, May 4, 1990.

98. Chuck Ayers, interview by Craig Simpson, Aug. 16, 2007.

99. David Lowenthal, "Past Time, Present Place: Landscape and Memory," *Geographical Review* 65 (Jan. 1975): 31.

100. Foote, *Shadowed Ground,* 3.

101. Richard Bentley, interview by Gina Bodra, May 3, 1990.

Index

Abell, Chris, 107
Abraham and Isaac (Segal), 12
"Abraham's Sacrifice of Isaac" (Segal),
  199–200
Abrams, Lynn, 19–20, 215–16
activism: African Americans' students,
  36–38 (*see also* Black United Students
  [BUS]); differing memories of KSU
  students', 35–46; KSU students', 32–33,
  36–39, 43, 58; KSU students' against rules
  and regulations, 39, 43; of labor unions,
  34, 145; links among students, soldiers,
  and workers, 145–46; student, 34, 49
administration, KSU's, 31; assumptions and
  misconception of, 68, 93; commemorations and, 184, 186; decentralized decision making of, 38–39; memorialization
  and, 184, 189–90, 199–200, 202, 212; not
  providing narrative of shootings, 181–82;
  protesters and, 40, 43–45, 83, 92, 170;
  response to Tent City, 195–96
African American studies, 41
African Americans, 35–38, 41, 42. *See also*
  Black United Students (BUS)
Agte, Barbara Becker. See *Kent Letters*
Ahern, James, 184
Akron, Ohio, 51, 164
Akron Beacon Journal: investigation into
  shootings by, 152, 158–59; printing
  Justice Department's summary of FBI
  report, 161
al-Kafiz, Ibrahim (formerly Dwayne
  White), 42
Alewitz, Mike, 16, 39, 47; on lack of leader-
  ship, 98–99; on political meaning of
  events, 80–81, 145, 218
allegations. *See* rumors

Allport, Gordon, 24–26, 70
Alspritch, Harry, 201
alumni, 202, 207–8
ambiguity, and rumors, 24–26
American Association of University Professors (AAUP), 153
American Civil Liberties Union (ACLU),
  172, 175
American Legion, Ohio Unit of, 13, 207
amnesty, in protesters' demands, 83
antiwar movement, 93; after Laos invasion,
  183–85; counterprotesters and, 145; ef-
  fects of radicals in, 96–97; government
  efforts to defuse, 55, 145, 186; influence
  of KSU shootings on, 145–46, 184, 218;
  at KSU, 39, 58–59, 61–62; in May 4
  Visitors Center exhibits, 214–15. *See also*
  demonstrations
Appy, Christian, 137
armored carriers, National Guard's, 78,
  86–87
arrests: of BUS members, 183; of SDS protesters, 44–45; of Tent City protesters, 193
Arthrell, William (Bill), 81, 192, 195
Ast, Bruno: criticisms of memorial designed by, 208–9, 211–12; in Memorial
  Design competition, 13, 206–7; memorial designed by, 14, 209–10, *210;* scaling
  down memorial design to limit cost, 13,
  207–9
audio quality, in Oral History Project, 6
Auld, Jeff, 184
Ayers, Bill, 14, 213
Ayers, Chuck, 7, 43, 58, 124; on draft lottery,
  54–55; interpretation of shootings, 105,
  221–22; interviewed by FBI, 160–61; on
  May 4 rally, 59, 95; on Music and Speech

241